I first witnessed Lori's connection with the floor, and today I see that same deep ali.......... ... ... coaching practice. I'm thrilled that others will now get a chance to meet Lori on the pages of her book. In it, she takes the reader from her dancing days through her process of becoming a successful business coach, and in doing so, she explains the transformative model she developed to support thought leaders in embracing true freedom. Her client stories reveal how her Clearing Process can release your most authentic self in your business and your whole life. I wholeheartedly recommend this book to anyone who has ever doubted that success and authentic transformation are possible.

LYNNE TWIST
Founder of the Soul of Money Institute and the Pachamama Alliance, and author of the award-winning bestseller *The Soul of Money: Transforming Your Relationship with Money and Life*

This book beautifully invites all of us to become aware of the way we think and concisely shows us why our thoughts shape our lives. Lori has done a remarkable job in connecting her years as a dancer, choreographer, and nonprofit leader with the leadership practices and conversations that have the power to transform the way we do business. This is a book for anyone on the journey to a better business and a more fulfilling life.

SANJIV SIDHU
Founder and CEO of tech companies, including i2 Technologies and o9

It's not often a book gifts you with amazing ideas about business while completely drawing you into a narrative with its soulfulness. This is that book. I gasped out loud, laughed, stayed up late reading, and jotted ideas for my business on every horizontal surface I could find. Dancing Naked changed my mind; changed the way I lead and manage; and changed my life. Lori Darley is a voice of authenticity and brings conscious spirituality into lives and companies. She teaches us to live, consciously and authentically, in the moment, fully in command of all we have the potential to be. I found her advice to be profound: "Every time one person suspends her own point of view long enough to listen to someone else's, without judgment, we are one step closer to peace." The world needs Dancing Naked.

TONI PORTMANN
CEO and executive chairman of the board, DHISCO, Inc.

dancing
naked

dancing naked

*claiming
your power
as a
conscious
leader*

LORI
DARLEY

with
Aleksandra Corwin
Agata Antonow

Publisher	*Corey Michael Blake*
President	*Kristin Westberg*
Executive editor	*Aleksandra Corwin*
Editor	*Agata Antonow*
Editor	*Alison Hennessee*
Creative director	*Sunny DiMartino*
Project management	*Leeann Sanders*
Facts keeper	*Mike Winicour*
Proofreading	*Jonathan Hierholzer*
Last looks	*Adam Lawrence*

Writers of the Round Table Press
PO Box 511, Highland Park, IL 60035
www.roundtablecompanies.com

Printed in the United States of America
First Edition: October 2016
10 9 8 7 6 5 4 3 2 1

Library of Congress Cataloging-in-Publication Data
Darley, Lori.
Dancing naked: claiming your power as a conscious leader /
Lori Darley with Aleksandra Corwin and Agata Antonow.—1st ed. p. cm.
ISBN Paperback: 978-1-939418-87-6
ISBN Digital: 978-1-939418-88-3
Library of Congress Control Number: 2016953711

RTC Publishing is an imprint of Writers of the Round Table, Inc.
Writers of the Round Table Press and the RTC Publishing logo are
trademarks of Writers of the Round Table, Inc.

*Some names and identifying personal details have been changed
to protect the identities of those involved.*

Contents

part 1: claiming my power

part 2: claiming your power

This book is dedicated to my mother,
Lois Ellen Meehan Darley, *who always aspired*
to be a writer and, in truth, wrote her entire life.
This one's for you, Mom, wherever you are.

And also to my husband, **Larry,**
for his unconditional and unbridled love.

Foreword

When Lori first told me her book would be titled "Dancing Naked," I had to smile. It certainly sounded like the woman I have been honored to call friend and colleague for more than two decades.

Dancing Naked is a manifesto for true freedom—the freedom we all aspire to as individuals and business leaders. We all want to live our fullest and most passionate lives, unencumbered by limiting beliefs and setbacks that seem to prevent us from fulfilling our destiny. I have seen for myself the profound transformations that dancing naked, Lori-Darley-style, can encourage in businesses and individual lives.

My first impression of Lori, when I met her years ago, was a burst of energy and color. When she walked into my North Dallas office suite, she carried herself with a confidence trained into the bodies of dancers.

"So you're a dancer? What's that like?" I asked her.

The passion and energy with which Lori spoke of dance was contagious. It became clear that for Lori dancing was not just movement on a stage; it was about connecting with the audience in a deep and meaningful way. Later, when I got a chance to see her perform, I felt as though all of us in our seats were having a conversation with her through music and movement. Something profound was being imparted in what I would come to recognize as Lori's loving approach to creating a truly engaging experience for her audience. This was truly *art*—Lori put the audience in the dance.

Over the years, Lori became a close friend. Eventually she realized that while she loved dancing, it was time for her to move on. It would be a frightening step for many, but Lori dove into the process with her inspiring blend of fiery talent, charm, and perseverance. She worked with me at the Transitions Institute, which I founded, and through our work together she created and pursued a career as an executive coach. Over the years, Lori moved from being a student of mine to being a masterful thought leader in her own right.

Lori continues to use the dance between herself and others to communicate. She does not tell her clients what they "should" do but encourages them to stretch their limits. Even when the process is uncomfortable or challenging, her loving energy is fully present for everyone she works with.

Just as she found dance as a child, Lori has intuitively found her rhythm in coaching. She has not left dance or the stage; she has found a new way of communicating and showing the love she feels for people—the same things I noticed when I first sat in the audience watching her perform.

Because of Lori's approach, this is not a prescriptive book. Authentic shifts do not come from a rote exercise in a notebook; they spring from an internal well. It is important to make a connection—to our past and current narratives, our vision, our possibilities—to truly uncover our path. Lori's book begins with her own story, which reveals how Lori was able to navigate this journey. The second part of the book shows Lori in action, supporting businesses and executives as they make authentic shifts. This section is filled with ideas that can be applied immediately on the path to transformation.

I am excited for you as you turn the page to share Lori's story and explore The Clearing Process. As her friend and colleague, I can't wait for you to get to know this extraordinary individual and her transformative work that allows us to express ourselves in a powerful, vibrant connection with others and the universe.

DAVID ZELMAN, PHD
Founder and CEO of Transitions Institute, Inc. and author
of *If I Can, You Can: Transformation Made Easy*

Acknowledgments

My biggest thank-you goes to my husband, Larry. For all the times I was crumbling while writing this book, he brought me back to life. When I was at a loss for words, or a title, or just plain lost, Larry brought his genius to the table and helped me find my way. He is my everything. For his limitless love, belly-aching humor, and commitment to love me as he loves the world, I am forever and ever grateful.

David Zelman's impact on my life has been immeasurable. His wisdom and incredible generosity of spirit have supported me during my entire coaching career.

Karen Zelman is the embodiment of unconditional friendship and love. Karen's beauty and light beam inspiration and compassion to everyone whose lives she touches, and there are many. She and David are family.

Special ultra-thanks to my collaborators, editors, and writers: To Aleksandra Corwin, for her amazing questions, incredible gifts, patience, coaching, and deeply grounded wisdom. To Agata Antonow for her unique viewpoints delivered with such grace. And Alison Hennessee, for her outstanding attention to detail.

Amy and Avram, John and Liz, Simeon and Ela, and Willa and PJ are the loving family who bring their infinite grace, love, patience, and empathy on so many levels. And of course, my mother and father, who gave me the greatest gift of all. To them, I extend deep love and gratitude. My amazing nephews and grandnephews—Chris, Will, Jack, Ari and Ezra—are sources of inspiration and energy. I'm so excited to share a slice of this life together with all of them.

My dear, dear friends for life whom I consider my chosen family, including Robin Parker, Denise Jayroe, Steve Potts, Randy and Terri Potts, Ellen Pincus, Randy Hunt, and Bobbi Van. They have always been there for me.

Pam Dougherty offered profoundly clarifying editorial support in the early, early iterations of *Dancing Naked*. I couldn't have gotten here if she hadn't been there with me.

Teresa Barker is another writer/doula who helped prepare my body, mind, and spirit for what was to come. She helped me write the book I was meant to write.

The entire RTC team.

- First and foremost, Corey Blake: for his vision, support, and huge spirit, and the laughs that always help me keep things in perspective
- Keli McNeil: for keeping me on time and on point with all the many projects we have completed together
- Sunny DiMartino: for her brilliant visuals that inspire me every day
- Leeann Sanders: for the big-picture vision and for being a flawless keeper of process integrity
- Kristin Westberg: for keeping the vision flourishing

Brandy Barnes rocked the social media run-up to this book launch and kept me sane as she created an entire universe for us to play in.

The incredible women in my women's circle have listened endlessly to the ups and downs of this process. Mati Vargas-Gibson, Adrienne Palmer, Cris Robinson, Christine McGuire, Terri Seltzer, and Brandy Barnes all have my gratitude for their generosity.

LeeAnn Mallory, Carol DuBose, Kay Caldwell, Kay Lisch, Cindy Hardesty, Kathy Light, Patrice Wheeler, and Laura Atterstrom, to name but a few, are my coach friends who have supported me along the way.

My clients have entrusted me to dance in partnership with their lives and businesses. They have helped me evolve in so many ways.

A gratitude beacon to Jenny Fowler and Maria Enriquez, who help me keep everything in its right place, especially my sanity.

So many amazing people at Social Venture Network have shaped my life, including Madame Lori Hanau, Sir Jerry Gorde, Libba and Gifford Pinchot, and Josh Knauer.

Special shout-out to Mike Rowlands. No words are adequate for the multitude of ways he has supported this vision.

Lori Link was my first career coach, and worked with me for over fifteen years. She truly linked me to my Lori-osity. I am forever indebted to her for her wisdom and deep caring.

Sharen Bradford's beautiful eye in capturing, through her photography, the fleeting nature of our dancing journey has always been an inspiration to me. Toni Portmann encouraged me beyond comfort to stay true to my most authentic and original impulse to share my story. My thanks extend out to both.

Lynne Twist believed in me when this project had barely begun. She is who I want to be "when I grow up"! I stand in awe of her powerful and ongoing commitment to the extraordinary capacity of humanity.

These acknowledgments would not be complete without expressing my sincere gratitude to the women who gave me powerful opportunities to grow as an artist and a leader, and who inspired me to perform at my best. Thank you to my fellow cofounders and co–artistic directors of Dancers Unlimited Repertory Company: Jane Evelyn Chalk Davis, Patty Delaney, Patricia Dickinson. And also to my dear friend and loyal partner in the dance, Micki Saba.

Thank you!

Prologue

At my Baltimore workshop, I asked the participants to enter the room without making a sound.

"Welcome to The Clearing Process," I said once the group was assembled. "To begin, I'd like for you to just start to walk into and around the room in silence."

I started to walk, spine straight and fluid, around the room. "As you walk, move into soft focus. Connect to your breath. I'd like for you to just notice the shift of weight on the floor, the quality of your breathing, anything that's held. Now let me hear your breaths."

Immediately, the room was filled with the soft sounds of aspiration and footfalls as we all slowly walked around the room. I kept the cadence of my voice measured and soft, but clear enough to carry. As I moved and spoke, I felt myself slip into the familiar comfort of leading a group of people who were present in their bodies. Decades of training kicked in; it was like sliding into a well-practiced and well-loved dance.

I did a quick scan, taking in people's postures. I've always said, "Once a dancer, always a dancer." I knew I would change when I stepped away from dance and started coaching; what surprised me was how much stayed the same. As a dancer, I was always aware of my body—when you're being twirled six feet off the ground by a partner or leaping through the air on a dim stage, you have to be—but I realized that as a coach I was just as aware of the body, both mine and those of my clients. My clients' movements and postures provided potent clues to their attitudes, ideas, and realities, and most weren't even aware of it. Changing the way they worked with their bodies could often bring about multidimensional shifts in other parts of their lives.

When I looked around, I noticed that many people weren't yet fully present. One man near the front was clenching his fists with enough force that I could see his knuckles turning white. A woman to my right had her shoulders hunched up near her ears. She was so tense she was only taking thin little sips of air from her upper chest. Mike, a longtime friend attending this event, was attentive and expectant, but his arms were tight to his sides; a tall man with a warm smile and brown hair, he was slightly hunched forward, as though listening intently. Beside him, a petite woman was tilted to the side, one foot tapping, seeming at once fatigued and anxious.

Whatever stories these two were telling themselves—*I'll never get it all done* or *I can't handle this* or *Why is it always my problem*—they were enacting those narratives in their bodies, reinforcing thoughts that may or may not have been true. And I was willing to bet that neither of them realized what they were doing.

"Now, as you walk through the space, I'd like for you to connect with your eyes with anyone else in the room."

The feel of the room shifted again as everyone focused outward and on others. In some cases, the contact was friendly, in others almost wary, in some flirty. Each set of eyes contained a different expression.

I walked among the attendees and made contact, too. I wanted others in the room to keep track of the changes they were experiencing. On top of that tall order, I had to make the group more comfortable with each other so they could work together from a space of authenticity.

"Notice as you connect with your eyes—has the quality of your breathing changed? Stay in touch with your breath as you continue walking, and now I invite you to connect with the people in the room with your hearts."

It was fascinating to watch. The pace slowed. Making eye contact with the eyes comes naturally to most people, but how do we connect with our hearts? How do we accept an invitation like this—to connect with others in a way that can feel vulnerable? A few people placed their hands over their hearts, a few people moved closer when making eye contact, a few looked unsure or nervous. Eyes, sure, but hearts? Uh-oh.

I only let the squirming continue for a little bit before moving on. "Now, pick up the pace a little bit. Connect with your elbows."

This brought some laughter—maybe relieved chuckles in some cases. People got closer to bump elbows and some tension dissolved with the simple, childlike gesture. At the same time, the intention of the exercises was anything but childish. Everyone in that room was preoccupied with to-do lists, deadlines, and all of the responsibilities that come with being leaders in the business world. By asking them to walk in silence, direct their focus softly inside, and connect with others, I was asking them to be present, to check in with themselves, and to integrate all their experiences. We connected with feet and hips, and finally I thought we had relaxed around each other enough.

"And now shake it all out," I directed. "Shake your whole body. Take a deep breath in with your arms over your head, and take your seats."

The quiet and focused energy in the room was a stark contrast to that morning, when I had woken up in a tangle of bed linens, my heart beating fast. I'd just been visited by the old friend I call the Actor's Nightmare, the one familiar to anyone who has ever created and shared new work, who has ever offered themselves to an audience—the one that reminds you of all the many ways there are for you to fail. At one point, that dream would have brought me to my knees. But I knew better. It was all just old patterning, and I didn't have to listen to it.

After all, I was prepared. This was the work I had spent a lifetime preparing, and now I was officially presenting it to a large audience for the first time. It was the launch of my new business, Conscious Leaders, and the introduction of my new process, The Clearing—the very work you're holding in your hands now.

As a reader, you have a distinct advantage over the attendees at the workshop. You're about to read about the entire Clearing process; at the Baltimore workshop, however, I had only an hour and a quarter—enough time to start work on Clarity, the first step of The Clearing. But I knew that insights could happen in fast and unexpected ways with this process. I was ready to serve my audience and help them gain clarity in ways that would transform every area of their lives—all in the limited time we had together. It was a tall order, but I had worked for this moment, and I had the focused, intense strength of someone about to step onto a stage.

I tuned in to my shoulders, lowered them away from my ears. I breathed deeply, feeling the air as it filled my diaphragm and lungs, watching my chest rise and fall. I uncrossed my legs, planting both feet squarely on the floor. I allowed myself to realize that the future would unfold as it would unfold. I could only focus on the present. I finished my coffee, thinking about how many times as a performer I had faced similar moments. This day in Baltimore wasn't just me coming full circle. It was me launching my life from the most deeply authentic space I had ever known.

Many people's stories of reinvention begin with the boring corporate job and then work their way through a dramatic turn before reaching a climax in which the entrepreneur's business takes off or the artist within emerges. Those are great stories. But mine is different.

You could say I was born into the art of movement, first squeezing my chubby feet into pale pink ballet slippers at the tender age of four. The need to be seen and acknowledged—to be perfect and belong—propelled me from ballet and modern dance to the world of coaching and facilitating. It was a circuitous path, through a series of crazy left turns, up hills and down, through cleansing crucible fires. More than once, I reached for roles that failed to materialize or danced into leadership positions that were thrust upon me before I felt ready. Perseverance and commitment to consciously directed thought transformed that small ballet dancer into someone who feels at home offering support for the giants in boardrooms.

While I waited in the dim hallway outside the conference room to take the stage as my most genuine self, I thought, *Every moment I share, every conversation I have today will contribute and bring value to each person's experience.* The declaration helped me focus.

God knows I had prepared for the launch of The Clearing. I had rehearsed with the same passion and dedication I had once poured into performances in New York, Tokyo, and Moscow. I had staged two pilot programs in Dallas and had sought out rigorous feedback from professionals. I was ready, and I wasn't alone. Though in a literal sense I might be the only one standing at the front of the room, in truth I was buoyed up by all the loving support I had received from coaches, trainers, pilot audiences, and my husband. Leading this group of executives today, I'd stand tall and proud, knowing that this supporting cast hovered in the wings, encouraging me with the power of their belief. With a smile on my face and a laugh in my heart, I opened the door.

Once I had gone through the first exercise of inner focus and connecting with eyes, elbows, and hearts, I clapped my hands, eager to get started. "I'm Lori Darley, and for the past sixteen years I've been coaching and training leaders, business owners, and entrepreneurs." I paused and took a deep breath, looking around the room to connect with as many eyes as I could. "I deeply honor and respect what each of you is doing in the world. My company is Conscious Leaders, a coaching and leadership development firm."

I gestured for everyone to stand up, and I started quickly shifting my weight from foot to foot, waving to the audience to join in. "For right now, let's get a little more present in our bodies." After I could see color start to fill in some of the faces around me, I added, "And since Halloween has just passed by, I want us to connect to the image of bones. Rattle your bones!"

I demonstrated, letting my posture relax and shaking myself out, hips, arms, legs, and all. "Rattle your bones and imagine there are ball bearings in your skull and you want to move those ball bearings around. And there are ball bearings in your hips and ball bearings at the end of each fingertip and in your knees. Just shake all those bones around."

At first, some of my audience snuck peeks at each other and shuffled from side to side, embarrassed and unsure.

"Come on," I encouraged them. "If those are ball bearings, they're a little rusty. Imagine *well-oiled* ball bearings."

That got another laugh. I began to shake more rapidly, my hands loose and snapping at my sides as my torso shook back and forth. Around me, people vibrated with more force, hips bouncing and feet moving. Soon, we were all bopping along, grooving together to some unheard but common music.

"All right," I announced after a minute or two, gently bringing my motions to a halt. "I think we've shaken things up enough for the moment. We're not done just yet—there's going to be more movement in a bit. But for now let's have a seat and give those bones a rest."

Participants sat back down in their chairs around the perimeter of the room. I could already see that some movements were freer, some expressions less pinched, and a smile of satisfaction curled up the corners of my mouth. If nothing else, the silliness of our skeleton shimmy had shaken some tension loose.

Once everyone was seated, I continued.

"When you signed up for this workshop, you signed up for The Clearing Process, an integrated process that allows us to tap into the wisdom of all four of our intelligences. Those four intelligences[1] are our intellect, or the thinking IQ; our emotional intelligence, or the capacity to work positively with our full range of emotions; our spiritual intelligence, or the capacity to connect with our purpose and higher self; and finally our embodied intelligence, or what I call our 'body wisdom'—billions of years in our DNA that we have access to if only we can listen." I noticed some people around the room nodding in recognition of these concepts.

---

1 In an alternate version of The Clearing Process program we include a fifth intelligence, which relates to a leader's awareness of the interdependent systems that impact organizational stakeholders.

"There are four conversational fields in The Clearing which harness these intelligences to varying degrees to help us find opportunities for action that were previously unavailable."

I pointed to the poster outlining the Four Cs:

CLARITY
a clearing for self-awareness
Your thoughts shape the way the world occurs for you.

COMPLETION
a clearing for peace with the past
Put your past in the past—where it belongs.

CREATION
a clearing for an expanded future
Every moment is an opportunity to create your intention and make impactful choices.

CAPACITY
a clearing for partnership, contribution, and scale
Growing a community of allies who wholeheartedly support your vision.

Intent faces scanned the poster beside me. Some people mouthed the words as they read; some began taking notes; some just furrowed their brows in obvious confusion. My smile widened as I told myself the story *I* needed to hear. Participants may have not yet understood, but wasn't it wonderful that I had the chance to guide them?

"Today, we're going to be talking about Clarity, but before we do, let's talk more about what The Clearing is as a whole. A clearing for me is an expanded possibility. Like when you open a door and suddenly a completely unfamiliar landscape appears, calling you to step onto a path that you didn't know existed. Maybe you didn't even know the door was there."

I thought of how as a little girl, all I wanted was to make my parents love one another. So I danced, because dancing brought them together. Then the dance shifted, and as I grew I found myself dancing so I could express myself. Eventually, hoping to create a home for others who shared that passion, I helped create a dance company. Dance had morphed again—into a community. I loved being with other free spirits who used their youth in service to this art form. Throughout all of these permutations as a dancer, I reflected, each shift represented a path I had never dreamed of before—the opening of a new door to reveal new vistas, new roads.

Some heads in the crowd were beginning to nod, and I went on. "Or we can put it a different way: The Clearing is like a camera lens. Things are out of focus and look one way, but you can make the choice to bring that lens into focus and see things through the viewfinder that you didn't know were there."

For me this meant finally stepping away from a disastrous first marriage, closing the door on my pride and joy—my dance company—and years later taking on my first coaching client. Each of these developments had required me to change my vision—which wasn't easy—but when I did, I'd been rewarded by seeing through lenses that made the world I thought I'd known strange and new and full of possibility.

"We already have experience with this, most of us. We round a corner and meet someone new, or we become parents, or we launch a business. Well, The Clearing helps us to consciously invite large-scale possibility."

I wanted my audience to feel this at a gut level. Over the years, I had attended many self-actualizing workshops, seminars, and events. I'd sat where this audience was now, completing worksheets and scribbling down notes. I'd become a student, studying the nature of being a human *being*. Along the way I learned that the body could be an answer—it could access a level of wisdom unavailable to the thinking mind alone. When the body got involved, it could provide breakthroughs that happened beyond language and intellect; they happened at the muscular and joint level. I wanted to give this audience a taste of that power.

"Today, as I said, we're going to be exploring the first C: Clarity. Before we make a conscious choice, we need to enter a space of Clarity. We need to understand where we are, what stories we're telling ourselves, and what's holding us back. Our bodies hold big clues to those questions, and I've found just tapping into our bones and sinews can help people make seismic shifts—transformations that affect every area of our lives."

It was time to move out of the warm-up stage and into the Clearing work. "I'd like us all to stand up," I said. "We're going to move through the room again, but this time, I want you to move into the space of your whole body. Notice how the weight shifts from foot to foot. Notice your posture and your breathing. Take note of your body."

I looked around the room as people rose from their seats and started walking. People were moving slowly, deliberately. One man in a blue sweater was taking measured, careful steps, lifting each foot up and down as though his shoes were as heavy as bowling balls. A woman in a gray sheath dress and flats was almost gliding about, her shoulders back and her long red hair swinging loose over her shoulders. Mike was walking forward deliberately, his shoulders back, his steps measured.

After a minute, I spoke again. "And now I want you to imagine that you have eyeballs and sensors connected to every part of your body, front and back, as if you can see and *feel* in the three hundred sixty degrees all around you, in every direction. You're aware of all of the energies in the room. You're so bold you could even walk backwards and not bump into anybody."

The whole group sped up as one. One serious-looking man with gray hair and a look of concentration had his arms out to his sides in an airplane pose, and his wedding band glinted as he banked left and right on his flight through the room. The woman in the gray dress was whizzing by people backwards, her elbows slightly out to keep balance. She didn't bump into anyone, as though she really did have sensors in the back of her head.

I could tell from the group's movements and expressions and from the tingling on the back of my neck that the exercise was working. My audience was tasting what it could be like to move beyond the cramped confines of ingrained thought patterns, to use the body to access expression and power you didn't know you possessed.

"And if you feel like it, make a sound," I told them. Several people whooped, which led to laughs all around. Then there were soft hoots and a few siren-esque wails. It sounded like either bedlam or a very wonderful party.

"Okay, everyone, let's shake it out."

We all shook and rattled our bones again. This time we fell into it easily, swinging our hips and arms. There were no rusty ball bearings left in *this* room.

To prime the participants for what was coming next, I now took them through even more focused physical work to help them get present in their bodies. I asked audience members to move through the room and respond to the names of emotions that I called out by taking a shape. I knew this was a powerful primer for connecting with sensations in the body, and for the work still to come. Things had been going beautifully, and my next exercise would be even more concrete; I wanted the business leaders in the room to see that my work had practical applications in the boardroom.

I clapped my hands again as the noise level in the room tapered off. "We're going to switch things up. I want each of you to think about an issue in your business or in your personal life. It can be a problem, a quality within you you'd like to develop, an idea you're considering—anything you want to work on."

The words settled down over the group like snowfall. Silence. I took a few steps back. It would have been all too easy for me to jump in with some prompts or suggestions, but I let the moment linger. I'd learned that so much could happen if I was willing to sit with the silence.

While I waited, I watched. Some participants stared out the small windows or down at their feet while they thought. Others seemed to know immediately what they wanted to work on and watched me with determined expressions, waiting for the next step.

"Okay, everyone have their issue? Great. We're going to focus our attention on the topics you've come up with. To do that, we're going to pair up and work on physically manifesting the issue as it feels right now in our bodies. Just take a shape in response to your thoughts about the issue—no matter what they are."

Based on past work, I figured that many in the audience would pick an area where they were afraid of failure or where they were already experiencing discomfort. Though those issues were often tough to acknowledge, never mind resolve, they were exactly where I liked to begin; from those challenges come the greatest growth. I knew this was true not just from my profession but from my own experiences. I had failed miserably—or was it beautifully?—in my life. I failed my way into a second marriage that was a gift from the Universe. I failed in my earliest attempt at corporate training. I misread people. I made assumptions. I second-guessed myself and faked my way to making it. But every experience taught me something new about myself. And stepping into these experiences—especially the painful ones—pushed me forward.

There was hesitation among the pairs in front of me—some awkward smiles, some nervous chuckles. Working with a partner provides a witness, which usually deepens the power of the experience. Even though I felt vulnerable about the issue that my question had brought to mind for me, I decided to demonstrate. Pulling Mike from the audience, I faced him, and in my best drama queen voice, calling upon the years I spent on stage, I flung my body back dramatically like a swooning nineteenth-century heroine. I put my wrist to my eyebrow in my best "woe is me" posture and yelled, "I can't believe this is happening to me! I'm writing this book, and I'm scared, and I don't know what's going to *happen*!"

I let myself feel all those swooping feelings of failure—the feeling of being dropped from four hundred feet with no parachute. I let myself feel the possible embarrassment of not completing the book; I let myself experience the burn of rejection as I imagined not finding an audience or publisher; I let the anger of a bad review crawl its way up my calves. I held the pose for a moment, then straightened up and returned to normal, dropping the over-the-top performance that would have made any soap opera diva proud. "Okay?"

There was laughter and clapping, as well as a few shouts of "encore." I took a bow and continued with the instructions. "And after you express your problem as it is now, I want you to express the problem dramatically, as if you were powerful and the problem were solved. Like this."

I held up my arms in a warrior pose and tapped into what I would feel when my book was done. I let the pride, satisfaction, and accomplishment seep into my lungs and stomach and throat. I let my fingers feel the smoothness of the cover and the airy whiff of a turned page when I opened a copy. I made a declaration of intention, of power: "If not me, who will do this? I'm ready. I'm here. I'm present."

Mayhem broke out during the exercise as the audience tried the same thing. Laughter, shouting, emoting. In the back, someone was howling with unrestrained delight. I can only imagine what people walking past the room thought. Yep, coaching and breakthroughs can sometimes look like a complete breakdown.

I walked around the room, proud as I watched my audience throw themselves into the exercise. I walked by a woman with her hair in a chignon. Her face was twisted in a grimace, and she clutched her sweater around her torso protectively as she called out, "I want to start this business. I want it so much. Why don't I follow through? I keep getting in my way. I'm scared. It's lonely in here."

Yes, people were gaining insight, slowly, one word and over-the-top gesture at a time. Some were hunched over, some were angry and letting themselves feel it—maybe for the first time.

Mike was in the center of the room, and his body was slumped forward. "I hope this person gets along with me. I hope they like what I say."

He shifted forward, his body stretching out into its full over-six-foot frame. He lifted one foot and put it down, not with a stomp, but firmly, confidently, as though he were anchoring himself deep to the core of the earth. His neck elongated and his shoulders and arms relaxed.

"I have the mic now," he proclaimed, his voice now clear and resonant. "And I know I believe in what I say."

He paused in the exercise and shook his head, turning to his partner. "Am I sensing this right? I feel taller when I imagine the problem solved."

His partner nodded. "Your body language is completely different. In the first pose, it's as though you're *trying* to make yourself smaller."

I looked around at all the audience members in their poses. This was it. I was seeing my work in action. We'd gone through only one step in my transformation process, but even with some work just on Clarity, people were opening doors and surveying roads to unexpected destinations. Everyone was holding up that camera, adjusting the lens, one finger poised to capture familiar images changed by new light and new shadows.

When I was a dancer, I didn't know what I didn't know. I didn't know I wanted to be invited into other people's lives and businesses and asked to show them a way to become fuller versions of the human beings they already were. I didn't know that my years experimenting in theater would give me a glimpse into the human heart. I didn't know that most people want to know how to be happy or that being a human being is mostly about *being* (and doing is secondary).

For years, I had danced in performances on stages where I felt as though I transcended the limits of my body and my daily life. I became ten feet tall and pure possibility. And now here I was again, showing people a version of that transcendent dance, a version that didn't require the dancer to be graceful or flawless but rather authentic and vulnerable. I was letting all of us dance without self-consciousness and endless overthinking, without the stories we tell about the future that keep us stuck in the past. I was letting all of us dance naked.

• • •

I wasn't the only one affected by that workshop. After we'd completed the last exercise and I was circulating among the audience members chatting and catching up, Mike approached me to touch base about a project for millennials that we had talked about in the week before the conference. While we were talking, he thanked me for the workshop and asked to follow up. Shortly after I returned home from Baltimore, he called.

He didn't mince words. "From the work we did in those sessions, I found I wasn't inhabiting four inches of my height."

"I saw a little bit of that during the workshop," I said with a broad smile. "Congratulations on reaching your full height."

We laughed for a minute before he got serious. "I spent a lot of time thinking about it, you know. I realized that when I go through my everyday life, I slump over and slouch. Then, when I'm speaking publicly or helping someone, I stand up straight. When I'm leading a training session, I feel at my most powerful and authentic."

"Interesting." I thought about it. "So when you help others stand tall, you stand taller yourself."

"Yes. When I have the mic, I feel completely different in my body. Like I'm breathing deeper and taking up more space."

This assessment certainly tallied with what I knew of Mike. I had met him years before at a Social Venture Network conference and had done some one-on-one advisory work with him just a year before in San Diego, supporting him as his business went through a transition. I had seen him speak and knew he was a force to be reckoned with. When he addressed big groups, his passion about sustainable business shone through; he made each audience member feel like he was talking directly to them, yet his voice reached out to everyone. I had seen him fire up artists and business leaders through his social venture work and consultancy. After he stopped speaking, the room crackled with passion and energy. Yet he was never boastful or full of himself.

"Why do you think you hunch over?" I asked him.

"It only happens in my job as CEO and in my private life."

I waited, sensing there was a story there.

Mike went on. "I guess I'm a tall guy, and I don't want people to think I'm towering over them. But when I think about it now, it's a false sense of humility. This is my body, how I was born. I shouldn't have to change that."

"How does your posture play a role in your job as CEO? What do you as a hunched-over CEO look like? What does it mean? How does it feel?"

Mike paused for a long time, and I let the silence extend as he thought. "You know," he finally said, "I guess I do feel hunched over as a CEO. The cofounders left a few months ago and now I'm the only leader up there, the one handling everything. I don't think I've fully stepped into those shoes yet. In my mind, I haven't become a CEO of the company yet. I didn't realize that I was hesitating, but at some level my body did."

I nodded. "That makes a lot of sense. The body knows much more than we give it credit for."

Mike had worked on self-actualization for years, so it was natural for him to turn to coaching to continue that work. Clarity had allowed him to see a block, and gave him the incentive to start working away at the mysterious case of his changing height.

"I think I want to be liked and needed, and it's frustrating because I thought I had worked past all that," he explained. "But I still have that desire for acceptance, so I unconsciously make myself smaller. And it's not just my body. I've been writing down other ways I'm not showing up at my full height. I noticed I'm not making the 'big asks' in business. I'm not pushing for better terms in negotiations or shying away from to making direct requests. Last week, I needed someone to fix a report they had created, but stopped short of asking them to stay late—even though they're the ones who made an error with the report in the first place!"

Mike took a deep breath. "I've been working on myself for years. Where is all this coming from?"

"You're right," I said gently. "You *have* been working on yourself for a long time, and you've done great work, but that doesn't mean it's done. Life is like a spiral. Old stuff can revisit us again from new angles, or new stuff comes up. We can't just 'fix' things and call it done. We're always evolving and growing. Sometimes growing gets a little messy."

A few weeks later I sent Mike an email to see how his resolve to live into his height and power was going. *Are you typing tall today?* I teased.

His answer pinged back on my phone: *Yep, no need for a growth chart for this guy. Take a look at this.*

On my screen was a picture of Mike's business card. Beneath his name and the logo of his company, was his job description: President and CEO.

I read on: *Last week our company worked on job descriptions, and I decided to step fully into my role and embrace what I am to the company now. Thank you so much, Lori. That Clarity exercise and our phone call made such a big impact—much more than I expected.*

I stood up taller then, too, remembering my Actor's Nightmare the night before my Baltimore presentation. Starting work on Clarity was as far as we'd gotten in the workshop, and it cheered me to think Mike had gotten so much out of it. It made me eager to take clients along the entire path of The Clearing.

I saved the picture of Mike's business card on my phone. I wanted to keep it handy, so I could look at it whenever I needed a reminder of how one insight could transform an entire life.

Author's Note

The experience in Baltimore was a testament to and a culmination of years of transformation, commitment, and practice, all of which led to a new level of freedom of expression in my work.

This book is for people who want to make real changes in their businesses and their lives. The work I am inviting you to explore in these pages has had immense positive impact on the bottom line of many companies—but it is also about much more than numbers on a spreadsheet or in a bank account. My clients are often high achievers who are looking for fulfillment in the full range of their lives, who appreciate the value of connecting with people and having a larger vision.

The clients I've worked with who've been the most successful have come to recognize this truth: your most powerful resource is you. Sometimes I work with sustainable businesses or social entrepreneurs and sometimes with more traditional organizations focused on products and profits. But even the most traditional leaders I work with are willing to consider unconventional methods, and in doing so, they can transform their lives and companies into spaces with unlimited potential.

If this sounds like you, welcome.

So if you're ready for the promise of this work, which takes your uniqueness into account and allows you to live to your fullest potential, sit down and breathe deep. We're starting with my narrative so you can see how I achieved my own clarity, completion, creation, and capacity—and so you can see how these principles developed in my life and work. Then I will share a few of my clients' stories to give you insight into how I support others in claiming their power and how you may claim your own.

I invite you to visit my website, http://www.consciousleaders.us/, and join the discussion. Here, you'll learn more about the concepts you read about in this book, and you'll get more exercises and hands-on resources to take you further on the journey. Use the downloads on the site to continue exploring your own talents and actions. If I can be of help, please reach out to me via my website, and I look forward to our paths intersecting.

Here is my invitation to you as you turn the page:

Let's dance.

part 1

claiming my power

Chapter 1   *first steps*

When I think about my first steps on the path that led me to where I am today, I think about my mother and father. They were both so bright, filled to the brim with possibilities. They had graduated from Cornell (my mother summa cum laude), where they were both Mensa members, and had met in the theater department. Dad went on to get an MBA from Harvard, and then worked for General Electric Company on a project developing the nuclear propulsion jet engine. My beautiful, talented, and deeply intelligent mother became a homemaker.

My parents had Amy first, and I grew up looking up to my sister, with her natural talent for dance and her perfect marks. We lived in a split-level house in Schenectady, New York, along tree-lined streets that glowed at night with the bright yellow lights from our neighbors' windows. In those days, Schenectady had a main drag, a shopping district with its looming Woolworths, and the Proctor's Theater block, where older kids would go see films. Most of my world, however, took place in Woodcrest, part of the suburb of Niskayuna. I'd walk under the elm and maple trees that lined Van Antwerp Road, or my mom would drive me by the Mohawk Golf Club, with its deep green grounds. It was the setting for a childhood straight out of a picture book: blue sky, tall trees, warm houses—everything in its place.

I got enrolled in dance classes at age four. My sister had been dancing for a year or two already, and I was desperate to follow in her satin footsteps. In the mirror at home, I squeezed my rotund little torso into a leotard, not aware yet that my body wasn't perfect. I stood teeter-tottering in first position, and it *hurt*. In ballet's first position, you ideally turn your feet out—out, out, out completely until your Achilles tendons are back to back, pressed against each other. The instructor knew that for my young feet such extreme turnout was difficult, and for me even getting halfway there seemed impossible.

I did not have the natural flexibility, especially in the all-important back and hips, that girls who were natural dancers had—girls like my older sister, Amy, who made everything look easy. Nor did I have the endlessly long legs, the pencil-thin arms, or the pregnant foot with a high arch that could become a dagger of perfect toe point.

At home, Amy sat me down on the living room floor with my legs stretched straight out. She had a perfect bun as she sat behind me and pressed her knees into my back, pulling my arms up over my head. My lower back was so weak I could barely sit up straight, and my hamstrings felt as stiff as cinder blocks. Amy tried to help me stretch, but all I remember was pain and her frustration that my body wouldn't do what she thought it should.

"Sit up straighter, Lori," she'd encourage, not unkindly. She'd slide into the stretch herself, showing me how it was done. On her slender body, the stretch seemed to spool out and roll down her dark leotard, but when I tried to follow, the muscles in my thighs jumped and I could feel dampness spreading along the back of my neck as I tried to school my features and body into the right position.

"A little bit higher." Amy inhaled evenly beside me as I worked to keep from suffocating. I wanted to be like Amy—you would too if you lived with a charming firstborn ballerina down the hall. And yet I wanted to be apart from her. I wanted to glide across the mirrored dance studio and have everyone clap for *me*. I pushed my body a little harder.

After ballet classes, Mom would drive us home in the big Chrysler station wagon and Amy and I would race up the walkway, where Duffer greeted us at the door, barking joyfully. Daddy would be sitting in the living room, tie loosened, a glass of amber scotch at his elbow.

"How was 'belly' dancing today, girls?" he'd ask as the two of us crowded in the doorway, our mother right behind us, her cool, perfumed hands on our heads. Daddy would laugh at his usual joke, and Amy and I would race to him. He'd sometimes scoop us up, lifting me so that I could rub his bald head and take in the familiar smell of cigarettes and scotch.

While Daddy was always laughing or looking off in the distance while jangling his keys in his pocket, Mom fascinated me. She was smiling and sweet, but even at that young age I sensed something upsetting under the surface. One evening, when I was about five, I sat and watched her put on her makeup before an evening out; the small powder brush filled in her eyebrows, and the slow drag of lipstick turned her smile a different color. She emerged gorgeous, victorious. Her thick brown hair had soft hues of auburn in it, and her wide-set eyes were carefully made up to look dramatic. With her prominent nose, oval face, and fair, freckled skin, I thought she looked like someone from the movies, and people did often say that she looked like the classic film star Greer Garson. She was wearing a long green dress that made her skin glow. It was cinched in at the waist, like many dresses in the 1960s. She pulled stockings up her legs, bunching the soft fabric up in her hands before smoothing up and up, her reddened lips pushed out into a pout of concentration. The fabric caught the edge of the tiny topaz ring she wore, and a thin tear formed up one side along her left calf, like a scar.

"Goddamn." My mother's breath drew in a quiet hiss. "Dammit," she added after closer inspection. The word cut through my concentrated viewing of the makeup tubes. She rarely raised her voice, but while she pulled the ruined stocking off her foot, I slid from the room.

There was a war with undefined lines that seemed to be simmering somewhere in our house. My mother waged war on her body, dieting and pouring herself into awful nylon girdles with miles of endless fasteners that promised a different silhouette. She squeezed herself into a marriage that in some alternate universe promised companionship and pleasure, but she remained a 750-watt light bulb that almost never turned on.

The requirements for entertaining Dad's business guests were endless, and usually she made the grade. She taught me how to set the table and eat properly with a fork and knife, one hand held awkwardly in my lap. One night, she was rushing around making lasagna, moments before the delegation was to pull into the driveway. The house was spotless, and I had been banished to the top of the stairs. My mother, in a long dress, was carrying the heavy glass tray of food to the dining room when she stumbled. The impossible happened—tomato sauce and cheese and meat spilled out onto the pale dining room carpet. She lost her grip, and the dish flipped completely from her hands and landed face down. She froze. On the stairs, I tensed, wide eyed.

"Damn." She looked down. "Damn, damn, damn, goddamn!" she hissed, just as tires hit the driveway. We made eye contact for a moment across the high-ceiling living room. She crouched and with quick, constricted movement of her arms scooped the avalanche back into the dish. The small topaz ring she always wore sparkled under the dining room lights as she worked.

My palms began to sweat and I backed away. I wanted to slip into my room and pull the bedspread up high to block out the anger of those quietly spoken words. At the same time, a magnetic fascination held me still; what would my mother do next? How would my father react? Mom turned and ran to the kitchen, coming back with a large dish towel. She threw it over the red disaster and put on a bright smile as she swung the front door open to greet the guests.

"Change of plans, gentlemen," she announced coolly, as my father eyed her through narrowed lids. "The lasagna decided it wanted an introduction to my French crème carpet, so we'll be heading to the steakhouse instead."

She laughed uproariously as she tucked her purse under her arm and sauntered out as if this had been the plan all along. The guests laughed, too; who wouldn't? She was a born performer, her wit and charm serving her well in ways she probably never planned. The only person who didn't seem delighted with her was the one she most wanted to impress. Even though Dad covered for her in the moment, I imagined that he tucked that scene into the secret space of his heart that held the long list of all his disappointments, the many ways his marriage, his career, his life hadn't turned out as he'd planned.

Even though there were fissures in our family, there was also love. When I was six, a change came over my mother. Her stomach grew rounder and rounder, and she eventually sat Amy and me down to explain that we would soon have a little brother or sister.

"Doesn't that sound nice?" she asked us.

I wasn't sure what to say. I had seen school friends get excited about having a new baby brother, but I eyed my mother's swollen ankles and excited face with some trepidation at first. What would the new Darley be like?

One morning, my mother was whisked away to the hospital. Amy and I sat in our fuzzy slippers in the living room, waiting for news, our toys spread out before us. Aunt Cora, who was actually my mother's aunt, stayed with us, but she spent much of her time in the kitchen with a cigarette and a cup of coffee. We could hear her voice as she talked on the phone.

Finally, late in the evening, we heard the unmistakable sound of car tires on our driveway. The flash of headlights worked its way around the perimeter of the living room.

"Daddy, Daddy!" we shouted when our father walked in, looking drawn but with a smile on his face.

"How would you girls like a baby brother?" he asked.

We didn't get to meet John until the next day, when Dad drove Mother home from the hospital. When she stepped in through the front door, she was carrying a small, crying bundle.

Leaning over, she let us look at the tiny red face. "Amy, Lori, this is John."

Thrilled, I peered at the small human being that was now part of us. John seemed unimpressed, and he needed a lot of care. I hovered near the edges of his crib and watched with delight as he mumbled, yawned, ate, burped, and was changed into miniscule blue onesies.

With Mother and Dad watching nearby, Amy and I leaned over him, making faces and noises, trying to get those wandering blue eyes to fix on us. After a week, he finally locked eyes on my exaggerated grin and the weird buzzing sound I was making to get his attention. Looking right at me, he giggled out loud and I turned to Mom and Dad.

"Did you see? He laughed!" I was enchanted and looked back at the surprised face and the big loophole mouth.

John became the fun sidekick for Amy and me. With his hurricane cowlick, a little swirl right at the crown, and his giant eyes, he was adorable and would coo after us as we invented new ways to make him laugh or created new games to play with him.

With the new baby, our family was complete. Mom had more to do than ever before, then and in the years that followed. I watched her and adored her as she went about her work. I peeked over her shoulder as she folded white sheets and small sweaters week after week, as she put bandages over my little brother's scrapes and cuts, as she made meal after meal, the apron tucked tight around her girdled waist. In the evenings she was bent over hardcover copies of *Siddhartha* and *Psycho-Cybernetics*, long before they were cool. Sometimes she sat writing in her own journal, the endless cigarettes and heavy ashtray always by her side. One year, she enrolled in the Famous Writer's Course by correspondence, and I became used to seeing her with her papers spread out before her, a Bic ballpoint poised in the air as she gazed out the kitchen window, presumably searching for the right word. She went on to write an article in the *Saturday Evening Post*, and much later would coauthor a book titled *Careers for People Who Love to Travel*, but her dreams of writing never went beyond those two pieces.

Other times, I watched her trying her hand at the occult art of automatic writing. Sitting at the kitchen table with a pen and notebook paper, she would relax and let her hands draw large loops on the page. Occasionally, if she was patient enough, she thought she would receive messages, but they rarely meant anything to her. Words would seem to form out of the scribbles —but were they really words at all, and what could they mean? She didn't do this very often, but she had enough belief behind this strange practice to keep her at it on and off throughout my early childhood, until one day she got a message that seemed to come from her sister. When the word "Marj" appeared to form in the loops and swirls on the page, she dropped the pen and pushed back from the table. Her older sister, Marjorie, had died when they were very young, and Mom never got over the sense that it should have been her. The message frightened her so much that she never attempted automatic writing again.

My mother only occasionally went to church, but in addition to the automatic writing and journaling, she tried yoga and other methods of what we today would call self-actualization. What was she seeking? Happiness, probably—like most of us. She believed there was a mysterious force that connected us all, that the occult somehow proved the existence of this connection, and that the mysterious force could be harnessed for good or ill. She believed in magic and the "good outworking of events." But I think that the closer she came to actually connecting to that mystery, the more uncomfortable she became, whether those truths came from the "other side" or simply from a realization from her heart. Call it positive thinking, a belief in affirmations, prayer—all of these things add up to what I know today is the power of intention. She just didn't realize she was doing it.

She believed that anything was possible. She believed that we could be anything we wanted to be when we grew up. But as time went by, it seemed that she began to believe these things for her children, not herself.

For herself, she seemed to believe in her role as hostess, and the times I saw her shine were during my parents' scotch-fueled cocktail parties. I remember the eagerness on my mother's face—the rapture—when my father swept her into his arms for a foxtrot around the dark wood-paneled library. I don't remember my parents touching at any other time, and when I saw them like that, it was the only time I felt relaxed. They held themselves beautifully against each other, and my mother's smile lit up the room.

They looked as though they were in love, and my mother could safely release her dangerous inner flirt, the facet of her identity that skimmed just below the surface when she played the part of charming hostess. I was so proud of them when they danced. I was proud to have parents that were in love. When they danced was perhaps the only time they were.

They should dance together all the time, thought my six-year-old brain. Dancing was obviously the road to happiness.

Usually, I crouched at the top of the stairs or peered through the slats of the library's double doors to catch a glimpse of the adult wonderland I was forbidden to enter. On those rare occasions I was allowed to join the grown-ups, my dad would let me put my feet on his and would dance me around the room to Dixieland jazz. On my tiptoes on Daddy's feet, I wasn't stiff, unbending Lori, nor was I Lori who didn't read as well as Amy and had to study hard for every test on spelling or fractions or state capitals. I was the charming princess and the star of the show. I'd smell the perfume that the women wore and wish I was wearing a pretty dress. I'd hold on tight, trusting his feet to carry me through the steps, never wanting the music to end.

I tried to keep the music going in my own way. Sometimes, I'd come home from school, fling my plastic satchel on the floor, and flip through my parents' records, frantically looking for intense music that fit my mood—Rachmaninoff, Tchaikovsky, flamenco. I'd pull the slick record from its sleeve and turn on the record player. In the quiet of the house, it made a scratchy noise just before the needle touched down to make its mark. I'd put the music on and whirl and whirl, trying to see how long I could spin, expressing something with my body that I could not say with words. When my feet would not hold me up another minute, I'd collapse into the wingback chair in the living room, the music still swelling all around me.

Of course, in dance class this type of undisciplined whirling was just not allowed. My first dance teacher was, by any criteria imaginable, the most beautiful princess I had ever seen. Miss Danzig wore a pink leotard, gathered at the bust by a matching velvet ribbon, with a black chiffon skirt. Sometimes we younger dancers would call her Miss Sandy. She had jet-black hair styled in the famous 1960s bouffant, and she wore thick black eyeliner. She was in her midtwenties, and I was too young to understand that her hourglass figure was a curse in the dancing world—to me, her full breasts and round butt made her the epitome of womanly allure. I thought she was perfect; I was too young to understand the pressure ballerinas face to be slim, straight lines.

She ran a dance studio out of the basement of her mother's home in the working class part of Schenectady. The concrete walls were painted ballet-slipper pink, with exposed cinder blocks around the edges. It all felt like chiffon to me, as if the walls themselves could bend and stretch, reach for the stars, like I would soon be doing three times a week in class. Pen-and-ink drawings of the five ballet positions alternated with poster-sized black-and-white photographs of the New York City Ballet.

The older Danzig, Miss Sandy's mother, had bright blue eye shadow layered just above her black false eyelashes. Her hands had long, brightly painted fingernails, and her skin persistently remained a dark mahogany, even when snow piled in high drifts outside the studio and the sun only shone anemically through the windows. I'd wave to her—or rather to the freshly teased, frosted head of hair that I would see barely peeking over the top of her reception desk's high ledge—as I made my way downstairs to prepare for class.

Jostling for space in front of the mirrors in the small dressing room, our group of six-year-old aspiring prima ballerinas approached our first test—building the perfect ballet bun. Wielding hairspray, bobby pins, hairnets, and rubber donuts that helped us create lush buns out of wispy hair, our group of eager students tamed our manes. I'd solve my short-hair problem with a hairnet and a pink headband before stretching on my second-skin pink tights, black leotard, and leather ballet slippers. I'd suck in my belly and look in the mirror one final time before moving to the holding bin to wait for class.

Inside the actual studio, Miss Danzig formally greeted us all. I had fallen completely under her spell by the second class. In that mirrored space, we soon learned that Miss Danzig's attention was won by the smoothest hair, the brightest face, and the longest lines a little girl could make with her body. We'd all strive for perfection, using little plastic flower combs and carefully arranged leotards to show our dedication.

The studio was lined with mirrors that had strong wooden barres at the midpoint. They were simple wooden bars, but as with most things in ballet, we used the French words to refer to them, rolling the *r* in words, just like Miss Danzig. We would line up at the barres to stretch and to move through the poses under Miss Danzig's sharp eyes. Moving into the center of the room, we'd slide our feet along the wood floors as we went through practice, working to position ourselves just right on the studio floor as the fluorescent lights shone down on our faces and surrounded us in special pools of ice blue.

"All right everyone, now, *tendu*! Stomachs in, looong line with the leg. Turn out the left foot!" Miss Danzig's voice rang out as we moved into the jump, trying to point our feet as sharply as possible.

"Positions, please."

I probably spent a whole year doing nothing but *pliés* (bending the knees) and *tendus* (extending the leg out so only the toes touched the ground). Then I worked my way up to plié-tendu, eventually starting to *sauté* (jump). Year after year, I poured my body into leotard and tights and leather slippers, learning steps and routines. I worked on standing straighter, pulling in my stomach more, sliding more effortlessly into the positions, pliés, and bends. It was all about perfection.

When I was ten, I auditioned for and was cast in George Balanchine's *A Midsummer Night's Dream*. I had been dancing for years by then, pursuing my dreams of ballet, but being cast to dance at the Saratoga Performing Arts Center was a huge deal. Balanchine was the undisputed father of American ballet. He was the founder of the New York City Ballet, serving as artistic director for over thirty years, and was at the height of his power at the time—a living legend. Balanchine created *Midsummer*, among the first American full-length ballets, and every single ballerina at the summer dance program was dying to be part of it. The first opening night was in early 1962, and by the time I got my chance in 1967, the ballet had run through several successful productions.

I had been cast as a butterfly, which meant I would be on stage with "real" ballerinas from the New York City Ballet. At nine years old, I was now one of "them"—a dream probably held by thousands of little girls.

There were several groups of children in that production, all of us part of Balanchine's vision for the ballet. We attended our first rehearsal with hearts thumping in our chests.

Standing in the wings with the other children in ballet slippers, I watched Balanchine stalk around the stage, talking to the ballerinas in his Russian accent. He spoke fast and gestured large. The "real" ballet dancers did everything he said, as soon as he said it, scrambling into place the way we children did when the ballerinas spoke to us. We might have been in awe of the ballerinas, but they were clearly in awe of Balanchine.

There was a huge ballet company for the elaborate production, and even more people backstage creating the intricate costumes and stage sets. There was also a sizable children's corps de ballet, so I got to meet girls from all sorts of backgrounds who had gathered together to dance. We'd cluster together and stare at the older dancers as they talked and practiced.

After practice and during breaks, I got another glimpse of ballet—one far from the practice room mirrors. The ballerinas, who moved like delicate flowers and fairies in clouds of soft, pale fabric, were completely different offstage. Leaning against the outside of the building, they slouched in their coats and tutus. Hands on their hips, cigarettes between their fingers, shoulders curved over their thin, sunken chests, they gossiped and swore and complained. Their voices carried all the way to where I was slipping into the practice area to warm up.

But even that sharp contrast between the fantasy of the stage and the banality of real life couldn't break the spell I was under. I fell in love with everything the theater could give me—the lights, the smells, the sweat, the street language. It was a secret society that demanded everything you had to give.

Once the curtain went up on opening night of *A Midsummer Night's Dream*, I felt all eyes on me. The expanse of blackness in front of me left me awed, while the stage lights buzzed with electricity that overwhelmed my senses. I couldn't have been more conscious of every movement, of every expression. My actual part was very small. Along with the rest of the tiny ballerinas, I would dance out on stage, "fly" around, and then hold poses for a long time near the principal ballerinas, our colorful costumes trembling. I was a butterfly all right, and I had a whole swarm of them flitting around inside me; but their nervous message told me that all was right with the world. As I would one day help my executive clients understand, nervousness was a sign of taking big steps and big risks—the kinds of steps that lead to the limelight .

I was amazed by the music, which swelled loud on the dim stage, and by the full impact of every element of the performance finally coming together in a way that I hadn't yet seen, not even in dress rehearsals. The lights were perfect, illuminating Oberon in his muscled glory and the head butterfly in all her colorful delicacy. The bright colors of the vines and Oberon's chairs almost glowed, as ethereal as if they were truly from a fairy realm. I had spent months watching Patricia McBride and all the other dancers in leotards, laughing and frowning and dancing. I thought I had seen them in all their moods. But in that moment before the curtains went up, they were transformed.

It was the first time I truly got a glimpse of the magic of performance. Just as the ballerinas had become their characters, I was not just Lori, a middle child with an everyday life running around with her big sister in the backyard. I was also a butterfly, trembling in the breeze in a world where fairies were real.

I had been told that my smile was powerful, so I beamed it out to everyone as an act of love I hoped would never end. What was even more special for me—besides the dancing and the live orchestra, which accompanied our every move—was this feeling of being in the presence of legends. I hoped with all my heart that their mystical powers would rub off on me. Back then, ballerinas seemed like whole other creatures to me, and I never questioned the pecking order that made them famous and me a butterfly in their elegant shadow.

The emotion that is most present for me when I think of that New York stage is love. I felt deeply, deeply connected to everyone in the house. I felt like we—the performers and the audience—were all working together to build something that wasn't there before. When I danced or practiced alone, I might feel a little like a ballerina, but stepping on stage after working with stage set designers, choreographers, and premier dancers, it was clear that the charged, dreamlike atmosphere only happened because all of us somehow connected to create one beautiful, grand thing.

There is one moment—a few seconds, at most—about that performance that stands out above all others. I was surrounded by famous ballerinas, balanced on my toes on a glossy black floor. I danced my steps and stared out at the audience, which spread out before me like a dark sea. From the stage, the audience was mostly shadowy shapes, but sometimes when I let my eyes sweep over the seats, the lights moved just right and I could make out individual faces.

At one point, my eyes rested on a man. I thought he was a businessman because he was wearing a beautiful suit in a deep charcoal, but in reality I had no idea who he was or what he did for a living. For one moment, though, our eyes met and held. I remember thinking I saw a glimpse of green in his eyes, which were wide open, his face filled with awe as he took in the dance. I was aware that he was seeing me, that in some way our performance was affecting him, was changing him.

It was perhaps a tiny moment of foreshadowing; years later, I would routinely face businesspeople from a stage, but not in a butterfly costume. As an executive coach, I used words and my understanding of minds and bodies to get that same reaction—that emotional tempest that presaged a new way of thinking and doing.

It's not just that I learned to perform on a stage as a dancer and later returned to the stage as a coach. No, the connection between dance and coaching is much stronger for me. I realized early on in my coaching career that there's a direct connection between the work of a ballerina—all those hours spent mastering the mind and body to perform incredible feats—and the work of an executive.

It is a connection I learned to explain again and again. Business leaders I worked with sometimes saw their work as largely being focused on the mind. Their heads were filled with ideas, innovations, and contract details. All too often, their bodies were just the well-suited vehicles to get them to the next meeting. I learned to point out that our bodies are much more than that. Just as I had learned in dance that to perform was to transform, I was able to show executives that paying attention to their bodies could help them expand their idea of what was possible.

It became my calling to teach leaders to use their bodies and their minds in the same mindful, disciplined way—to step into new opportunities with the same grace and strength dancers use to defy gravity and float through the air, transformed.

Chapter 2

beyond ballet . . . mental stretches

Ballet was my first love, but by junior high I had started exploring other avenues of creative expression: modern dance, comedic performance, singing. My mother was patient and encouraging with all my passions, driving me tirelessly to lessons and applauding in the audience. Although in many ways my mother lived a small, trapped life, she told me I could be anything. Over time, I came to articulate that disconnect: we all make choices, and I would make different ones than she had. On the nights I performed, I couldn't imagine living my mother's life. When I stood in the bright lights of the stage, the thunder of applause all around me, my small body felt tall. But in the wings, adulthood was waiting.

Just as I was beginning to hit my seventh-grade stride in Schenectady, Dad became part of Telesignal, a subsidiary of Singer. Soon after that, he joined management at Worthington Corporation and we moved to Long Island. Our family was clearly moving up in the world—all our new neighbors had money, and the neighborhood was full of tweedy dads and overtanned yacht-club moms—but I wasn't sure how I felt about it. Schenectady had felt like home; here I didn't know whether I'd be able to fit in.

Dance became my anchor after the move. Right away, Mom found a new studio near our home, and we drove over to check it out. The surrounding scene was pleasant enough. A quaint deli sat next door, and across the street, white sails puffed out in the wind on Huntington Harbor.

But the eighteenth-century house looked like it had been dropped in from a horror movie set. The deep maroon paint was dark in patches and the narrow black roof sagged in the middle. The trim had once been white but now looked dingy and tired. The house was tall and narrow, all peaks and lines, and the creepy effect was heightened by the thinning grass and a small copse of trees around the structure, which just obstructed the view. It reminded me of the mansion in *The Addams Family*; but without the faces of my favorite characters peering from the windows, it was far less charming. I wanted to turn back, and Mom's glance told me she was having the same doubts.

My foot hesitated on one of the steps. *I could turn around and walk back,* I thought, imagining making my way through the January cold to the familiar comfort of the blue Volkswagen hatchback. *I could go home,* I thought, feeling a slight pang at the thought of the new house, with some cardboard boxes still unpacked and its corners unexplored. But just then, I heard it on the breeze: a faint whisper of Chopin waltzes coming from inside the strange house. That was enough to propel me up another step and then another—all the way to a door with flaking paint, paint which fell serenely to the rotting floorboards when we knocked.

What struck me first was the stench of cats kept in captivity. The smell of dander and stale urine made me weak in the knees, assaulting my nose. I glanced at my mother; she hated cats. I saw that she had to square her shoulders and grit her teeth to enter. Her head held high, she kept her face stoic. I fought down my nausea and we walked into the studio.

At the end of a hallway dense with aspiring young ballerinas, all in familiar pink tights and black leotards, sat Betty Orlando. She looked like a three-hundred-pound marshmallow topped with the smiling face of a cherub. Her eyes were a mess of black eyeliner and gloppy mascara. Her lips, barely visible beneath the folds of her fleshy face, were painted with bright pink lipstick. On this freezing day, she wore a thin pink cotton dress with a lacy, button-popping bodice that looked homemade. Her hair was piled up in a bun, upper lip moist with sweat, and her large hands held a tiny tutu: Betty sewing a costume—the first of countless times I would see her doing so.

"Hello," she breathed out with effort when she saw us. Her exhalations made the papers on the desk rattle. "Welcome to the Orlando Ballet Company."

I looked around the derelict room, wondering to myself where the actual ballet classes were held. I had left a studio in Schenectady large enough to accommodate forty dancers to a class, in big rooms with enough space to execute ten *grande jetés* across the floor. I saw no space for such dancing here. Then, through a small doorway, I saw eight or nine dancers crammed into a pre-Revolutionary parlor, all of them intensely focused on a combination of steps.

"Oh, Vinnie, my husband, told them to practice that," Betty told us with some pride as she fixed the shiny gold trim of a headband and handed it back to one of the tiny ballerinas standing across the desk. Vincent Orlando, she told us, was the choreographer of the ballet company and her partner in the company.

"Vinnie's just down the hall," Betty said, pointing. Taking this as an invitation, we walked along the short hallway, where more tiny ballerinas in pink were waiting for their next class. Mom and I veered right, following the general direction where she had pointed, and peered past the dust swirling everywhere. We could hear Stravinsky's *The Firebird* coming from a record player and could see a dressing room where an ancient, unused piano leaned against a wall.

Sometimes, you can turn a corner, round a bend, or walk through a door and find your entire world changed. That was about to happen to me.

We entered a small room, maybe eighteen by twenty feet, with wooden floors that were at least a hundred years old. A young man accompanied one of the most perfect dancers I'd ever seen in a duet, and standing against the wall watching them was Vinnie, who would change the very way I thought. The beautiful dark-eyed girl looked a few years older than me and danced as though she were part of the music. She had everything that a ballerina should have—the long, strong legs; the thin, sculpted arms; the distinct vertebrae; the effortless flexibility. After each lead, she landed with feather softness. On a stage, her movement would have looked and felt weightless, but the floors were so old in that studio that I could feel them buckle. I sat down opposite the dance to watch.

I didn't even glance at my mom, but some soul cry in me spoke out: "I want to dance here because this is what this man produces." In that moment, I didn't even register the chaos around me. No number of hidden cats or rickety floors could keep me away.

Betty's husband, Vinnie, was short, with slick dark hair curling under his earlobes. That perfect ballerina, I later learned, was Anita Seigel, one of Vinnie's favorite dancers. Fifteen at the time, she had the ideal legs and feet that I had only seen at the New York City Ballet or in pictures. She had dark skin and dark, long, thick hair that effortlessly stayed in a neat bun. In the two of them, I saw something I wanted to work toward. The next few years of my future were decided right then.

Two days later, I was enrolled in my first class in that tiny, smelly studio. I never saw, only smelled, the mysterious menagerie Betty kept in an undisclosed corner of the labyrinthine house. The amount of cat food consumed on those premises was unknowable, but one year the company used empty cans to construct a huge Aztec-style sun, a set piece for one of Vincent's Haitian-style ballets. Easily five hundred cans were used to build that sun— no doubt a small dent in the studio felines' food consumption.

I had studied there for less than a year when I was invited to be an official member of the Orlando Ballet Company, which was a small group of preprofessional teenage girls. This was also the place where I would begin my spiritual journey. Here, I would discover the power of thought and how it could be applied to the practical realities of life. I would learn not only that I could create my own reality but the steps to actually do it.

Vincent didn't just teach ballet and choreograph masterpieces. He was an avid student of metaphysics, and introduced us to the teachings of Seth. Years before Abraham Hicks, Seth was a disembodied personality channeled through Jane Roberts of Elmira, New York. Roberts published *The Seth Material* in 1970, claiming the book was dictated to her by the being named Seth. At the time, the book was making rounds as one of the most influential texts on metaphysics. Years later, I would work with clients who asked me about the Law of Attraction and *The Secret*. Before all those books, back in 1970, there was Seth.

I first saw *The Seth Material* casually placed on one of the side tables in the studio. I was toweling myself off after a strenuous practice and reached out to take a look as I caught my breath.

"What's this?" I asked another one of the dancers.

Chris was warming up to rehearse his duet with Anita. He glanced at the title and laughed. "That's something you're going to be hearing a lot about. Vinnie talks about it with the members of the company."

The Seth Material, Seth Speaks, and *The Nature of Personal Reality* became required reading for anyone who wanted to dance with the Orlando Ballet Company. In the 1970s, many people were still seeking their truth and pursuing the stoned-out epiphanies of the decade before. A dose of metaphysics with my *balancé* didn't seem that unusual. I listened to Vinnie talk about it and by the time I was sixteen I was diving into the material on my own and was soon completely absorbed.

The Nature of Personal Reality was a type of quantum physics primer. It explained, in simple terms, the nature of the quarks —the subatomic particles considered to be the building blocks of all matter—and how human thoughts influence quarks to create form. The way we think, in other words, can affect the physical reality around us. And because we have control over our thoughts, we have control over our reality. I devoured these concepts and immediately began to apply them to my teenage body. With each thought I attempted to transcend my DNA and shape-shift into the image of the "perfect ballerina." I also began to recognize how I could influence my own moods and bring my best to each moment. Daily I sat in a floral chair in my sister's bedroom while she was out and chanted, "I am tall, thin, and beautiful." Before performing, I would tell myself that the audience loved me and try to fill myself with confidence. During ballet class, I spent each exercise chanting something similar in time with the music.

To both my mother's and Seth's credit, I was encouraged at an early age to believe that I could shape my body and spirit. My mother read *The Seth Material* at the same time I did, and we spent hours discussing our love for these new ideas.

Flopped on my bed, I'd tell my mom about another Seth quote that Vinnie had shared: "If you want to know what you think of yourself, then ask yourself what you think of others and you will find the answer!"

Mom laughed and fixed her hair. "I think that man at the gas station was lovely. Does that mean I'm lovely?"

We both laughed, but then Mom got a faraway look. "It's a nice thought. That if we're kind to others, they see the kindness in us, and if we see others as good, our own goodness glows a little brighter."

I wasn't sure whether kindness glowed in me, but I was aware that the Seth material was changing the way I danced.

While I never grew taller than five foot four, my new way of thinking did have an impact on how I perceived myself and, subsequently, how I moved my body. Moving "as if" I had long legs translated into a more energized stretch in elongating my line. Considering the stiff and inflexible body I was given as a child, my progress was slow, but steady. Each time Vinnie told me "excellent," or I landed a little softer than before, I felt a spark of pride and attributed it to the work I was doing with my mind as well as with my body.

I didn't know it yet, but that work would be the foundation of my work as an adult. Learning the power of my choices and my inner dialogue to change the way I danced left a lasting impression.

One day I was sitting in the studio, waiting in between classes and chatting with the other girls. As always, Betty was sewing some pink, frothy material and some of us dancers were stretching. Vinnie was sitting back and reading to us all from *The Nature of Personal Reality*: "The private experience that you perceive forms your world, period. But which world do you inhabit? For if you altered your beliefs and therefore your private sensations of reality, then that world, seemingly the only one, would also change. You do go through transformations of beliefs all the time, and your perception of the world is different. You seem to be, no longer, the person that you were. You are quite correct—you are not the person that you were, and your world has changed and not just symbolically."

His voice was soothing and helped distract from the smells of the house. That day, after we had finished the adagio and allegro work in the studio,

Vinnie sat back down in the corner, lit the cigarette dangling from his mouth, and quoted the books some more:

"You must watch the pictures that you paint with your imagination," he intoned, looking at each of us in turn.

His words resonated with me in a way I couldn't quite articulate then. I massaged some feeling back into my leg and wondered about that notion. What pictures was Vinnie talking about? Was he referring to my memories—snapshots of beloved faces or exciting moments? Or did he mean the pictures of things that weren't real, at least not yet, like the image I saw when I dreamed of executing the perfect *balancé*? A few of the other dancers sat around, half listening as they tried to calm their breathing.

Unfazed, Vinnie continued with his favorite quotes: "When your ideas about yourself change, so does your experience. You get what you concentrate upon. There is no other main rule." Across from me, I caught the eye of another dancer, who was listening as eagerly as I was. We smiled, both of us part of a weird close-knit family.

That day and many other days, I walked away not only with aching muscles from hours of practice, but also a mind buzzing with ideas and questions. My body was learning to dance, and my mind was acting as the greenhouse for ideas that would serve me throughout my personal and professional life. I was learning about the power of my body, not just to create dance and to defy gravity, but to help me get in touch with emotions and change the emotional states of audiences. At the same time, I was learning that my internal dialogues could influence what was possible for me.

The freedom I felt with the Orlandos changed the way I approached performance; I wasn't dancing just to perform or to get attention but to connect with others so they could discover their deepest passions and most authentic self-expression. I believed that dance had the power to transform everyone who joined in the experience—dancer and audience could both understand wisdom that could be conveyed only by the mind and body working in concert. When I was on stage, I felt as though I were not just dancing but moving beyond the physical. I was young and starting to feel that I could really do and be anything I wanted.

Vinnie's metaphysical explorations resonated with a lot of us at the Orlandos' studio, but that didn't mean some of my peers weren't also investigating other methods of succeeding in dance. The pressure to be both slim and strong meant that many young dancers went far beyond chanting mantras about their size. Attempting to override the genetics that put the Balanchine body out of reach for all except the very few, they'd skip meals or slip laxatives in their bags; and it wasn't uncommon to walk into the studio bathroom to hear someone heaving in the far stall. Of course, I often wished for Anita's perfect looks and even flirted with what today would be considered dangerous eating habits, but I never fell down that rabbit hole. Part of it was the Seth material, but part of it was a burning desire to continue exploring how I could move beyond the limits of height and shape and size. I was fascinated that my body, with all its flaws, could make me feel so amazing when I danced.

• • •

So much of that formative time was spent learning to express my deepest, innermost self to an audience of onlookers. There were the boundaries of me, demarcated by my shoes or the hem of a gauzy costume, but there was something more, beyond my legs and arms and even my mind, that desperately wanted to be seen.

I became aware of this when my baby brother once asked, "Why do you dance?"

I looked at him, the little boy always watching his sisters race off to dance class, and wondered how to explain that when I danced, I was more than the sum of my bodily parts and more than a daughter, sister, and student. Dance let me express something in movement that I couldn't articulate in language. Dance was becoming a spiritual practice for me, and eventually a professional one as well.

In the end, I didn't tell him all of that. I scooped up his little body and danced him through the living room, asking, "Isn't this fun?" until he giggled.

Here's what I never told him: In my everyday life, I wanted to be perfect for others, but it was different on stage. In front of an audience, if you try too hard to please, you "lose your feet"—dancers' terminology for fumbling on stage. It took me years to discover how not to lose my feet. While performing meant knowing the steps and getting physically ready, stepping into a costume and assuming a part, finding my feet started with my mind. It was the silent spark I found with the audience, communication at its most powerful, preverbal state. It wasn't about trying to be perfect for them but about trying to *connect* with them. I think my brother saw, and others see, dance as a natural talent and something that happens in the body. But I had learned it all starts in what you tell yourself, and in the possibilities you create with your internal narrative.

I learned this almost by accident, in part by listening to my dance teachers' advice and in part by noticing the differences I felt while performing when I thought in different ways. When I thought about the audience and what they meant to me, I connected with them more deeply and didn't have to worry about losing my feet. I told myself that everybody loved me, that they loved to watch me perform, and I let that feeling circulate in my being. This was not an exercise in ego; it was about making the performance about a specific feeling—a connection—rather than a sequence of steps. When I shifted how I thought and put love and confidence into my mind while dancing, the way I interacted with the audience changed. I danced better. I was more relaxed. Eventually, approaching my performances with this mindset became a way of being in service to the audience.

I didn't know it then, but this was the basis of what I would teach business leaders years later. Being a coach is also a type of performance, and in that context, building rapport with the audience is even more important. To make an impact and to reach people, you need to be able to connect, even more so than as a dancer. In my work today, I need to think beyond the performance—beyond the notes printed on cue cards—and to the *purpose* of what I'm doing. Each time, before I start coaching, I think about what I am to my clients and try to circulate love toward them. I commit to being a resource, and support them as they re-source themselves. At the same time, I become a source of support.

Sometimes, people ask me a variation of the question my brother asked all those years ago: What does dancing have to do with executive coaching? One thing I learned early on in my coaching career is that the skills professional ballerinas and modern dancers have are the skills executives often desperately need to learn.

I often wish I could zap CEOs and entrepreneurs to an afternoon at Miss Danzig's studio. They could learn a lot from that petite woman about playfulness, creativity, and their bodies. Business leaders, for example, need discipline in order to pursue their goals, and few arenas teach discipline as well as ballet. Professional ballerinas have some of the hardest lives on the planet, watching what they eat, rising at 4:30 or earlier, and pushing their bodies to the very limit and beyond.

It's not just discipline, though. Ballet dancers need to be aware of their bodies at all times, to tap into everything the body does. Some CEOs I have worked with tend to ignore their bodies, even though the body provides vital clues. When a ballet dancer feels tension in an ankle during a jump, they know that means something. When a business leader feels tension in their stomach during a contract negotiation, they too should be able to recognize it and know that it means something—but all too often, these feelings get waived off.

Dancers also understand how small changes make a big difference. The same steps for two different ballerinas look completely different. A fraction of an inch when dancing can mean a perfectly executed jump or a serious injury. Executives sometimes don't realize that their tiny decisions—standing taller in a meeting, shifting weight from one foot to the other, clenching a fist under the desk where no one can see it—can have direct impacts on how they interact with others and how they are able to step into opportunities.

Paying attention to the body can help create a whole new level of awareness for anyone in business. It's what I've been teaching for years.

Even as a child, I started to develop the idea that we are all here by agreement and that we are somehow inexplicably connected. That the way we experience our lives is mostly of our own projection and reflection. Sure, we experience events and circumstances seemingly outside our control. But the stories we tell ourselves about those experiences—and the way we respond to them—are our own creation. And the story I came to tell myself about my art was this: I wasn't just dancing for an audience; we had come together to create something bigger.

I gave the audience dance, but I also demanded attention. It was not about upstaging other people, but more about the intensity of my commitment to do this work in front of these people.

"Look at me!" my soul cried. But also, "Look at me being of service to you. Look at me be this extraordinary gift, and know that you are, too."

It was a message that not everyone absorbed. In the 1990s and beyond, I would work with business founders and leaders who had never learned this dance between themselves and their "audience"—clients and employees. They experienced their relationship as transactional, rather than transformational. They told themselves stories about why they were underperforming or burned out or unhappy. They were still stuck in the self-perpetuating trigger responses of their bodies, and in their reactions to events. I would invite them to a place where they could be more conscious about what they told themselves and how they interacted with others. When they did that, amazing things happened. Companies grew and leaders were able to enjoy their calling.

When I see clients tap into this full expression of their ability, there's a magnetic force to their words and actions, a pull that draws in followers, collaborators, admirers. In more recent years, I've had the feeling many times as a coach and speaker; but it was as a young girl that I got my first taste of what it was like to harness my own power. Here is the scene: I stand in front of an audience at the Orlandos' studio, a crowd of fellow dancers sitting cross legged on the floor, Vinnie leaning against the fireplace in one of those parlors, everyone watching. In an instant, my moves are more than the culmination of dance steps. Each time my feet hit the floorboards, the floors of that old building buckle and dust motes dance in the air. Yet each time I land and leap, each time I twirl, I am an endless spiral of potential. I am no longer a girl, no longer a beginning dancer: I am growing into my skin, into myself. As I complete the final turn, my audience begins to clap and cheer. My heart is beating fast and I am fully in the moment, fully in command of all I have the power to be.

Chapter 3

a dance of friendship

By the time I graduated high school, I had been with the Orlando Ballet Company for five years. I had danced in countless local performances and earned the praise and respect of my teachers and peers. The previous fall, I'd applied to Northwestern on a whim and eventually got a fat envelope in the mail. I'd also gotten into Cornell, my parents' alma mater, but decided I wanted to forge my own path, so I headed off to the Midwest to major in theater.

There, I'd refine my acting and singing skills, and I'd certainly dance. But I wasn't going off to join a "big" dance company or perform in a defining role. I was grateful for all that the Orlandos and my other dance teachers had taught me and for the many opportunities my parents had been able to give me. And I wasn't blind to the fact that I did have talent as a dancer. I also knew, however, that I would simply never be a ballerina. Even at an idealistic eighteen, I knew how cutthroat that world was, how few people succeeded. No matter how much talent I had, I'd be competing against dancers who not only had talent but had also been born with the right legs, the right feet, the right bones. As for modern dance, at the time I simply didn't know enough about it to envision a path to professional success in that arena.

And then there was the simple fact that I was scared. Like so many teenagers, my life had always followed a clearly prescribed course, and the logical next step was college. Pursuing a life as a professional dancer would have meant diverging from that norm and putting my whole heart into dance. At that age, I just wasn't ready to commit to my passion—to myself.

So I figured I would step out of the dancing world with a bang. My cousin Mark Damisch invited me to join him behind the Iron Curtain. Mark was a concert pianist and Northwestern student. His idea was to create a cross-cultural dialogue through a piano concert tour, and he asked whether I could dance to some of the music.

In 1975, the Cold War was positively frosty. News reports about the fall of Saigon and the end of the Vietnam War that April were interspersed with reports about the Khmer Rouge taking power in Cambodia. The US and Soviet space programs took part in a joint flight and even shook hands in space, but on the ground there was still plenty of mistrust. The fall of the Soviet Union and thawing relations between West and East were still many long years away.

Despite all that, I told Mark I'd go. On June 16th, 1975, Mark and I boarded TWA flight 707 and flew over the Atlantic, landing in Heidelberg. It was both greener and more crowded than I had expected. Houses from centuries past crowded together on narrow streets, but green hills rolled beyond all that architecture. Mark and I walked along the banks of the river Neckar and crossed the old stone bridge to get a closer look at the water. From Heidelberg, we explored other German cities, including Bonn and Frankfurt.

It wasn't until we got to Berlin, though, that our real adventure began. In the other cities we visited, we were free to look around and I still felt safe. There were the usual tourist stops—museums, cathedrals—that I expected from my first real trip to Europe. It was crossing into Eastern Europe that I was worried about.

We arrived in West Berlin. That part of the city looked much like the other German cities we'd visited, but I knew that was about to change. We went to Checkpoint Charlie, the infamous crossing point in the wall that divided the city. There, so many East Germans had made insane attempts at passing through this physical representation of the Iron Curtain, hiding in compartments beneath trucks or trying to scale its impenetrable walls. The checkpoint consisted of a small white guardhouse with a jutting roof. We looked at the stark black-and-white sign in front of the checkpoint and read the chilling words "You Are Leaving the American Sector" as we handed our papers to the stone-faced official behind the window. Then we proceeded toward "no man's land." Guards surrounded us. Their hats shielded their eyes, as if to draw attention away from their faces and to the rifles slung over their backs.

We were going in, not trying to get out, which was unusual in and of itself; most of the guards were facing east, focused on catching anyone trying to make a bid for freedom. As we progressed eastward, I felt the miraculous protections of being a US citizen fade, step by step by step.

All of a sudden, I heard a loud popping, a metal-on-concrete sound. I froze as all the guards swung their guns in one motion, and I found myself looking into the barrels of several weapons. No one said anything, and tension danced across my nerve endings.

Not daring to move a muscle, I glanced at Mark out of the corner of my eye. He was sheepishly looking at something on the ground. I followed his gaze to spot a strangely familiar white, blue, and orange striped can. A can of Sure deodorant had fallen from Mark's overstuffed backpack.

I couldn't help the nervous laugh that escaped me, and beside me, Mark tittered, too. Pretty soon, everyone was laughing—even the guards. I didn't mind that the guards were laughing at us. After all, they say there are no accents in laughter, and it was better than being taken by Stasi agents and thrown into an East Berlin prison. In that moment, the divisions between us melted away; we were all just human beings laughing at the nearly fatal packing of a clumsy American teenager.

Red faced, Mark put the can of deodorant back in his pack, and we continued our walk through the checkpoint. I felt like I had walked into a black-and-white movie reel. Everything was gray, and there were no new buildings. The billboards and bus stop advertisements disappeared. It was as though time had stopped here after 1945. Brick buildings that faced the Wall were still crumbling from the bombs dropped in World War II. No effort had been made to cover up the bullet holes from battles thirty years before.

We made our way to Dresden on the old-fashioned trains that ran east. Once in the German city, we stayed in a youth hostel and argued well into the night with the hostess and her college-aged son about the definition of free speech.

"Free speech should be the basis of any society," Mark told them confidently, his dark hair and eyes glinting under the lights.

In his thick German accent, Jurgen, the hostess's son, explained to us with that unflappable Soviet-era logic that "Ve haf free speech. Da government tells us vat books ve can rrread and ve can fffreely choose vich of dos books ve vant to read. Zat is all da free speech ve need!"

There was no convincing him otherwise. No matter how loudly we made our arguments about freedom, Jurgen and his mother felt they had a wealth of freedoms bestowed upon them by their government. But as we sat on the hostel's lumpy sofas and talked late into the night, we were at least able to laugh about it.

The next day, we were yawning as we caught our train. Sitting in a rail-car, about to pull out of a train station in Dresden and headed for Warsaw, I stared out the window at a landscape of endless gray buildings. I had a bottle of cheap red wine, a few sausages made of some kind of mystery meat. Mark was next to me, and the two of us were anxious beyond belief, excited and a little scared about the next stage of our journey.

Beside me, Mark was absently tapping his fingers on the armrest, as though playing a piano. The train started to wheeze and pant like a large iron beast, getting warmed up for the journey ahead, and I braced myself for the inevitable lurch forward. The announcement system came on suddenly, and Mark's hands stilled as the voice boomed out over the train station speakers: "Achtung! Achtung!"

Again on the loudspeaker—"Achtung! Herr Damisch! Herr Damisch . . . !" I glanced at Mark. I didn't understand the rest of the announcement, but there was a sense of urgency, and I understood that Mark was being told to get off the train just as it was about to leave the station.

My heart rate sped up. I didn't know any Russian, Polish, or German, and I was relying on Mark's grasp of those languages to help me understand the world around me. The loudspeakers crackled again, telling my cousin—my lifeline to safety and sanity—to GET OFF THE TRAIN. NOW.

Mark raced to the front of the train and hopped off the platform while I gripped the fabric armrests with all my might. The train was pulling out in minutes. My head was spinning. Would he be back? Should I get off the train, too? Or should I go on to Poland without him? I glanced at my wristwatch. One minute to departure. The train expelled another big pant of steam and a shrill whistle. I started to gather my duffel and sweater.

Just as I was ready to leap off the train, my heart about to pop out of my chest, Mark jumped back on and collapsed on the seat next to me, breathless.

It turned out that Jurgen and his friends from the youth hostel just wanted us to stick our heads out of the train at the next stop. They wanted to say goodbye but had missed seeing us off. *Well,* I thought, *East Germany may not have free speech, but the officials are flexible enough when it comes to delivering personal messages.* I willed myself to calm down, and by the time we got to the next stop, I was able to wave and smile along with Mark at Jurgen and his friends, who were standing at the platform and waving with enormous enthusiasm in a crowd of dour-faced travelers.

As the train chugged east, my chest was light despite the increasingly barren landscape outside. Mark and I had already made a connection with people here. I started to believe that when a person takes time to have a conversation with someone he or she disagrees with, we are one step closer to fulfilling our human destiny. Every time one person suspends her own point of view long enough to listen to someone else's without judgment, then we are one step closer to peace. My worldview would continue to expand every day of that Iron Curtain tour, but even by day three I was beginning to recognize the power one person can wield when she acts with clarity, intention, and consciousness.

We traveled through Poland as well as Germany. We performed in almost every city we stopped at for audiences of every demographic—students, gray-haired grandmothers, civic leaders, and the merely curious. A West German daily newspaper described me as a "Terpsichorean, barefooted talent," and an audience of students in Kiev gave us a standing ovation. When I glanced up at the end of every dance, I'd see faces smiling in wonder, hands clapping in that familiar gesture performers everywhere crave. At home, I would look up "Terpsichorean," hoping it was something complimentary—and it was: it referred to the muse of dancing and choral song.

Despite the general culture shock, our trip for the most part ran smoothly—until we reached Moscow. There we checked into the Metropol, an elaborate pre-Revolution building that had stood unchanged since the 1800s and would look much the same twenty years after our visit. One of the staff watched us check into our room and gave us a piece of advice. "Do not brush your teeth with tap water. Use vodka. Much safer."

We felt the chill of the Cold War on more than one occasion during our stay. At one point, we were told that a reporter wanted to interview us. Mark glanced at me, and after a moment's hesitation, I shrugged an assent. Why not?

The reporter turned out to be an unsmiling man with a stiff walk and iron-gray hair that matched the surrounding landscape. He met us in the lobby of the hotel and barked questions at us, writing down our answers in a notebook.

"You here for performance?" he demanded.

We nodded.

"What you see here in Russia?"

"The hotels are lovely," I told him. "The architecture is beautiful, and there's so much history."

"This hotel? From 1912," he grunted at us, before diving back into his notebook.

He fixed his eyes on us again, watching our every move. "What you tell friends about riding carriage in Moscow?"

We hadn't been in a carriage in Moscow, so we were not sure how to answer that, or a few of the other questions he barked at us. Finally he told us that his article would come out in a year, "maybe more"; nodded to us; and marched off in his stiff walk.

Back in the hotel room, Mark and I speculated whether we had just had a visit from the local secret service. Mark laughed about it, saying we had "survived the KGB," but my smile felt a little forced. As I rinsed out my glass to brush my teeth, careful not to let any water linger, I hoped neither of us would get arrested.

The performance at the House of Friendship Moscow was daunting. Though we were told that our small audience of fifteen comprised artists, politicians, and engineers, we found out months later that many were actually KGB, the Soviet secret service. I had been feeling sick that morning, so I wobbled as I walked into the House of Friendship. We were led to a room where a few of the younger students in the audience moved aside some of the chairs to create a dance space.

The secretary of the House of Friendship walked up to us as the chairs were being arranged and the audience was milling around. An interpreter—a tall, thin woman with dark hair and red lipstick—stood by his side. Mark and I looked at the secretary and he smiled wide, brushing down his dark suit. He said something loudly in Russian and looked expectantly at the interpreter, who look at us and spoke.

"Welcome to the House of Friendship. We are very happy and honored to have you dancing with us."

As soon as she stopped speaking, the secretary shook hands with Mark and gallantly kissed the back of my hand before speaking again. "We will bring both our countries closer together. With beautiful dance," the stylish woman interpreted as the secretary beamed at us.

It was soon time for the performance. I danced bare-legged to the strains of American composer Norman Dello Jollio, my stretchy modern dance skirt whirling around me as I swished and turned in angular movements. Mark played and I danced with all the passion I could before this audience, who were familiar with the highest standards of Soviet ballerinas.

The music stopped, and Mark and I looked out at the tiny audience in their folding seats. There was a beat of silence followed by applause. Some of the older people clapped politely, if coolly, but the younger people were more effusive in their praise. One younger man, his smile wide, kept clapping and clapping until I thought his palms must have stung.

While the applause was still fading, an official in a dark suit came up to the stage and the audience fell silent again. In hesitant English, he spoke to the room. "We are proud to welcome American dancers to House of Friendship."

He turned to Mark. "For you," he intoned, handing Mark two square items. "About the Bolshoi. Soviet ballet. For your dance. For your cultural understanding."

I glanced at the items Mark held. Two books—one on Russian culture and society and a rare volume about the Bolshoi ballet.

The official took a bouquet of flowers from an assistant's waiting hands and presented them to me with a flourish. "For you," he said as I took hold of the stems.

After our return to the States, Mark discovered that the FBI had files on us. In fact, the State Department interviewed him three times, I suppose to make absolutely certain we hadn't leaked state secrets. I suppose it didn't occur to them that two seventeen-year-old students *had* no state secrets.

Years later Mark told me, "When the FBI came to see me, they mistakenly recorded my major as political science. No wonder we can't find weapons of mass destruction."

After Moscow, we went to Budapest and then returned to the West through Vienna. It was like waking up in a Technicolor dream. After weeks of a black-and-white existence, the sight of neon signs and billboard advertisements was a visual and spiritual recovery. It did my soul good to see color and familiar slogans for Coke and other products. It was just that little bit more like home.

We were scheduled to travel to Spain, but the country was marching toward democracy and there were labor strikes and protests at the universities. Some of the country was under martial rule. We sat in our hotel room in Vienna, watching television and letting the exhaustion sink into our bones. We decided to trim our adventure back to eight weeks instead of our projected ten.

"Home," I exclaimed in bliss. I was looking forward to seeing my parents, friends—even the boyfriend who hadn't written to me the entire time we had been away even though we had arranged for mail to be delivered at several general post drops.

On one of our last days in Europe, I retreated under a gazebo in a park to read my mail. I recognized my father's controlled penmanship, and as I opened the envelope, my heart raced with worry. Had something happened? I had never received a letter from my father. What was he going to tell me?

I was in for a complete and happy surprise. My father had used whatever influence and connections he had in New York to obtain a 35-millimeter film version of an episode of *The Harry Reasoner Report*, the CBS precursor to *60 Minutes*. This particular episode was filmed earlier in 1975 at the Orlando Ballet Company. In my first network appearance, I was rehearsing in the familiar black leotard and pink tights in Huntington Harbor.

It was the most eloquent expression of my father's love I had ever experienced. Moments before, I had been feeling alone in the universe; I was miles away from everything I had ever known, and my head swam with scenes of fear, the image of Checkpoint Charlie and the guns of the guards clear in my mind, even weeks later. Yet, thanks to my father, I was able to turn my mind from those images to the beauty and human connection that had been just as prominent during my travels. And even more poignantly, my father had reminded me of the constancy of his love. Recognition, achievement, and success seemed possible in the future that stretched out so mysteriously before me.

The truth was that at that point, I felt deeply uncertain about what lay ahead. The constants that had anchored my life thus far were changing: My family was in the process of moving to Dallas, so the now-familiar house in Long Island was no longer a haven. My sister had gotten married in the woods of Long Pond in Massachusetts the summer before I started my freshman year at Northwestern University in Evanston, Illinois, so she had her own family and concerns. I was moving away from the Orlandos, and for the first time since I was a small child I wouldn't be spending all my free time heading to a dance studio; I'd be heading to college classes, instead.

No matter what the future held, however, I flew back to the United States with a new awareness and understanding. Fending for myself during my trip behind the Curtain proved to me that I could be my own person, and staying relatively calm when faced with both guns and foreign audiences showed that the Seth training was not in vain; I was able to make choices about how I thought, even when I was afraid or in unfamiliar environments. Choosing to focus on what I could read rather than all the unfamiliar words around me, or choosing to laugh rather than cower in fright when Mark dropped a deodorant can and we found ourselves looking into barrels of guns—these were turning points for me. I learned I could consciously choose my responses, even in such moments of fear and uncertainty. I also learned that dancing for overseas audiences was just as exhilarating as dancing for American ones; the magic was universal.

Chapter 4

running from my voice

I started college in 1975 and spent my freshman year living in the Residential College of Philosophy and Religion. Unlike traditional dormitories, the residential colleges let students from similar disciplines share the same housing. I was a theater major, but I loved bantering about the meaning of life or Ram Dass with the students in my residential college. At the same time, there was always that certain tension that cut through every conversation I had: Were the other students smarter than I was? Better read? It was as though I put pressure on myself to feel pressure. I was telling myself stories, and they were shaping who I was and how I was reacting.

That fall, walking through the ornate ironwork arch at Sheridan Road and Chicago Avenue, the entrance to the university, I watched my fellow students. They seemed much more confident and focused than I felt. They moved with purpose, flirted, and laughed with each other, creating immediate circles of friends, and I wasn't sure I fit in with any of the varied clusters of kids striding across the lawns or sprawled under the trees.

I was homesick, trying to make do in an unfamiliar place, and the weather wasn't helping. I wasn't used to the frigid winters, the vicious winds off the Great Lakes. As the days grew shorter, I would huddle in my coat and walk home in the dark. Temperatures dipped to the teens, and some days they crawled into the single digits. I learned about wind chills, which made the already-cold temperatures feel even colder. On some days, the wind made it feel like minus seventy. Miss Sandy, Vinnie, and all those nights spent in front of audiences in New York seemed a world away. Rather than falling into the welcoming embrace of a ballet studio, I made my way through the foreign curriculum of my freshman acting classes. I threw myself into the work and took acting seriously, discovering in the process that there were parallels between dance and drama. The familiar stage was still there, the audience, the costumes, and the movement of the body. I became serious about mastering the steps in this new field.

The third floor at my residential college was coed. I had made sure to live in a coed dorm, but I discovered the idea was much better in theory than in reality. In high school, I'd had plenty of interactions with boys, but the boys from my classes hadn't lived down the hall from me, where they could give me sly grins on the days I got my timing right and they shuffled across the halls in towels on their way to the shower. On the one hand, I had gained new confidence from my summer abroad, and I flirted outrageously, reveling in my ability to make anyone laugh. But as I chatted and giggled, a small part of me stood apart, uncertain and wary. Yes, I could start a conversation with the cute boy down the hall, but I was still shy. That part of me hadn't changed, and while I might tease a prospect about how funny, smart, and sexy he'd have to be to get me, I was still fundamentally insecure.

I flirted like my life depended on it; maybe it did. During my freshman year I engaged in habitual mating rituals in search of myself and my spirituality. Sometimes I acted like the girl who only knew how to put the pedal to the metal. Brakes—what brakes? Boundaries? Weren't those imaginary lines drawn on maps between countries? Not something I had much experience with. If I drew lines in relationships, the boys might not like me. At the time, I couldn't articulate the motive behind my intense desire to please, but at its core, that drive was fueled by my tacit assumption that others' needs were more important than my own.

The iconic sign of the theater is two masks, one crying and one laughing. They represent Thalia and Melpomene, the muses of comedy and tragedy. Seemingly opposites, they are two parts of a complete whole. Such opposites existed in me. I was both shy and outgoing, both confident and unsure, afraid of rejection. Both sides existed in me in their entirety.

Maybe because theater embodied these dichotomies, I loved acting and threw myself into the challenge of it. How could I dive into a character's perception of reality without first examining the forces that influenced the playwright's interpretation of their personality? Just as I would one day ask executive clients to dive deep to find what brought them to a particular moment in time, as an actor I had to excavate until I was able to create a character. Acting was about feeling and sensing the way a character would interact—and perhaps allow the audience to interact—with their perception, their approach and feelings about the world around them. My body and voice became a vessel that allowed for that intuitive and analytical process to unfold.

In my Voice for Performance class, final exams were a monologue. I spent weeks preparing mine—from *Romeo and Juliet*—for our professor, Gail, and the rest of the class. I poured my heart into the scene, in which Juliet receives the poison that she will take on that fateful night, knowing she will wake up in the family crypt.

In the first moments of the performance, I felt a little unsteady—anxious about the despair I'd have to display for my peers. But by the time I reached the final lines, I'd forgotten that anyone was watching, forgotten that anything outside the words still existed.

"Come, vial."

When I'd rehearsed, I'd considered playing Juliet as a scared teenager, squeamish about the bodies she'd see in the crypt, but now I found that I was embodying grief, resolution, and fear, and also courage. My voice made it clear: This character was no longer a hysterical teenage girl. Here, in the quiet of her room, Juliet was a woman, and she was choosing her destiny with clear eyes.

"What if it be a poison, which the friar subtly hath ministered to have me dead." The words came out cracked and broken, but utterly clear. I slammed my hand onto my chest, pushing in sharply with the heel of my palm as if to crush the breastbone. I'd have a bruise for weeks afterward. "Upon a rapier's point. Stay, Tybalt, stay! Romeo, Romeo, Romeo! Here's drink. I drink to thee."

When the last words left my mouth, I let out my breath and waited for the polite applause of my classmates. There was only a very loud silence.

Oh no, I thought. *Did I blow the scene?* I stood there, feeling drained and a little shaken, wondering where I had gone wrong.

After what felt like many long minutes, Gail spoke. "Never in my career have I heard a better interpretation of that scene by professionals or otherwise."

I didn't know what to think. With nothing more than the power of my voice, I had commanded the room and rendered a group of theater majors silent. I had even scared myself a bit.

Gail turned to the next actor to perform. "Next."

The actress looked at Gail and at me, wide eyed. She shook her head, refusing to go on. The next actor after that refused to perform, too. I was the last monologue of the day; none of my classmates wanted to follow my performance.

You would think that after discovering the power of my voice I would continue to throw myself into theater and acting, trying to get big roles, trying to harness the lightning of performance. Instead, I hid. I went to classes and did my homework. I went home and studied. I went out with friends. What I did not do was audition. In fact, at Northwestern I was only in one performance—and that was as a dancer. In spite of the magic of that classroom and the Shakespeare performance, it would be years before I tried to audition for anything again. I was running from my voice and, with that, was silencing access to my personal power. I may have ignored boundaries in my relationships with boys at my school, but when it came to boundaries in my school life, I was throwing up entire walls between myself and success.

Why did I hide? I loved acting and the validation of Gail's words, but the response also scared me. Delivering the scene tapped into a huge power, into feelings that went beyond who I was. It was like riding a tidal wave, in a more personal way than even dancing had been. And I felt scared to step into the limelight with acting.

Over the next year, I would feel the cold a little more keenly when I returned to Illinois after every visit to my parents in Dallas. When I was in Texas, I found myself driving past Southern Methodist University (SMU), peering at all the greenery of the main quadrangle and at the rounded dome of the Georgian-style campus hall.

In the end, I decided to apply to SMU. For my audition for the school's theater program, I decided to perform a scene from *Who's Afraid of Virginia Woolf?* I stood in front of the blue halogen lights of the classroom stage, the professors of the theater department silhouetted in front of me, and gave it my all. But I was just a nineteen-year-old without the worldly experience to comprehend Martha. My voice was thin and soft where it should have been jaded and bitter. My body was infused with too much hope, and every gesture radiated optimism and naiveté. I moved like what I was—a young woman on the cusp of life—rather than someone whom life had repeatedly ground into the dirt.

When I came to the end of the piece, I took a half step back and waited.

There was a note of amusement when one of the professors spoke. "I admire your courage, Lori, for taking on such an *ambitious* role."

It wasn't exactly effusive praise—nothing like the words Gail had spoken in that dusty classroom during finals week in Evanston—and sure enough, I didn't get into the theater department. Looking back years later, I would ask myself, *What was I thinking? How exactly does self-sabotage work into my success strategy?* Why would I try on someone else's voice rather than letting my own shine through? Was I still scared by that experience with Shakespeare, where the power of my voice had rendered an entire classroom silent?

I've learned to be a little kinder to younger Lori. She was still making her way in the world, and self-sabotage was her way of playing safe and staying in the comfort zone. I could have taken on a challenging part I understood and gotten into the program so I could use my voice, but I didn't. I avoided owning the talents and gifts I had been given.

I applied to the dance department at SMU instead. It was almost a whim, but they didn't even require me to audition. I was accepted, and now, thanks to an impulsive decision, I could leave the relentless cold of the Great Lakes and move closer to my family.

• • •

It was December 30th, 1977. I was a junior at SMU, and my friend Janie and I prepared for another night on the town. Disco was at its height, and Club Elan was the happening joint in Dallas—famous for its glamorous women, backgammon tables, and black Russians served in frosty glasses. The backgammon tables buzzed with activity, and as usual I couldn't wait to get on the dance floor.

Janie and I often got together when her parents were out of town. We'd party hard, then bring our dates home to her parents' sleek modern abode. I was brilliant at burning the candle at both ends—go to school by day and party till four a.m. several nights a week. There's talent in that.

Danny saw me walk in that night. I was dressed in a long, silky floral dress, not exactly the attire Dallas women wore in the late seventies. Most of the other women wore hot pants or slinky black dresses. I was more the East Coast hippie—but with shaved armpits.

After a couple of hours of drinking and dancing, the music toned down. The easy notes of the Bee Gees' "How Deep Is Your Love" floated across the floor, and suddenly this good-looking Marlboro man shyly approached and asked me to dance. I rarely turned down an invitation to dance, so without hesitation I joined him on the floor. As the Bee Gees sang "We're living in a world of fools," we danced close. I never for a second suspected the next thirteen years of my life would be affected by that choice.

I should say what we really did was hold each other and shift our weight from foot to foot, like a couple of seventh graders at their first school dance. He wasn't much of a dancer; I probably should have taken that as a hint that we weren't a match. But in the moment, desire overrode any internal voices indicating that I might want to take a step back.

In the cold light of the next morning, he hardly spoke, and I thought I had a strong, silent type on my hands. My attraction stemmed from some urban-cowboy fantasy I didn't know I had. He was tall and muscular, with a chiseled jaw and a Tom Selleck mustache. Though he wasn't graceful or poised, he was quietly powerful, even the gentlest movement underscored by strength in reserve.

Who was this man? It took a little digging to find out. My first impression of strong and silent had been mostly right, and he didn't readily share his inner life. I did, however, discover that while Danny wasn't interested in dance, he was just as invested in physicality as I was, and in his body as I was in mine—but his dreams involved a major league baseball diamond rather than a stage.

"I'm in training to go to spring tryouts," he told me the night we met.

A few days after that first night of dancing, we went out to see a movie. *Rocky* had come out the year before, but it was playing at a local theater and Danny was eager to see it again.

"They shot this movie in twenty-eight days," he told me on the way to the show. "Can you believe that? And the whole story reflects Stallone. The movie executives wanted to cast someone else, but even though it was his first script, Stallone insisted that he star. He wasn't going to let anyone else do what he needed to get done."

Rocky—including the theme music by Bill Conti—would become the backdrop of my relationship with Danny. I eventually lost count of the times I heard the familiar lyrics: "Getting strong now / Won't be long now / Getting strong now."

"Wasn't that great?" Danny asked me as we left the theater. "He overcame everything and showed everyone."

Rocky was the classic story of the underdog, and I didn't need a psychology degree to see that Danny identified with the idea of someone—especially an athlete—overcoming doubters and achieving success. Over the years, we would see all of the Rocky movies together.

I didn't imagine the first day we met that Danny would stick around, but a year and two months after our initial meeting, Danny proposed to me, on Valentine's Day, at a local steakhouse known for its trapeze-swinging barmaids. We set the wedding date for the following December, after I graduated from SMU.

I wanted to be in love and have a home of my own. Yet I noticed early on Danny's anger and his jealous rages.

"Who was that?" he'd demand after seeing me talking to a male dancer or fellow student. He'd toss drinks and shout, and I would walk away, the two of us trapped in our own repetitive dance steps.

Besides Danny's temper, there were other signs this was going to be a troubled relationship—signs I might have noticed if I'd been willing to see them. When Danny and I made our first obligatory prewedding visit to Midlothian to meet his mother, Ruth, and his stepdad, Chuck, I was shown a stack of family photos. One of them was a chilling photograph of a man in full Marine Corps dress, stone faced with eyes like a dead fish. The photo made me deeply uncomfortable, mostly because of the blank expression on the man's face.

Still, I wanted to be polite around Danny's family, so I picked up the photo, turning to my husband-to-be.

"Who is that? I didn't know you had a brother!"

"Why, that's Danny, Lori!" Ruth replied, laughing.

I frowned at the picture. "No, it can't be. It doesn't even look like you!"

It really didn't look like the man I thought I knew. I will never forget the cold feeling that swept over me when I looked at the photo.

On the drive home, I grilled him. "Why didn't you tell me you were in the Marines?"

He said nothing—just kept his eyes locked on the road ahead.

I stared at his jaw, watching the way the muscle jumped under the skin. "Did you go to Vietnam?"

A long pause. And then, "Yes."

That weekend I wanted to know everything. Where was he stationed? What years was he there? What did he witness? I was full of questions.

He answered with horrific stories. At times his eyes filled with tears. He told me about a horrific torture scene and the racial tension among the ranks. He even told me about a racially driven murder that had supposedly been perpetrated against a fellow Marine.

It wasn't until after we divorced that Danny's father told me that Danny had been in the Marine Corps but had never served in Vietnam. What was the truth? I never found out for sure, but I believed Danny's father. I thought Danny must have been so ashamed at having never set foot in Vietnam—when other Marines hadn't even made it back—that he acted as though he'd served there.

At the time, however, I took all his stories at face value and tried to help him with the pain he obviously felt. I forgave him the drinking and the sometimes violent outbursts. After all, he was a hero and obviously his experiences had scarred him deeply—or so I thought.

And there was plenty to forgive. It was not unusual for Danny to come home in the small hours of the morning, drunk and raging.

One night, he came home stinking of booze.

"Lori, I think I killed a man," he slurred as he fell into our bed.

I was immediately awake, all the fog of sleep cleared by Danny's declaration.

"What? Danny, what are you talking about?" My heart pounded and my palms started to sweat.

But I wasn't about to get a reaction. Danny had passed out cold, snoring. I stayed awake into the morning, unable to sleep.

The next morning, he was hungover and irritated. "I was just drunk, I didn't mean it."

I didn't know what to think. Had he hurt someone? I stopped asking questions, already aware that there were no answers for me. I prayed and walked on tenterhooks for a few days. When no police arrived at our door, I took a deep breath of relief. Of course my husband hadn't killed anyone. He wasn't perfect, I told myself, but he wasn't a murderer. I was safe, or as safe as I got in those days.

I had learned to choose how I thought, and I believed that my thoughts influenced my reality, so why had I chosen this man? It's a question I've circled back to again and again. At the time, I thought I loved him, and there was a certain drama and excitement in what I saw as a passionate relation-ship. When Danny picked me up and twirled me around, he reminded me of the nights my parents had danced and I had watched. Sometimes he would sweep me up in a passionate kiss I felt right down to my toes and I'd remem-ber again the first night we had met, when he had seemed so mysterious.

In many ways, though, I was also molded by social pressure. Yes, I could choose, but all around me I saw evidence that I was supposed to choose family and married life. My wedding day, after all, was supposed to be the happiest day of my life—or so various relatives and magazines would have me believe. So I ignored any misgivings and marched on toward marriage.

The day of our wedding dawned cold. In December 1978, one of the worst ice storms Dallas had ever seen was on its way. It started with a gentle snowfall that covered the city in a veil of white, and soon layers of ice, sleet, and freezing rain covered the entire city in deadly sparkle.

But we had planned a wedding, no matter the weather, so the day con-tinued on in a mad scramble of odd intimate moments and complete chaos. Amy and I huddled in the bathroom by Mother's study, giggling like children and curling my hair. In my dress, my hair half done, I whirled around the liv-ing room, singing "I Could Have Danced All Night." The lights kept flickering, and we were locked out of the church at first, so my mother was worried about getting the decorations up in time. But eventually we were able to get into the church, and in a flurry of activity the space was transformed into a festive tumult of pale winter flowers and draped tulle. We all breathed a sigh of collective relief. We were as ready as we could be.

Then the organ music swelled, and I was walking down the aisle, watching the faces around me in the soft light, and Danny, strong and handsome in a suit at the altar. My white dress, the one my mother had worn for her wedding, spun around me, and I walked slower under its weight.

The reception was at the house, and forty people crowded in, the lights still blinking madly. Boots Randolph was playing on the hi-fi, and I caught glimpses of Mother whirling by and Amy dancing along, smiling. I went upstairs to change into my going-away suit, only to return to redo what felt like the hundreds of buttons on my wedding gown to take pictures with Danny's family in the dress.

Then we were off, running for the car through a crowd of smiling, laughing faces. We drove through Texas snow and stayed in a hotel, waking the next morning to find that the storm had gotten worse and everyone—including my mother—was scrambling for an electrician because power was out in vast swaths of Dallas.

• • •

I was a married woman, but things with Danny didn't change for the better. Danny was traditional—and in some ways, so was I—but Danny acted as though dancing was something I did in addition to the most important role: being his wife.

"What's for dinner?" he'd ask, confident in the assumption that I'd be the one cooking for both of us and doing my wifely duty by having hot meals ready for him. In retrospect, the most troubling thing is that as much as I railed against it, I would serve dinner each night, increasingly docile as the years went by.

Of course, few stories are one-note tales. Danny wasn't a monster, and I wasn't a wilting violet who'd entered into a marriage with no way out. There were times when he was loving, times when we had fun together. *Rocky* continued to play a role in our marriage. After the movies were available on VHS, we'd sometimes sit on the couch together, eating a snack, watching Stallone train with Mickey.

By the time we had been married for a while, Danny's dreams of playing major league baseball had ended, and he had tried unsuccessfully to launch a pro golfing career. While each disappointment made me lower my expectations for the man who had been so charming when I first met him, Danny clung tenaciously to his idea of big dreams coming true. Watching *Rocky* again and again, he had a template for someone overcoming every obstacle to succeed, even if Danny seemed less and less dedicated to enacting that script for himself.

And as for me? Well, I wasn't exactly grasping my future with both hands, either. I thought my mother hadn't fulfilled her potential, and I had been determined to make my own way, but here I was in the same posture, staring down the pots and pans in the sink.

Chapter 5

professional shoes

What did the future hold for me after college? I knew that in some way it would involve dancing. I had just graduated from SMU with a bachelor's degree in dance. Most of the dancers from my class hoped to enter a dance company, and I was no different. Before my marriage, I had already been looking for a job, and one day when I came home, Danny was waving an envelope. I had been accepted to the Repertory Dance Company of the Southwest. I enjoyed performing with the group, but less than a year later, I began to imagine a new plan.

One sunny Texas afternoon, I met my dancer friend Pat at the San Francisco Rose, a popular hangout for SMU students. We drank wine and talked about the expanse of life before us. We tossed around the idea of forming our own professional dance group in which we could follow our artistic vision, performing shows we'd choreograph ourselves. My dancer friends and I often talked about this dream, but usually it was just idle dreaming. Tonight, however, as the evening waned, the discussion became more serious, more pointed. This time, I realized, we were really going to do it.

It would take us two years to gather together the money, the space, and the chutzpah to start, but start we did. Ten of us worked together to cofound Dancers Unlimited Repertory Company (DURC) in 1979. At first, we had just $400 in our shoebox, donated by an arts-loving oil tycoon, P. L. Moore, who had also helped start the 500, Inc., a Dallas foundation dedicated to supporting the arts. We had no idea what we were signing up for, but soon we had enough cash to get a running start.

All dancers need a place to hang their shoes, but our budget for studio space was small. Our first home was on Main Street long before Main Street was cool. Before anyone thought it even bohemian to be there and before the West End, Deep Ellum, and Uptown, we carved our place in downtown Dallas. Back then it was still considered dangerous to walk solo in our neighborhood, and the chic nightclubs and pubs of the area were still decades away.

That's what allowed us to get the studio on the second floor above the Schick Shaving Center for a song. It was a hot hunk of real estate for sure. Those dusty ten thousand square feet held decades of memories from a past that few in Dallas knew existed. It had most recently been an occult bookstore called the Witching Well. Our very conservative, very Texan landlords tried to reassure us that their tenants had been white witches, doing, well, that *good* kind of magic. But as we scraped up the wax drippings from the center of a large pentangle still quite visible on the middle of the floor, we wondered. Had this place been home to animal sacrifices? Were goats involved? Or just simple, down-home, Texas-style exorcisms? I could almost feel the heat rising from the wax. *It's okay, it's okay*, we reassured ourselves. Nothing a thorough sage-burning ceremony couldn't cure.

In what would become the women's dressing room, we found a nice Formica counter with a row of phone jacks beneath it. Apparently, back in the fifties, the place had been home to an illegal bookie joint. Our dressing room formerly housed a row of telephones and probably a line of seedy men taking and making bets on horse races.

On the third floor, tiny rooms were lined up like dominos next to the studio. We gazed at the old USO and Arthur Murray dance signs and wondered. It turned out that back in the 1920s, the tiny rooms had housed "working girls," and not the kind who answered phones or typed up letters in the steno pool.

We had just signed a lease on our first home—a whorehouse, a bookie joint, and a Wiccan bookstore.

Throughout the 1980s, we would add our own patina to that historic building, adding layers of dancers' sweat, ambition, and squabbles to the hallowed floorboards. What did we know about starting a dance company? Not a thing, but we were full of the passion and confidence of our twenties, and the 1980s were just starting—a fresh decade for all of us. Over the next years, the founders of DURC would be rivals, coworkers, and confidants, as well as sometime-friends.

In a way, the company and we, its founders, went through the adult version of the Terrible Twos. Just like toddlers, each of us insisted it was "all about me," acting out to get what we each wanted rather than finding ways to pull together. We squabbled as we tried to define our vision, and made mistakes along the way. Maybe we needed to go through that sort of early temper tantrum, just like any small child working her way through the stages of development. Or maybe it was a matter of us doing better once we knew better.

At first, we dabbled in every type of dance, eventually settling into modern dance pieces (with some jazz and ballet numbers thrown in). Hanging on to male dancers and funding was a struggle, and sometimes we all juggled a second or third job to make ends meet. Despite the struggles, we were pioneers in the Dallas arts scene. We hired dancers, choreographed unique performances, and put on shows.

My life began to settle into a new pattern. Every morning, I'd go to work at a real estate management company to copy, staple, and file invoices for five dollars per hour. Then I would walk into the studio, do a few preliminary stretches, turn on the power to the stereo system, and, if it was my turn, begin to formulate today's warm-up class.

Dancers arrived, repeating the same routine, catching up on their romantic dramas, financial challenges, and maybe a few reflections on the previous day's rehearsals. Once the daily chatter died down, we'd move to the pieces we were developing for performances.

There was a lot of dreaming involved in being a young dancer. I dreamed then that one day, I would become the Baryshnikov of modern dance. My soul purpose, I thought, was to use dance to bring the world some insight that would forever change the way people lived. I wrote in my journal that someone, somewhere, in some darkened performance hall, would witness a moment on stage so profound, so evocative, that they would make a shift at the cellular level.

Something of that young artist is still alive in me today. While I didn't become the Baryshnikov of modern dance, the fire inside still burns—the desire to make a difference, the commitment to using all my gifts and talents to serve that end. That fire also burns so that I can support others in using their own gifts at the highest level.

Of course, running a dance troupe wasn't all grand dreams for the future. Mostly it was hard work—rehearsals that stretched into the wee hours as we labored over every step, and teaching aerobics classes at a local gym so I could be paid to do my cross-training sessions. There were also worries about money, bad dance partners, and torn ligaments, and days when I wondered why I was even a part of DURC—much less one of the founding members. But most of the time, even on days when I questioned everything that had brought me to this point, there was the saving grace of the work and dance. I'd stand there in an empty room, music playing, and begin the practice. Because that's what there was to do. That's what was in front of me. It was my church, my ritual, my process, my prayer circle, my running group, my home.

Sometimes, however, even the work couldn't save me. I sometimes stepped into the role of the enforcer, trying to keep everyone focused on dance—no easy task. One day, I was trying to sew curtains to make an informal performing space in our studio. One wall of the studio was covered with mirrors that we faced every day for class and rehearsal. We thought if we covered the mirrors with curtains, we could perform facing the opposite direction and seat an audience of maybe thirty people in folding chairs along the wall. I was trying to whip up those curtains, and the performance was in a few days. I was already grumpy when one of the dancers, Norma, announced that she had to go home.

"Got to get to my real job tomorrow," she told us cheerily.

I snapped.

"You think you can just show up and dance? This is a cooperative effort, and I'll be goddamned if anyone gets to leave for their fucking beauty sleep!"

It wasn't my finest moment. But those were the days when I thought it was all about proving to each other how dedicated and committed we were.

One night a couple of years after the company's founding, as I drove home from a long day's rehearsal, I saw smoke rising over the tree line. At first I ignored it; some house fire in the distance, I reasoned. But the closer I got to my apartment, the denser the smoke became, and when I turned onto my street, my way was blocked by a cavalcade of fire engines. Wrenching the car into park, I hopped out and ran up to the nearest fireman. He looked at me. "Sorry ma'am, you can't pass. This area's cordoned off."

"But I live here!" I shouted over the din of the sirens.

The fire turned out to have been in my neighbor's apartment, so my home wasn't burned. But it wasn't completely spared. The firemen had entered my apartment with an axe and covered everything with plastic tarps to protect against water damage. Though the fire hadn't touched my possessions directly, they were all darkened by a layer of greasy soot. Danny wasn't home and wouldn't come home for hours, but my dancer friends showed up that night to comfort me and celebrate the fact that we were alive.

Something good for Dancers Unlimited came from that dance with fire. There was something about that night, that event, that pulled us together. Something magical seemed to push us on, holding on to the possibility that we could successfully and collaboratively lead our shared creation. At the time, I was working on creating a dance for the company, and that night provided the inspiration I needed. "After the Fire" was performed for years and was even licensed by other companies.

During my twenty-year tenure with Dancers Unlimited Repertory Company, the project I remain most proud of is our holiday series. Admittedly, a primary reason for doing the holiday series was that it always attracted city and state funding, and there was never a time we couldn't use more cash. All sarcasm and cynicism aside though, the dancers truly loved this time because as artists, we loved to entertain, and entertain we did. We pulled out our most lighthearted, child-friendly pieces, dusted them off, and performed them for a variety of audiences, from the economically disadvantaged to the socially elite to the terminally ill. We commissioned a dance work from a choreographer out of New York who was known for his comedic talent, and we were immediately sold when he proposed choreographing to the soundtrack of the old Warner Brothers and Walter Lanz cartoons, like Bugs Bunny, Elmer Fudd, and Woody Woodpecker. One part involved the three of us on our knees performing a Radio City Rockette–style kick line. Step kick, step kick. Maybe because they were performed at Christmas, or maybe because they made us get completely in touch with that child that exists in all of us, these performances always bring back fond memories.

But despite the magic of performances and work I loved, by the late 1980s, DURC was changing. The core of the company began to split off, and our friendships teetered on the brink of collapse. In 1987 we lost the studio; even in the still-seedy downtown neighborhood, continuous lack of funds had put the space we'd come to call home out of our reach. The building would stand empty and bereft of music for years before it was torn down to pave the way for downtown Dallas's redevelopment. From then on, the remaining founders of DURC worked mostly in high schools and colleges for the performing arts, and occasionally a more memorable opportunity would present itself, like the year we performed at the Brooklyn Academy of Music with a live orchestra.

How does a dance company, in which the members make their careers working together and trusting together, come apart at the seams? For us, it started with life changes. Some of the founders wanted to start families or pursue other careers. The constant worries about money didn't exactly create the most stable work environment, and as our founders got older, some realized they would not be dancing forever. Some moved away, got married, or just started dreaming of things besides dance steps and leotards.

Dancers Unlimited, an incredible and maybe impossible vision begun with ten naïve dancers, eventually evolved into a company led by me. Me. I was the one left standing, and our shared vision of creating an innovative dance company putting on cutting-edge performances evolved into my solo dream.

By the spring of 1990, I had taken up the mantle as sole artistic director of Dancers Unlimited and was working on my first major project alone at the South Dallas Cultural Center. The SDCC was in what was then an industrial district, and in that small urban theater I decided to create a program that would serve the underserved.

Children from schools often too impoverished to attend regular performances in bigger, more established theaters were bussed in so they could see dance. I had a grant to help me transport students from elementary schools to the SDCC for shows. The money, as always, only went so far, so I had volunteers on hand to help corral the children. I was focused on my role as performer and manager, and I didn't really meet many of the volunteers—until one of them approached me after one of the shows. He was wearing jeans and a Hawaiian shirt. His long brown hair was curled around his ears, and he sported a full and distinguished beard, brown like his hair but salted liberally with gray. Like all the other volunteers, he'd just spent the last few hours getting dozens of schoolchildren from a bus to their theater seats and back to the bus, but somehow, he didn't look impatient or tired. His expression was warm and open, and there was a genuine smile just visible below his mustache.

"Thank you so much," he said, his smile widening. "The work you're doing here is amazing."

I stared at him, a little surprised. I shook his offered hand with my mouth slightly open, scrambling for a reply. By that time, we had put on several shows and I was usually the one thanking volunteers, not the other way around.

"I'm Bill," he went on. "I wish my two sons had an opportunity to study with you. I've always wanted to give them dance lessons."

"Really? That's great!" I said. Inside, I was thinking, *You want to teach your boys to dance? Wow! Now that's an evolved man!*

"Yeah, I think dance lessons would be amazing for them, would teach them a lot."

I nodded and moved to roll up the dance floor padding that we had put down for the performance.

"Here, let me help you with that." And suddenly, Bill was there, shoulder to shoulder with me, chatting about his sons.

That was it. With a simple act of kindness, Bill had captivated me. For the next few days, the feeling of his arm against mine lingered with me as I danced, as I dressed, even as I dreamed. While Danny snored beside me, drunk, or as I fell asleep while he stayed out all night, I would remember Bill's kind words. I couldn't think of the last time Danny had said something kind, and the passionate kisses from before our marriage were long gone by then.

A few days after I met him, I dreamt Bill was dressed as a carnival organ grinder, complete with a trained monkey on his shoulder and a metal coin holder for making change. When I woke I knew Bill was my "change man," my companion through a period of transformation. I'd already known that a change was inevitable, whether Bill was by my side or not—it was *my* change, after all—but I was grateful for this dream-world sign that I wouldn't be making the journey alone.

The night after my dream, Danny came home drunk and passed out, sprawled face down on the bed we shared. For long minutes I sat beside him, listening to his wet, heavy breathing, recoiling from the sour tang of bourbon on his breath, in his clothes, from his pores. Finally, feeling disgusted and soul-sick, I threw the comforter off and swung my legs over the side of the bed. I padded barefoot across the hall to the spare bedroom, with its narrow bed and its gauzy curtains blowing in the breeze. Sleep wouldn't come, so I grabbed my journal and a black felt-tip pen. In the quiet of that room, I couldn't hear Danny's snores or smell the alcohol. I could hear only the peaceful scratch of pen on paper and smell nothing but the ink. I poured out my soul:

> *I am filled with sadness, grief, and confusion. I feel certain I want out of my marriage because of who I am when I am with Danny. I feel dirty, wanting, unfulfilled—wanting to be understood. I am selling shares in compassion. Isn't that what we all want? To be understood and feel loved?*

In the rhythm of writing, as my words splashed out against the stark page, I connected to some higher source, my God, my Spirit. The details were unclear, but I knew more absolutely than I knew my name that I was done with this relationship. I had reached a fork in the road, and I knew that when I walked out of the house the next morning, I wouldn't come back. I had no plans beyond that.

I packed my dance bag the next day and left as usual, calling goodbye to Danny, even though I knew he was still sleeping it off. But I wanted to be able to tell myself I'd said goodbye. After a day of rehearsal, I planned to go to a friend's house, but Bill was there in the parking lot when I came out of the theater.

He took one look at my face and immediately seemed to register my anxiety, sadness, and exhaustion. He tilted his head slightly, then said, "Would you maybe like to go to dinner?"

We ended up at a small place serving Mexican food, with drinks in bright blue glasses. We sat outside, and I stared at the last sips of my white wine. "I think I just left my husband."

It was the first time I had said those words out loud. Bill didn't say anything, just gave me a sympathetic look and nodded. I knew that he understood. My voice, direct and guided, belonged to a woman I barely knew. A "me" was emerging that both exhilarated and scared me. And he got it. All of it.

Bill was no stranger to transition, he explained to me. "A year ago, I was sitting at home and felt this pain in my chest. I couldn't breathe. It went away, but I thought I had had a mild heart attack. Everything changed for me then. I was putting in long hours at my video production company, but I wasn't getting anywhere. My second wife filed for divorce, and I'd just had it. I sold what I owned. None of it mattered that much. And I stayed with friends for almost a year. At first, I didn't know what to do."

"So what did you do?"

Bill got a soft smile on his face. "I got serious. I sat a lot, in meditation mostly, and spent a lot of time thinking about what I would do, how I would contribute, and wondering about the nature of the universe."

Nice work if you can get it, I thought. I felt that I couldn't do that, with bills to pay and an apartment to find. What I didn't know was how much of Bill's knowledge I would absorb over the next four years he and I were together.

I had left my home with little more than the clothes on my back. Strategic thinking was not a gift of mine back then. I didn't have a plan or a course of action—only an intention: to keep following the voice I'd just begun to hear—*my* voice. I had given my voice away temporarily in college, when its power had scared me in a dusty college drama classroom, but it was coming back with a vengeance. It was not to be ignored, and I was ready to follow where it led.

That first night away from Danny, Bill became the hospice for my marriage. I was in the midst of producing my first major evening performance series at the Undermain Theater in Deep Ellum, so at rehearsal, I was composed, using my regal dancer's posture to take advantage of every inch of authority and poise I possessed. But as soon as I left the theater, my spine slumped and my shoulders curved inward, sheltering the ache in my chest. I crashed my way through those first few weeks of being separated. I slept at the theater. I slept at friends' homes. I stayed at the La Quinta Inn right around the corner from our house. Life was unsettled and I wasn't sure what would happen next, but there was still the sense of relief at finally having left. I had left without telling Danny, and I worked hard not to run into him. And Bill made me feel less untethered in the world. I might not have had it all figured out, but I had my work and I had love. Bill became my course leader, my guru-on-demand, and the boyfriend who wouldn't go away. We were together more days than not, and when we were together, we were talking—not extraneous chatter just to fill the silence, but serious, soul-to-soul communication. If we weren't diving down into the deep seas of the cultural conditioning that had brought us to that very moment in time, we weren't doing our work. And our work was to not only move through our day-to-day, but also wrestle with the deeper questions and bring that curiosity to everything we said and did. We talked about spirituality and self-actualization work consciously, but it also flowed naturally into our conversation because we were both interested in personal journeys. Bill and I connected through kindness and a mutual love of self-actualization. Even then, I think I considered in the back of my mind that this was not forever and this wasn't quite what I wanted from my ideal relationship, but it was wonderful in its own way.

Once again, my work was the safety net that caught me. Even as I wondered about what steps I would take next, I moved forward with dance. That summer I traveled to seven cities on a dance convention tour. I worked for a major dancewear company that sold teacher training courses, videos, CDs, and a bunch of other products for the aspiring dancer that I deemed commercialized crap. I taught ballet classes and choreographed routines for the masses of aspiring dancers on top of a rickety platform in hotel ballrooms.

For two months after leaving Danny, I lived out of a suitcase while nursing a feeling that Bill didn't fit my picture of what my next relationship would look like. He was twelve years older than I was, had been through two marriages, and had two sets of kids. But though I may have had my doubts, there was no doubt that Bill had a huge influence on my thoughts and my later work—things I'm very thankful for. He read a great deal about developing the self, and it was through him that I met two key mentors for my work.

At the time, I hadn't yet completely developed the ideas that would drive my coaching work. I didn't fully see the ways I was constructing my life, choosing my thoughts, creating what I was moment by moment. I was still questioning, and it led to some intense talks with Bill.

"What is the nature of being a human being?" we'd ask one another, curled up on the couch, snuggled together and sipping cocoa. What made us human? What was the essence? Were there traits we all shared?

"Why do we think the way we think?" we'd ask over the kitchen table, wondering where these amazing ideas and thoughts sprang from. Human thoughts had caused genocides, built civilizations, invented cures for disease, and created reality television. Where did these thoughts come from, and why did people think the way they did?

Bill went from being my change man to a kept man on a dancer's measly income. Bill worked some of the time, but his employment was always more unsteady than mine. We negotiated everything from the start, leaving no stone unturned—from household tasks to sexual monogamy, which came later in the relationship. We developed a closer intimacy than Danny and I had ever managed. For the first time in my life, I began to say what I really wanted out loud. I could tell Bill I didn't want to serve dinner every night or move in together right away.

It was safe. I was safe. I realized that I could give voice to my deepest, darkest secrets. Danny had once said, "If I love you and you leave me, I'll hunt you down and kill you." His voice had the cadence of a joke, but there was a knife-edge under his words that had raised the hair on the back of my neck. So the newfound security and spiritual exploration was more important to me than Bill having a regular job. Bill contributed in other ways—and some of those things still remain with me.

I still have the photos he took of the dance company and of me; they're some of the best visual memories of that period of my life. I would be dancing or practicing only to turn and find Bill, his face obscured by the heavy black camera, intensely focused on me and the dance.

Of course, my life wasn't all glossy photos and spiritual exploration and domestic comfort. Danny didn't just drop out of my world without a trace. A few weeks after I'd unofficially moved out, I arranged with Danny to meet at what had been our home to pick up my stuff. I couldn't just show up un-announced. I'd gone to the house just days after leaving him, hoping to get a few of my belongings when he was at work; my key no longer fit in the deadbolt. Danny had already changed the locks.

My hand was shaking as I dialed Danny's number. While the phone rang, I closed my eyes and listened to my breathing, trying to find my voice, hop-ing to keep it steady.

When he answered, my tone was calm and even. "I just wanted to pick up some things."

"Of course." He sounded reasonable, and my pulse slowed. "Drop by; all your things are here."

He met me at the front door. Just as quickly as the door opened, he tried pulling me into him, into a kiss. The length of his body pressed against me. I shrank from his embrace, both attracted to and repelled by its familiarity. I was nervous but resolute. The plan was simple: get in, have a quick con-versation, pick up whatever I could, and get out.

Hah.

Just inside the doorway, I looked down at the old wooden hi-fi cabinet and saw a jagged knife sitting on top of it. Silent in its message but vibrat-ing with intention. Neither of us said anything about it, but that knife took up as much space as another person in the room. Danny didn't even glance at it, but the threat was clear: *You are my captive, and I will not hesitate to tear the softest tissues within you if you leave before I grant you permission.*

I felt like screaming, but I knew that fear would destroy me. I turned to a still place within me. Rather than reacting, I relaxed my body and told my mind that it would be okay. I worked on exuding calm. Today, I still teach clients the same thing—to catch themselves when they react emotionally to something and to choose a different reaction to get a different result.

How do you speak with the threat of harm and death only a step away, glinting at you? We talked normally, our words trite.

"How have you been?"

"I've been well, you look well."

All I really wanted was to sleep and for this to be over.

"I want you." Danny's whisper was a hiss, and I wanted to flinch from it, but that knife was still there. "Let's make love—one last time."

I turned my body away, not wanting to look him in the face. "I don't think that's a good idea."

The presence of that knife was between us, and I felt passive and impotent, unable to shout no, unable to push him away. Some small voice inside me said, *Don't resist; you will live through this.*

We had sex. And then, I slept. The experience was not devoid of pleasure, but the physical satisfaction was marbled with silence, fear, and shame. He called me names and almost spit out his disgust at me. I didn't say anything, didn't give him anything to react to. In the end, I managed to get out alive and with one garbage bag filled with clothes. That was the sum total of my marriage, all that I ever got before or after the divorce.

It wasn't the last time I heard from Danny. On opening night, I got a note backstage. I opened it up and stared at the words in Danny's messy script: *Give us another chance.*

I knew that Danny was in the audience, but when I scanned the crowd before the show, I couldn't see him. After the show was over, Bill met me at the side door with a smile and kiss.

"That was amazing! You were incredible."

I kissed him back, putting my arms around him and wanting to feel his warmth through my t-shirt. "I think Danny's here. I got a note backstage."

"Should we be worried?"

It turned out that we should have been. When Bill and I walked out of the theater toward the parking lot, Danny's beat-up Thunderbird screeched to the curb. In the driver's seat, Danny's face was shiny and his eyes glazed, his mouth turned down in a mocking sneer. Once again, he had that crazed drunken zombie look.

"Hey," he yelled. "I wanna talk to you. What are ya doing—where ya going?" He looked at Bill and scoffed. "Who the hell are *you*?"

All the times Bill and I had spent talking about how to overcome our emotions and live fully in the moment came to me. I breathed. I turned into a dispassionate observer and tried to tap into compassion, telling myself, *Danny is doing the best he can.* While my heart thudded, I looked up at Bill. His expression was placid and open, the only indication of distress a slight flaring of his nostrils with each breath. I was sure he was running through the same mental exercises I was.

When we didn't yell back, Danny got the befuddled look of the thwarted drunk, his mind probably too foggy to make any sense of what was going on.

"Fuck this," he screamed at us before he roared off. The smell of burning rubber and a puff of exhaust were the only traces of him left in the next few seconds. My breath, so measured while Danny stared at us, came out in a gust of relief. Bill grabbed me and pulled me close for a hug, both of us silent. Then we kept walking home. It was the last time I saw Danny.

Bill was nothing like Danny. He was interested in my work, in dance, in being together. He wasn't violent or jealous. It was a drama-free relationship, and from the beginning we negotiated everything together.

One morning, soon after my return from a dance teacher tour, we were sitting in the kitchen of Bill's latest housesitting gig, waiting for the coffee to brew. I'd had plenty of time to think about our relationship while I'd been traveling, and I'd reached a decision. I turned to him.

"I don't want to live together," I told him, as the smell of French roast filled the kitchen.

"That's fine."

For a moment, I wasn't sure he'd been listening—that was it? No argument? No conversation? But then he smiled, and I knew, as always, he had heard me.

"But I still want to build something," he went on, reaching for my hand across the scarred kitchen table. "I want to care for you and nurture you, see where this transformation of ours goes."

We did eventually move in together. Bill never committed any money to household expenses, but he said he would do anything else I needed to get done to make my life easier. We would explore our spirituality together.

"Okay."

With that agreement, I felt as though I were breaking some unwritten rule about finding myself in solitude. No one said anything and I didn't articulate it at the time, but in some way I thought I should be in mourning after the end of my marriage. I should be spending time alone. Instead, I was in a happy relationship. The last thing I wanted to do at that point in my life was to set up housekeeping with another man, but I created a bond that got me through some rocky times.

Bill and I had four years together, and I loved every one of them. Through him I learned to be completely responsible for the role I played in my life. But he was probably more friend than lover. We're still soulful but platonic allies, even all these years later. We have a lot to offer each other, even if romance isn't how our relationship works best.

So though Bill and I didn't turn out to be soulmates and I doubted my decision to be with him so soon after ending my relationship with Danny, now I think I made a great choice. Later in life I was validated again when a respected teacher said that the greatest work you can do is when you are in a committed relationship. Of course, the first and most important relationship is to yourself. But I knew I achieved clarity sooner when I got out of my head and into the truth-baring conversations of intimate relationships. We are not meant to be solitary creatures, and just like in dance, there is magic to be experienced by working together.

Chapter 6

aching goodbyes

When we found out my mother had cancer, it was a blow to the heart. When we found out there wasn't much to be done, it was a shard of ice to the soul. But my mother, who had always faced every event with humor and grace, was prepared even for this.

When the family arrived on an afternoon in 1993 to spend time with her, she looked serene, and a small smile curled her still-lovely mouth.

"I didn't know death could be so beautiful," she said almost wistfully as we all sat on the sun-drenched patio together and the hospice workers did their intake session. My mother was having a good day, and we had helped set her up outside, covered in soft blankets, so she could enjoy a little fresh air.

I didn't know whether death was beautiful. Mostly I was a whirl of emotions. Bill spent those days in Missoula with me and my sister and her family. My mother and father had divorced years ago and had each remarried, and my mother's partner, Alan, had been her primary caretaker during the year and a half of her illness. Amy and I did what we could to help, but we often felt helpless. We all started cocktails as early in the day as we could justify. Could we stick it out? Could we stay until she was gone?

When the nurses were absent, it took three of us—Bill, my sister, and me—to change my mother's gown. I tried not to look, tried to preserve for her the dignity she clung to, but I couldn't keep from seeing. Her body was limp and wasted, her hair patchy, one breast missing and, in its place, a puckered sideways scar. The nurse told us morphine didn't cause hallucinations, that the pain eats up the drug, but mother would sometimes come out of her stupor, look around, and start to scream, wide eyed: "They are here for me, but I don't know who they are!" My pasty New Age beliefs, my visions of bright white light—they vanished in the face of that fear. I could say nothing.

I also struggled to say the right words when I wheeled my mother into the bedroom for what would be the last time. She was quiet that day and it was clear she had something on her mind.

"I haven't really done anything or accomplished anything." Her words were slow and labored, and they broke my heart. I wanted to erase them from the air between us.

I walked around the wheelchair so I could sit down to look her in the eye. "You have accomplished and done so much. For me, for all of us. You've raised three amazing children. You've lived a good life. You've loved and been loved. So much." My mother passed away two days later, on a clear, dry Montana afternoon. She had slipped into a coma the day before, and the nurse had given us the signs to watch for—mottled skin, no more urine dripping into the catheter bag. I knew that her time was close; I'd prepared for this moment for days. Sitting by her, I could hear the oxygen pump hissing, the hushed voices of the hospice nurses in the hall.

Eventually, I lay down on the bed beside her. Each member of my family took turns being alone with her, like an assembly line of confessional clearings. When it was my turn, I sometimes talked and other times just listened to the quiet sounds of the room.

"Say all there is to say now," one of the younger nurses had told me when I arrived from Dallas, but as I spoke, I wondered if my mother could hear me. Was this an exercise in futility?

Still, I pressed my body to my mother's side, as I had done as a small child, and reached for the words inside myself—words I didn't need to speak out loud. *I love you, Mommy. I've tried to show you in all the ways I know how. Though I don't want to, I can let you go now. I want you to be out of pain. I want you to let go and be at peace.*

I felt self-conscious. Was I overdramatizing? I left the room. The four tenors sang at the top of their lungs from the TV. Bill, Amy, and I sat together. Even though we had been prepared, the gaping ache of grief threatened in that moment to overwhelm us. Music filled the house, but everything felt prickly and wavy. The walls vibrated. My heart ached.

The nurse called us back.

"I think this is it." She said it gently, with a tenderness I imagined she had honed over the hundreds of times she had said these words before.

We surrounded the bed and wrapped our bodies around our mother, enclosing her. Alan, her second husband and caregiver, handed each of us the words to "Amazing Grace," printed on pale paper. I tried to sing. I'd sung before, performed on stages, but at that moment my voice shook. The tears fell steadily and all of us were off-key. Gently, Alan told us to turn off the oxygen pump. Mother's breathing slowed, and she labored over each lungful. There was a long pause. Then another breath and the next. A pause again.

Then the incredible happened. One of us laughed. Can you believe it? We laughed! We thought Mother was playing with us, one last time.

Then finally the breaths stopped, and the room turned cold in one endless pause. I felt her spirit fly up, and I wailed. I wanted to give Mother my voice so she could straddle my cry on her ride into heaven. I wanted her to take a piece of me with her as she went, so I lent her my cries.

Alan told us it was tradition in many cultures for the women to cleanse the body. And so we did—Amy and I. We dressed her in her most feminine nightgown, cut up the back for easier placement. She looked beautiful, but I could not watch as she was rolled out of the room. I knew it would be the last time, but for dreams, that I would get to see her.

Yet perhaps some part of her spirit lingered or touched us. The afternoon she passed away, when we stepped outside in the sunshine, we were treated to the sight of a double-rainbow. It was rare and I had never seen one, yet there it was, in all its beauty at a time I desperately needed to hold onto the beauty of life. When Bill went out for a walk some nights later, he caught sight of a meteor. Twice in quick succession, the skies painted magic on their canvas.

I grieved for my mother for years. In some ways I still do, although now the sadness I feel about her is tinged with happiness that she was in my life at all. In the months following her death, when the grief made me ache as though I had walked face-first into a concrete wall, I realized it wasn't just that she was gone; part of what was causing my immense sadness was the disappointment she'd confessed to me at the end about what she felt was her lack of accomplishments.

Because of when she had been born, because of the social pressure to be the perfect mom and wife, she had never fully pursued her own passions and dreams. I know that my mother had felt she was passing away with the music still inside her, but the more I thought about it, the more I realized the music inside does not express itself through accomplishments. It is about being fully present and connected. And in that way, my mother had been a full symphony, sharing her music with us all.

This realization broke me free from the immobility and sorrow I felt in those first weeks after her passing. It made me want to step into my fullest life and support others to do the same.

But I couldn't plunge into a brand-new future just yet. My mother's death came just before another ending in my life, but this time, I wouldn't be saying goodbye to another person; instead, I'd be concluding a chapter of my own story. And I'd be letting go of a part of myself.

Chapter 7

dancing with romance

A dancer's professional life is essentially short. Even for a young person, the rigors of dancing take a toll, and as I entered my thirties I had to come to terms with the reality that I would not always be dancing. What else would I do? When would I know it was time to leave the stage for the final time? I had no idea, but I was definitely intrigued when Southern Methodist University announced its reinstatement of the Choreographic Theory and Practice MFA program.

I found out about the program when SMU contacted me as one of their former students and asked whether I was interested. I was still running Dancers Unlimited at the time, but as always, DURC was limping along financially. *Well*, I considered, *getting an MFA might help*. I thought having an advanced degree might be a safety net. If DURC finally gave up the ghost, maybe I could teach at a university. I didn't have any real idea of what a career shift like that would entail, but it was the closest thing I had to a plan B. It helped that SMU was willing to give me funding in exchange for teaching some undergraduate nonmajor dance classes. I didn't have any money at the time to put toward tuition, so this was a deciding factor in my enrolling in the program.

As an undergraduate, I'd zigzagged across campus attending classes across schools and disciplines. Now I spent nearly all my time in one corner of SMU: the Owen Arts Center. The entrance to the trio of buildings was white—white stone, white steps, and tall white modern columns, like frames for the performances and art inside. When I was there, I was a world away from the crowded streets of downtown Dallas, even though the school was still in the city. I took classes in criticism and aesthetics, dance history, and technique; I wandered the exhibits around the Meadows museum, and I rehearsed, but what I loved most about graduate school was the relationships I forged there.

There were three of us in the MFA program. Tina, Scott, and I had plenty in common, since we were all dancers; yet I was definitely the most mature student and the only one still unsure why I was there. I had a vague notion of teaching, but Tina and Scott had ambitions to dance. They had both gone to the prestigious Juilliard School in New York, and both were beautiful dancers. We spent time together, sweating, practicing, complaining in the way all graduate students do about long hours or classes.

But even though I had hesitations about my place in the program, many of the classes—both those that I took and those that I led—were exhilarating.

I especially loved teaching Dance Composition. I wrote the syllabus for the class and truly loved watching younger dancers create. Working with words, textures, art, music, silence, I would watch my students get inspired. Out of nothing, movement phrases would appear and would then be shaped into longer phrases. Pretty soon a scene or a part of a dance would emerge. Gestures hinted at the relationships between the dancers. We'd dance our hearts out, inspire each other, bring something to life that hadn't existed before class had begun.

During my two years at SMU, the chair of the dance program—who'd been appointed just before I began grad school—resigned. The school undertook a rigorous search to find a replacement, and eventually a longtime faculty member took over the reins. In the way of academia, there was a lot of drama and behind-the-scenes office politics. I remember making a call to a friend. I was so frustrated by the drama at the university, and a backlog of aggravation poured out of me in a flood of words and exclamations as I stood there, in a studio DURC was subleasing from the City Ballet in the Park Cities.

After the torrent had slowed, my friend let a few beats pass before he replied. To this day, I remember exactly what he said to me: "Instead of thinking about yourself as being outside the system, put yourself in it. Own your place and choose to be there, since you're there anyway."

That advice has stayed with me for life. Standing in that studio, surrounded by dust and the smell of sweat, I realized he was right. I needed to be present where I was, rather than wishing things were different.

I soon didn't have time to worry about wishing, anyway. During my second year in graduate school, I worked on my thesis, inspired by a very rare book of drawings of Isadora Duncan by the Spanish artist Josep Clarà. Duncan was one of modern dance's great pioneers. She was known as a barelegged dancer, which during the height of her career at the turn of the twentieth century was truly scandalous. Years before, I had devoured her autobiography, *My Life*, so I felt I knew her well. She was a free spirit, and her movement was wholeheartedly inspired by the natural world and her own breath.

For one of the pieces I would present as part of my thesis, I used the sketches as inspiration to create phrases emulating the moments in Duncan's dance that Clarà had captured. I had the drawings turned into negative slides, so the lines were white rather than black and were projected behind me as I danced. To the music of Chopin, one of Duncan's favorite composers, I tried to make manifest Duncan's eternal spirit.

The second piece for my thesis was a kind of first draft for what would later become a full evening piece performed by Dancers Unlimited. Using students and a production budget I didn't have to raise money for, I created the first iteration of "Shoppers' Guide to the Center of the Universe." This was the story of Armand and Eviana in the Garden of Nieman, who fall into Dallas, Texas, and enter into shopping hell. I had been inspired by Sherri, my partner for a short time at DURC, and I wanted to try my hand in comedy. It was rough and needed development, but the audience seemed to enjoy it, and it got a few laughs.

On closing night of the performance of my thesis work, we had a reception in the atrium at the Owen Arts Center. Faculty and students were standing around drinking cheap wine and making small talk. I was about to join Tina and Scott when one of my professors took my elbow. She told me there was someone she wanted me to meet, and led me toward a group gathered around a balding man with glasses, a blunt jaw, and a disheveled mop of dark hair.

It was Ron Protas. For a number of years, the dance department at SMU had been pursuing a relationship with the Martha Graham Dance Company. When Graham died in 1991, she named Ron Protas as heir to her estate. Though she and Protas had been close during the final years of her life, Graham's company didn't share the same fondness. First of all, he wasn't a dancer. And to make matters worse, he had a reputation for bringing artists to their knees with his cruel feedback.

Tonight Ron was a guest of the SMU dance department at the concert where I had performed my thesis dances. At the time, I really had no idea who he was, only that he wielded power in the negotiations with SMU for the rights to notate and perform Martha's works.

My professor introduced us, and we shook hands. I immediately noticed that despite his well-tailored suit, Ron's slouch made him stand out in a roomful of impeccably postured dancers. He gave me a long once-over, as if with one glance he could determine the entirety of my worth.

"Oh that Isadora piece was dreadful," he told me breezily. "You had absolutely no sense of Isadora's breath. But that shopping piece was really funny. Good moments there."

My face and neck flamed as I stared at him, unable to speak. The half-hearted praise of my second piece disappeared in his humiliating dismissal of the Duncan work. This was, after all, my thesis, the culmination of two years of work. I looked around at the faculty members surrounding Ron.

No one was smiling, but no one was meeting my eye or standing up for me, either. And without bothering to wait for my response, Ron turned away from me and to a clearly more interesting conversation while I slunk away.

The following week, I went directly to each of the three faculty members who had been there, asking why they didn't say anything. One responded, "Well, Lori, I didn't really see it as such a big deal. After all, he's insulted the greatest modern dancers in the world. At least you're in good company."

I didn't feel like I was in good company. I felt let down by people who were supposed to be supporting me. I eventually let it go, but I soon decided that the world of academia was not for me. The trouble was that I was almost forty at the time, and I knew the bloom was off my dancing rose. Though I was still strong and flexible, I didn't kid myself that I could keep up a full-time dancer's schedule for too much longer. If I wasn't going to be on the stage or in a university classroom, I needed a new plan—but I couldn't yet quite see what that plan was.

My dancing career wasn't the only thing drawing to a close. The start of the end for Bill and me came one night late in April 1994 when I met a fellow dancer and teacher for dinner. Lisa and I were deep into rehearsals for *Exports*, a show we were working on. I had just watched a recital at the studio where she taught and where we had rehearsed for years. After the show, we decided to grab dinner at a North Dallas bistro. I got there first, so I decided to just have a seat on my own. When I walked in, the first person I saw and the *only* person I saw was a man sitting alone in a booth near the door, waiting for his friends. This man had a light literally shining on his face and amber eyes that beamed right back at me. We smiled.

Damn, I thought. *I feel good.*

Once seated at my table, I ordered myself a glass of wine. Before it even arrived, Larry walked right up and introduced himself.

"When you walked in I thought you were attractive, and I wanted to meet you."

A bold first move, I thought.

I smiled, and we exchanged the usual pleasantries.

"Are you waiting for someone?" he asked.

"Yes," I replied, giving no hint as to the gender of my dining companion. I didn't really think about it at the time, but when Larry tells this story, he's quick to point out I was clearly keeping him guessing.

I told him about *Exports* and, not coincidentally, that I happened to have our recently printed flyers for the dance series. He asked where I lived, and I told him.

"Kind of a rough part of town, isn't it?" he replied.

"Not really," I told him. "I just surround it with white light."

His eyes widened at that, and his mouth curled into a smile. He walked away just as Lisa arrived.

At the end of the evening, Larry angled through the crowd to my side. His shoulder brushed mine.

"Can I call you?" he said, speaking softly under the chatter of our companions.

I didn't hesitate. "Yes."

Yes, even though I was still living with Bill. By that time, Bill and I had agreed that if either of us met someone and felt an attraction, we had permission to pursue the conversation, as long as we remained true to each other. Bill and I were committed to our relationship and to monogamy, but at the same time, there was no jealousy or unrealistic expectations. Conversations were allowed, as long as Bill and I talked about any attraction, but physical connections were off the table.

The following weekend, I went to Austin with another girlfriend. Before I left, I told Bill about meeting Larry, and both of us were fine with me potentially exploring that connection. When I got home from the trip, my bulky answering machine was blinking with five or six messages from Larry. I called him back, and a few minutes into the conversation, Larry began a strange line of questioning.

"Did you grow up in New York?"

"Schenectady and Long Island, mostly."

And then a few minutes later: "Did you go to school up north?"

"I was at Northwestern for a few years, but I graduated from SMU. Where did you study?"

I thought I had steered the conversation successfully to him, but he kept rounding back to those same probing questions about my past: "Have you studied abroad?"

I couldn't help but laugh. "Why are you asking me these questions?" Maybe I should have been wary. If any other man had asked me questions like that, I would have suspected ulterior motives. From the start, though, Larry made me feel comfortable. A strong, calm voice from deep in my chest assured me that this man was safe.

Larry went quiet for a minute. "I'd really rather not say."

"Oh, well, I really would rather that you did," I insisted, my suspicion growing.

My insistence is how I learned that six years ago, Larry had gone to a psychic in New York. Not just any psychic, either—she later became famous for helping the Westchester police department find missing bodies. She predicted that he would meet a woman by the name of Lisa, Laura, or another name beginning with L and that this woman would be his life mate. Two years later he went to another psychic in Dallas, who predicted precisely the same two names, and he became obsessed.

Larry told me he used to play the cassette recordings of the psychic visits side by side just to make sure he didn't miss anything. He said he'd searched for this woman for years until his business coach, David Zelman, told him to let it go, that he was missing all the great Penelopes from Pittsburgh! Larry had never given up searching for his soulmate, but he did release the need to fulfill the psychic's predictions.

I listened to his story with my heart pounding. When he finished, I took a deep breath. "That's really strange," I said, a tremble of excitement on the edge of my voice. "Because that night, when you walked away from the table the second time, I told my girlfriend, 'That's the man I'm going to marry!'" I laughed, hoping I hadn't gone too far. "I didn't even think about it. The words just . . . came to me."

There was another long pause on Larry's end of the phone, and he told me that the psychics had said he would recognize his future mate from the description they had given him and that this woman would recognize Larry immediately, intuitively.

We let that sink in for a bit, absorbing the shock. This was our first phone conversation, after all! I kept asking myself, *Is this guy for real? Can this really be happening to me?* Every few minutes, Larry excused himself from the phone to go to the bathroom. I puzzled over these frequent breaks, but didn't ask. After we had been dating a few months, Larry and I laughed about that first phone conversation, and he told me that he needed the breaks because his entire body had turned hot and his thoughts were running on one loop: "At last! I've found her!"

We decided to meet for dinner at Kathleen's Art Café on Tuesday night. The restaurant was on Lovers Lane and famous for its desserts.

After dinner, he took me to his home. There was real passion there, but I also had my agreement with Bill to uphold, so our playtime didn't go very far. Still, I felt like I was on a runaway train. In those first few hours together we sealed our fate. We figured we would take a shot to see whether there was anything to those psychic predictions made a thousand miles and several months apart.

I trusted Larry completely, though I couldn't articulate why, and I never questioned his story, even after my experience with Danny. It just felt right. By all standards, I had broken every rule in the book, and I didn't care.

Larry didn't just introduce me to love again; he would also introduce me to a man who would have a profound impact on the new career I was about to embark on. I met David Zelman just a few days after Larry and I had our first date. Larry was in the real estate business, and he invited me to his North Dallas office suite, where he mentioned his office mate led a consulting business.

"I want you to meet David," Larry told me.

He didn't tell me much more than that. I knew Larry relied on David for his business perspective, but he'd also valued David's input when he was trying to find the future wife two psychics had predicted. I knew David led transformational trainings and had a PhD in psychology.

I had no idea what I was in for when I strolled into Larry's office, glanced at the simple, gray, modern furniture, and sat down at David's desk. I waited. David looked at me, and I looked at him.

Then he spoke: "So you're a dancer? What's that like?"

Often when people led with this, they were either uninterested in the answer or only interested in hearing wild stories, but David looked genuinely curious. I answered with the enthusiasm dance had always brought out of me.

"It's exciting, infuriating, joyful, exhausting—it runs the gamut," I said with a laugh. "I think that's how art is supposed to be. I'm producing a concert for this upcoming June. It's a show we hope to take to Brazil, a kind of artistic exchange we have with another company. I'd love for you to see it."

"Well, then, I would love to attend." Then, his eyes twinkling, he added, "This story Larry tells me about your meeting is pretty extraordinary. What do you suppose it means?" He had the suggestion of an ironic smile on his face, but it didn't seem like his skepticism was meant to be insulting; he just wanted to know what I thought of all this.

"I'm not sure, but we thought we'd follow this path and see where it takes us." My palms were sweating.

"You're living with another man?"

It was the first time I got to experience the quality I've since come to admire about David: he gets right to the point.

"Yes," I said meekly. "But we're all talking about this and have been one hundred percent open about everything. I've never been in a situation like this before, so I'm not sure how to do this, but—" I held up my hands in a what-can-you-do gesture. "Here I am. We're doing it."

The meeting lasted maybe five minutes. I left after we exchanged a few more pleasantries; and as I walked to the car, I thought about how odd it was to be interviewed by Larry's business consultant. After all, I was the director of a dance company, a choreographer and dancer, and Larry and I were beginning a relationship, not a realty deal. What had just happened?

Afterward, Larry told me that as soon as I had gone, David had walked over to Larry's desk, folded his arms, and said, "Any reason why you wouldn't marry this one?"

My meeting with David had been for Larry, to help him make sure that despite the crazy situation with Bill, he was following the right path by pursuing a relationship with me. But the meeting turned out to be just as significant for my own path. I was stepping into a new world, not just with Larry but with my eventual transition out of dance. I didn't know it at the time, but in David I had found a guide who would help me on that path. For many years to come I would avidly study David's methodologies and his uncanny ability to draw out someone's essence in a few precise questions. The seeds of that transformation were already there in our first meeting.

A couple of weeks later, Bill, Larry, and I sat down in the duplex Bill and I shared. Larry and I told Bill that we had decided to pursue our connection and see where it would take us. We said we wanted to be together.

Bill was calm, but he doubted that my connection to Larry was as real and deep as we felt it to be. "This is an aberration," he said, without a trace of anger. "It won't last. But okay. Let's set some ground rules."

I rolled my eyes. Bill loved ground rules.

How is it possible to even have that type of conversation without delving into accusations and hurt? Falling in love while you're in a relationship is always bound to be messy, and there's a lot of emotional baggage about who gets to call the shots. But with Bill and Larry involved, it was the most evolved discussion we could be having about this subject. That evening we decided on a set of guidelines. Until we finished my current production—which Bill was helping me get to the stage—I would live with Bill. I would see Larry whenever I wanted to, but there would be "no exchange of bodily fluids." That was it. After the show, all bets were off.

And the rules worked. For the next six weeks, I spent time getting to know Larry, falling in love with him, while I continued to live with Bill, working with him on *Exports*. He helped me with the marketing and kept me sane through all the chaos of putting on a new show.

In those weeks, I marveled over how completely I could love both men. With Larry, I felt the fresh love of discovery and the promise of a future. With Bill, I was surprised by how much our love endured. I watched as he fulfilled his commitments to me, with steadfast loyalty and even with humor and irony. He supported me and kept inviting people to the show. He rubbed my feet after every rehearsal. When it was all over, he took full charge of packing up the apartment and helping me move out.

The last night at the apartment, surrounded by boxes filled with parts of our life together, I broke down and cried. I was ready to move on, and I loved Larry, but Bill had also deeply impacted my life. Moving out hurt.

Bill didn't say anything, but he crawled beside me on the floor and held me as I sobbed, patting my hair. I could hear his heartbeat under his shirt, the way I had been able to feel it every night he had held me close. As my sobs died down, some of my grief at the ending was filled with profound gratitude at all that Bill had shared with me. That gratitude continues to this day.

I moved in with Larry on a Fourth of July weekend. Texas does Independence Day large, and I unpacked with the sounds of cheers and fireworks in the distance. As I put away my clothes and carved out a space for myself in Larry's life, I had such a sense of coming home. With him, I was where I was supposed to be. I had these eerie déjà vu experiences in his home, which would soon become our home. I felt bathed in love, and a deep peace entered my heart. I could rest now and grow in new ways.

My first wedding may have happened at the start of a winter storm, but my second took place under a blazing summer sun amid smiles and laughter. It was the perfect culmination of a year of growth and loving.

We had decided to get married outside, at the Randall Davey Audubon Center and Sanctuary in New Mexico, where we exchanged our vows surrounded by the dense, hardy green of piñon pine and junipers and the craggy peaks of the Sangre de Cristo Mountains that rose to the east. I took greedy lungfuls of the crisp mountain air.

The night before, we'd all stayed up late at the rehearsal dinner, enveloped by the love of friends and family, who toasted us into our new life. Late that evening, I thought of my mother and some part of me reached out—my heart ached, wishing she could have met Larry and seen how happy I was now. I went to bed feeling as though in some way she was there, as though in some way we had spoken.

When I woke on my wedding day, I hit the ground running. There was a massage and the bustle of getting ready, culminating in a salon appointment for hair and makeup at noon. It felt like I was getting married for the first time, and the day was full of tiny miracles. There were even spaces of stillness. Once I was ready, there was time to relax and just enjoy the moment. Our friends and family had done a wonderful job of keeping Larry and me from seeing each other.

When I was looking out the window and hoping the weather would hold, Amy came into the room, holding an embroidered handkerchief of her daughter's and a small blue conch shell.

"Something borrowed and something blue," she told me, as I ran my hands over the familiar scrap of fabric and admired the deep blue of the shell. "I'm so happy for you, Lori," she said. We hugged, and when we pulled away, neither of us was dry eyed.

"Thank you."

Amy held out a small gift bag, and my eyes widened in surprise. "You didn't have to," I told her.

"This is . . . just open it."

Inside was the most wonderful surprise, and we cried together when I pulled out the small topaz ring that had rested on my mother's finger for so many years. Gently, I smoothed my fingers over the cool rectangular stone and the thin gold band. I slipped it onto my finger and felt the embrace of my mother's love, years after she was gone. I would learn later that Amy had told Larry she had been looking for the perfect time to give me my mother's ring. My wonderful sister had certainly done that, adding just one more amazing moment to a day full of them.

My wedding day was certainly full of happy tears, but there was a lot of laughter, too. Our photographer was Lisa Law, famous for her celebrity photos and her book and documentary, *Flashing on the Sixties*. She was hilarious, and we spent much of our time giggling as she shepherded us into poses, her camera lens clicking away. She posed us for boudoir shots first and then in all our wedding finery.

Then it was time to drive up to the Randall Davey Audubon Center for the ceremony. In my full wedding regalia, I insisted on getting into the driver's seat.

"It feels right," I told Sherri in the car, navigating my way around the turns. "It just feels really right to be in control and drive up to my own wedding."

In the end, we were having so much fun taking photos and laughing that I almost missed my cue. We heard the music stop and my bridesmaid and I scrambled into place. A huge smile was on my face. Under the sunshine, I walked up the slope and around the corner to the clearing where we were to exchange our vows. Larry gasped when he saw me, and as I walked down the "aisle" along the grass, I could see his eyes fill with tears.

"You're so beautiful," he whispered to me when I came to a stop by his side.

The sun kept peeking out as we were married, and I could feel its warmth on my face as Eileen, the woman officiating our ceremony, recited the words that would make us husband and wife. She recited Indian love poems, the beautiful phrases in perfect harmony with the green around us.

When it was time to exchange vows, I couldn't help but laugh when Larry promised he'd relinquish his need to be right, and he chuckled when I promised I'd keep my promises. Both of us looked deeply into each other's eyes. I wasn't just repeating words; I was moving into a shared future with him.

Our friends and family came forward to share their love, and then Larry and I made the mad dash to the car while our friends showered us with birdseed and bubbles, rather than the traditional rice. Someone had put two big hearts on the windshield, and Larry carefully helped me and my dress into the car, and we waved at the friends and family clustered around us, basking for a moment in our shared joy and their good wishes before we looked at each other. Ensconced in our newly formed world, we drove off into our new life.

Chapter 8

stepping into a new possibility

While my marriage with Larry was beginning, DURC was coming to an end. By the fall of 1999, Larry and I had already contributed tens of thousands of dollars of our own money to the company. There's no question that we were keeping it afloat, and the pattern was clearly unsustainable. So Larry and I agreed: if I could pull off that season's production without going into the red, the company could continue. But if the project lost money, it was over. It was our ultimatum to the universe.

I threw myself into that production. We ordered a glossy brochure celebrating our two decades. We hired the best dancers we could afford and a well-respected marketing director, whose primary job was to get butts in seats. We rehearsed hard and long, and as the show began to come together, I felt my passion for this art rising again. Energy and excitement made me squirm in bed as I played the rehearsals in my head. In the studio and on the drive home, my body hummed along with the energy.

But despite my laser-beam focus on the art, the writing was on the wall. The first of the production's many problems was its timing. We'd be performing for two weeks in December, one of the hardest times to put on a dance production. If you're not performing *The Nutcracker*, people aren't interested. There's too much else going on: traveling, family time, shopping. And in Dallas, a city known for its society functions, performances in December have to compete with holiday parties in full swing.

Then there were the dancers I hired. We could afford to pay them the standard rates for part-time dancers in a small company but no more, and I knew all too well that those wages were barely enough to survive on. I was also aware that a bigger dance company could offer dancers of that caliber more than we could. I liked to think I was able to attract what dancers I did based on our reputation as an innovative artistic organization, but even then, we could almost never afford understudies or backup dancers. What we paid stretched our budget to the limit. If someone was injured or just took off without notice, the entire production was in jeopardy. We all worked together and laughed together, soaking up the sweat and effort of dance with jokes and drinks after rehearsal, but underneath was the tension that this could all come down like a house of cards.

My own part of the production required me to dance closely with an especially talented dancer. Joseph was so talented, in fact, that I was surprised when he agreed to join the production for next to nothing. I soon learned, however, that Joseph wasn't quite the bargain I'd imagined. He came with baggage—and lots of it. He would disappear for days at a time. He was quite young, and dance was maybe not the only thing calling to him.

After one of his two-day absences, I scheduled a special rehearsal. We were practicing a comedy piece called *L'Anniversaire*, inspired by a Chagall painting of the same name. In it Joseph and I played two love-struck house servants, maid and butler, romping together while our employers were away. It was campy and raunchy and fun, and while it looked light to the audience, this dance required precise timing and superb partnering. I hadn't performed it for at least three years, so I was rusty. And I couldn't deny that I was getting older. The last time I had performed the dance I had been in my thirties. Though I was still limber at forty-two, things that had once been easy for me now required a little more effort.

Could I have hired someone else to play the role I played? Yes. Would it have all gone differently? Maybe. Since then, I've reflected on how driven I was to be the one to perform the piece. Part of me felt that it had to be me playing this role. After all, I was leading DURC and I was the dancer with the most experience. A big part of me also didn't want to spend the time and effort coaching someone else for the role. Now I know to question my assumptions about what can and can't be done, but back then it seemed obvious that I would be the one dancing the piece.

It was my job to teach the dance to Joseph and to know the crucial details that could make or break the production. Toward the end of that rehearsal, we'd made our way through most of the piece but still had the climax to go over. One of the final lifts required my partner to hoist me to a sitting position on one shoulder for a split second. Then, as he bent forward from his hips to make his back flat like a table, parallel to the floor, I was supposed to simultaneously roll backwards, so that we would be back to back: him facing the floor, me facing the ceiling. From there, he would grab my upper body and swing my legs and torso to the front of his body, ending the sequence in a "fish lift," my legs together high in the air, my face turned up adoringly to his. Basically, we turned into a couple of intertwined pretzels, all in about four beats of music.

On our first attempt, we successfully executed the shoulder-sit. But I didn't realize until far too late that I'd somehow forgotten to instruct Joseph to lean forward into the tabletop position. Oops. When I began to roll back in preparation for the fish, there was no broad, muscled back to catch me—only empty air. I fell through space for a fraction of a second and went crashing to the floor, landing with a thud on the right side of my head.

I blinked up at the ceiling.

"Are you okay, are you okay?" Joseph screamed from somewhere above me.

Was I okay? I wasn't sure. Could I move my toes? Yes. Could I move my fingers? Yes. Could I dance? Hmmm. There was a lot I wanted to say in that moment. *You dropped me! You went AWOL. This dance company let me down. The lousy attitude toward the arts in this city has stood in my way.* But there was nothing for me to do but get up and survey the damage.

I sat up and gingerly moved my head side to side. I was stunned, my head throbbing, and I delicately moved my fingers and toes. I counted three when Joseph held up his fingers in front of my face. I stood up with my arm around Joseph's shoulder, and we slowly and painfully walked out of the studio together. The whole time I hobbled away from the scene, I was trying to work up the courage to dust myself off and get back in gear.

I did go to a chiropractor the next day and took it easy for a while, but I got back into rehearsals soon after. We even performed the piece. I got back up on the horse pretty darn close to immediately, but when I stepped out onto the stage with my company, I couldn't quite shake the fear and lack of trust that had come from my fall. And beneath the surface, anger simmered. I may have blamed Dallas, DURC, and Joseph (maybe not in that order), but I knew deep inside that I had caused this. My fall became "the sign." If I ever needed an excuse to leave, there it was, sharp and sudden as a blow to the temple.

Being dropped on my head was only the beginning. DURC needed to put butts in seats, and that just didn't happen. The operating and production funds didn't materialize, and neither did our audiences—at least not in the numbers that would have made a difference. The marketers and fundraisers we'd hired to avert this outcome didn't pull through.

And the artistic director? Yes, I had failed too. I'd been so focused on the dance that I hadn't managed the people who were in charge of raising funds and bringing in audiences. I let the performance carry me away, and I didn't look to the logistics of making a success. We lost money. It was the end of DURC. I was going to walk away.

Once the decision to leave the dance company was final, I felt like a boat with no mooring, adrift. The process of taking DURC apart was so painful that I didn't tackle the task right away. I let the holidays come and go, let myself get swept up in the tide of tinsel and cheer and goodwill toward men. It wasn't until February that I was able to take a deep breath and start disbanding.

As in every disbanding, there was pain. I especially remember one dancer, Jennifer, who took part in that final production. She was intensely talented, and it was hard to tell her there wouldn't be more roles for her with us. Shortly after, I met her in New York City, and she admitted that she had been angry and disappointed about the end of DURC.

"There were a lot of people looking to you to create something there, in Dallas."

The words had a bit of a sting to them, and I felt the guilt of letting her and the other talented dancers go. One thing that helped soothe that hurt was knowing the dancers were all strong enough to forge their own trails. Jennifer landed a role in Robert Battle's dance company and went on to dance in New York.

Cutting the cord on DURC hurt. Mostly, it was a mercy killing. But as I drove away from the studio a final time, the building fading in the rearview mirror was like a piece of self I had abandoned by the side of the road.

• • •

As DURC faded from view, I became aware that waiting quietly in the wings there had always been the hint of another life. In 1997, before I had any plans to give up the company, I included networking as one of my strategies both for building a board of trustees for the dance company, and for helping me find supporters, fans, and corporate sponsors. In one of the groups I attended, I met Lori Link, an executive coach. The fact that we had the same name didn't escape my notice. In some ways she was indeed the "Lori link"—the bridge between the Lori Darley who led a dance company and the Lori Darley who would coach leaders. As DURC came to a close, I already had the coaching in place to support me in my transition.

Working with Lori Link made me see that I had adopted a type of habitual deafness. When it came to money, artistic suffering, and artistic entitlement, I refused to hear the internal conversations I was having about these areas. I would tell myself stories about money struggles or about artistic suffering and I'd reap the benefits. I wore my artistic suffering like a badge of honor. That was the payoff—I got to be the long-suffering artist and even feel virtuous for it. But now I'd reached a point where I could ask, *Why do I have to sacrifice? Who says I have to sacrifice?* I experienced curiosity about who

I was. If I was not a dancer and a choreographer, what else could I be? After telling myself that those things were my identity and my gift to the world, how could I unhook myself from that line of thinking?

Lori Link wasn't the only guide I had in navigating this transition. As he had since the beginning of our relationship, Larry wholeheartedly supported me as I explored the identity I had constructed so far and my evolving purpose in life. He knew firsthand what the process was like: he'd devoted himself to transformation, doing a tremendous amount of personal work through therapy and personal growth trainings.

During Larry's own development, David was always right there, helping him through the process. David wasn't just an office mate but a trusted adviser—as I had been too. Larry would talk with David about business issues he needed clarity on and then bring them home to discuss them with me. More than a few times, my opinions aligned almost exactly with David's.

For example, early in our marriage, Larry was thinking about signing on for a new project in his real estate business. He had researched and considered the pros and cons and had done his due diligence, yet Larry was still uncertain.

"Is it ridiculous to spend this much time considering one project?"

"Is it really about pros and cons?" I asked across the dinner table. "What are you looking to get from this arrangement, and how can you achieve that?"

Larry looked at me in surprise. "You know, that's almost exactly what David said. Almost to the word."

It wasn't the first time and wouldn't be the last time Larry said this, but I got curious. "What do you mean? How is it the same?"

"David asked me if writing lists of pros and cons really helps me. Then he asked me to write down what my ideal business arrangement would look like and how the proposed project would fit into that vision."

Interesting. I sometimes wondered whether Larry wanted to connect the dots and see similarities that didn't exist. At the same time, I kept those reinforcements close to my heart; the idea that a successful coach and I had asked the same questions or offered the same guidance would be a powerful confidence booster in my coming early years as a coach.

I learned most from Larry by observing. For example, when Larry was thinking about changing real estate companies, we went out for dinner with the owner of one of the companies he was considering. After our appetizers had arrived, and while we were sipping our drinks, I started to interview the man.

"I'm interested in hearing more about your company. What's your purpose for the business?"

The man looked flustered and fumbled for an answer, then quickly rerouted the conversation. No matter how many times I circled gently back to the topic—"What's your vision for the company? Why did you start this business?"—he seemed stumped. Maybe he had simply set up the company to sell real estate and make money. Everything in the company focused on those two goals, but during the dinner he didn't articulate even those goals.

At home, when Larry was changing for bed, he told me he wasn't going to work for that company, and my questions were a large part of the reason.

"I want my work to matter and make a difference, to be about more than making money."

Discussing these sorts of decisions together made me appreciate how conscious Larry was about the choices he made. And not only did he think carefully about his immediate professional choices, but he also made sure to continue his overall development as a businessman and a person. He went to conferences for Social Venture Network, a nonprofit organization for business leaders who want to make a difference, and worked with coaches to better understand himself and support his success. He was committed to working on himself and his business, and he read self-actualization books, worked with coaches, and attended workshops for business leaders. And I traveled that journey with him. Many nights, we stayed up late discussing what we had learned. We continue this work together in personal development to this day.

David, too, was a huge help when I decided to walk away from dancing. He helped me explore some of the ideas floating around in my head as I wondered, *What next?* With him, I brainstormed developing a one-woman show, becoming a writer/performer, or transitioning into a transformational coach.

With the help of coaches like David and Lori Link, the support of my husband, and the wisdom I gained from myself through journaling and reflection, it became clear that the answer had been there all along. Coaching was in my future, but I realized, too, that it was also in my past. The possibilities I loved about dance—of reaching people, making a difference—were also the types of connections that I would eventually make as a coach. I was already coaching and teaching dancers. In many ways, my life had been a long preparation for this grand leap. From the moments I had read Seth with the Orlandos, to the times I had watched my mother exploring her spirituality at our kitchen table, to the talks about Ram Dass in college, I had embraced wholeheartedly the journey to learning more about what existed beyond the flesh-and-blood of me, beyond the thoughts, beyond the body's seeming limits. I had been in a lifelong apprenticeship for the next part of my journey and I hadn't even known it.

Dance and movement have actually been a path to self-awareness and self-actualization for thousands of years. Many forms of tribal dance are intended to build awareness, promote healing, and strengthen community. Gabrielle Roth, a dancer and musician with an interest in shamanism, had been teaching people about using dance as a meditative practice for many years before I became a coach, and I was influenced by her work. I wanted to combine this appreciation for movement and the power of the body with real business results. I didn't want my clients to just feel better; I wanted them to experience new possibilities in their professional lives, too.

I became a coach at a very exciting time in the field. Eckhart Tolle arrived on the scene, as did Abraham-Hicks and Deepak Chopra and Marianne Williamson. At the time, the news was filled with stories about these teachers, Oprah reigned supreme over the idea of self-work, and self-help had gone mainstream. It seemed as though everyone was looking for answers and was talking openly about trying meditation, yoga, and other paths to find clarity.

To become a coach, I had to become my first and most important client. I dove in, becoming the most cooperative lab rat for the ongoing experiment called my life. I devoured books, including *The Last Word on Power: Executive Re-Invention for Leaders Who Must Make the Impossible Happen*, *If the Buddha Married*, and everything I could find by Thomas Leonard, considered by many to be the father of personal coaching. He also founded two training schools for coaches, and I took a number of online courses based on his ideas, including from the Graduate School of Coaching. I also read Peter Senge and other resources on systems theory. I set out on a mission to learn as much as I could about how our perceptual reality—our thoughts, beliefs, and conditioned ways of being—impacts organizational success.

David Zelman continued to be a beacon for me in this field. He eventually founded the Transitions Institute, where he has helped thousands of people realize one simple thing: they are most successful when their intentions and actions are aligned and in support of a future they are committed to and deeply desire. His Transitions work would have a significant impact on me when I first went through his process in 1999. I happily became one of his clients.

In early 2000, David invited me to participate in his Train the Trainer program for the Transitions Process. He wanted to give other coaches an opportunity to use this work in their own professional processes. I jumped at the opportunity. I was looking for a map. I wasn't sure what kind, but if I was going to coach people, I knew that the ontological framework was the playground I wanted to play in.

David's program delivered: the Transitions Process did give me a map, not just for how to become a coach, but for being a human being and navigating beyond our strong need to color within the lines. Even more importantly, it also gave me deep insight into human consciousness and offered a way to tailor my coaching work to make a difference for people in almost any scenario.

Train the Trainer was so much more for me than a two-month inquiry into how I could use these strategies in my coaching business. It became a fifteen-year mastery program that harked back to the old apprenticeship system. At different times and in different situations, David was part mentor, part tutor, and often a cocreator and coleader. He repeatedly demonstrated to me his astounding ability to completely reorganize my way of looking at the world and to inspire me to impact people in ways I never would have thought possible.

Working with David was exhilarating, but it also pushed me. David never let you get away with much.

"Write a list of your significant life events," he told us early in the Train the Trainer program. After we had scribbled for some time, he added, "Now, write down what each event means and why they meant that to you."

I was here to learn how to be a coach. What did my own past have to do with anything? I shifted in my chair, my pen hovering about the page. I looked up and saw David looking at me. I got back to writing.

As I finished that assignment, I figured we had to be done with the excavation; how much deeper could we go on our second day? But I was wrong. As soon as everyone had put down their pens, David was back at the front of the room, ready with new instructions.

"Okay, now it's time to start a new list. Write down all of your incompletions—all the people, events, and stories you carry around with you that keep you up at night or have you avoiding certain people."

When I complained to Larry about it afterward, he laughed.

"When I started working with David, he had me start with a list of incompletions. I didn't want to do it at first. I kept asking him how all that could matter to my business. But he told me he wouldn't work with me until I completed that list, so I wrote it down. And let me tell you, it opened my eyes. I couldn't believe all the stuff I was holding on to and the difference tackling it made—in my life and my business."

When David went over the lists again the following day, I got a sense of what Larry was talking about. I realized the lists were an entry point into the process of reauthoring a life. I first needed to take responsibility for making those events and outcomes mean what I said. One of the items on my list was DURC's financial woes. In my head, and on the lists, I blamed the Dallas arts scene and the donors who let us down. Working with David, I understood that I had to take responsibility for the company not really connecting to the sensibilities of the Dallas audience. This list-making wasn't a vent session; it was an exercise in Clearing—although I didn't know it then. To help others, I had to address my own issues and stop carrying my own unexamined luggage.

I still have those lists somewhere. They were fundamental in teaching me what I could teach others, but also in my transition to becoming a source of support for others. It's hard to give someone a hand when your fist is clenched around old fears and resentments. David showed me how to meet people with both hands open.

Soon after completing the Train the Trainer program, I was invited to become one of the faculty members at the institute David had founded. We became good friends, and Larry and I often shared family holidays and travel with David and his wife, Karen.

David was not my only guide and trainer. In 2004, I was already coaching and getting on-the-job experience, which would ultimately become my most important method for developing my coaching practice. But that year, another major influence came into my life.

I was working with coaches at a major Fortune 500 transportation company. The company was committed to developing its team and had invested in programs and sessions for its employees and leaders. I was one of the coaches involved, and from my peers I heard about a free event on Embodied Leadership at the Addison Conference center. It was being led by someone named Richard Strozzi-Heckler. I'd never heard of him, so I did a little digging.

My research showed me that Richard did coaching work primarily through the body, which intrigued me. I had worked with clients one-on-one and had led a few group coaching sessions, but our work had mostly used words, or what is known in the coaching world as a linguistically focused methodology. I asked my clients questions and we discussed the answers—or lack thereof. Instinctively, I had also done some work with the body, asking clients about tensions they felt in their body or encouraging clients to be fully present in their physicality. I had never, however, formally trained to coach using the body.

So I did what I realized later almost always turns out well for me: I showed up.

I walked into the large, carpeted conference room where the Embodied Leadership conference was being held and found a seat among other participants. My eyes were immediately drawn to the front of the room, where the business coaches stood alongside the consultants. Some of them were dressed in conservative suits, but they weren't what I had noticed. I was looking at the man standing in the center of the group.

Richard Strozzi-Heckler is a few inches shy of six feet, and very compact. But even around taller people dressed in fancier suits, he commanded attention. There was a sense of peace around him completely devoid of the restlessness most people exhibit unconsciously—picking at a stray thread in a shirt, shifting weight from foot to foot, avoiding eye contact with strangers. He stood centered and steady. When others spoke, he focused on their words completely, as if there were nothing more important to him in the world.

We began by standing in a circle. In his calm voice, Richard spoke about his journey of understanding the body's knowledge and his experience as a sixth-level black belt aikido master.

"Our culture has diminished the value of our felt experience," he said. "We're evolving into creatures with a highly developed logical mental process. But we're also cut off from our most primal access to wisdom." As Richard began to talk about the insights that can only be gained when engaging the body, and discussed using the body to open awareness, I was completely entranced.

The first exercise seemed simple enough. We learned that our bodies were barometers, and the dimensions of length, width, and depth had specific significance. First, we expanded our spines, focusing on length. This was a metaphor for our dignity and action—our sense of self.

Then we rocked back and forth on our feet, exploring the depth of our bodies in order to connect with our relationship to past and future. How were we leading into the future? What was our relationship with what went before?

"Focus on the width of your body," Richard instructed. "How do you inhabit the space to the right side of you? To the left side of you? Allow yourself to explore that now."

I swayed from side to side, aware as I did that others beside me were doing the same.

Richard added, "The width you inhabit is a metaphor for your relationship with others, with community."

As I absorbed his words and continued moving, I became keenly aware of the people around me.

"The body is a metaphor for our human experience. Nothing is possible without the body."

As Richard walked us through the exercises, I was completely focused on the idea that my body represented my access to what I was committed to. The quality of presence in my body impacted the results I could achieve or not achieve. Immediately, this idea slotted into place and I felt a deep connection with what I was learning. This made sense to me at a visceral level.

We learned about aikido, a martial art that Richard used as more than just a way of besting an opponent. In Richard's hands, aikido became a way to practice breath and intention, a way of using the body to make movements while also focusing on commitment.

I remember that halfway through that day, for example, we were learning a basic aikido move called the two-step. Essentially, you step forward and make a 180-degree pivot, a move that was pretty familiar to me, as a dancer. Elementary, even. We did it with partners, we executed it on our own, we each did the step on our own time. Because of the pivot, the move had a slightly swirling quality and a flow to it. Some people spun strong and others wobbled slightly.

After we had practiced for some time, Richard spoke again. "I want you to notice that even though each of you has been taught the same step, each individual's step is a little different, because the embodiment is coming through the movement."

Next, Richard had us declare what we were committed to during our two-step; so each time we took the step forward, we had to say our commitment out loud. Over and over as I moved, I said the simple words, "I'm a coach helping people explore new possibilities."

As we moved, Richard walked around the room, observing and commenting. When he walked up to me, he spent a few seconds watching in that calm and focused way.

"You know this work," he told me. I felt seen and enlivened. I felt what was possible.

When I got home that night, I still felt some of the energy of the movements, and I talked to Larry about it.

"There's something here for me," I told him. It wasn't a surprise to either of us that I quickly committed to a yearlong certification program in Somatic Coaching from the Strozzi Institute, the organization Richard had founded.

The term "somatic" comes from the Greek word *somatikos*, meaning living, pertaining to the living body in its wholeness. As soon as I signed up for the training, I knew I was opening something huge in my life.

The Strozzi Institute attracted people from all over the world. We met and trained outside Petaluma, California, a spot surrounded by ranches, rolling hills, and an occasional winery. Each day, I'd put on my exercise gear and walk along the rock paths to the dojo where we trained. I'd push open the heavy wooden door, with its large iron latch, and step into the still energy inside.

A dojo is traditionally a place of learning, or a "place of the way." At one point, dojos were built right next to temples in Japan, although today we tend to describe any space where martial arts are taught as a dojo. The Strozzi dojo was filled with sunlight and divided between a carpeted waiting area and a large gray padded floor where we did our exercises. The walls were covered with black and white Japanese characters.

This is where we centered ourselves. We grounded our energy. We gave and received feedback. We meditated and contemplated the poetry of David Whyte, Mary Oliver, and others.

For many days, we practiced with *jo kata*. These are thirty-one moves we executed with the *jo*, a Japanese wooden staff about five feet long. When completed, the movements are graceful and fluid, one long dance. We practiced together and separately, but it wasn't about balance or martial arts. This was an exploration of clues to our inner life, with our body helping us uncover what words didn't always reveal. How balanced was I that day? From what place in myself was I leading? What part of me was I leaving behind? The focused movements in that quiet dojo and my own deep listening to the clues of my body helped me see.

I met others while I studied with Richard and the other coaches. I connected with executives from the aerospace industry and global engineering firms, people with doctorates in integral theory and organizational development, and people just in transition. Each of us was on this journey, and I was blown away by the generosity of everyone there.

"Remember to stay balanced along the vertical line and from left to right. Drop your weight to the ground," our instructor told us before we began our practice. "Remember to connect to your commitments, your breath."

This was familiar territory from my dance classes, but the aim was completely different. Here, we were using the body to achieve clarity about a business approach or concept. It wasn't about performance or the body itself. The body served our lives and our vision.

"By training the body, we're learning to move differently in the world," we learned.

I felt completely at home. This was, in words, what I had felt in my heart all my life.

Just as I had already mastered how to direct my energy in the body to communicate stories in dance, this discipline trained practitioners to direct their energy to ground their commitments, blend effectively with others' commitments, and take a powerful stand for what was most important to them. Most importantly, this work gave me powerful tools when my clients were triggered by events or even their thoughts.

In addition to practicing in the dojo, we trained with somatic work. Again, we turned to our bodies, noticing where we were armored, where we stopped our breath, where we were holding grief. In doing so, we learned how to support coaching clients in uncovering the same truths in their own bodies.

Finally, in 2005, it was time for my exam. This consisted of standing in front of everyone and speaking what I had learned in a way that people would *get*. I took a deep breath, centered and anchored my body, and started to speak.

To this day, I don't remember much about what I specifically said, but I do recall it poured from me like a live poetry performance, the words drawn from some deep part of myself. When I finished, I looked around the faces in the class, feeling both drained and exhilarated.

After a beat, Richard turned that calm focus to me and repeated to me the words that had so profoundly touched me in that conference room many months ago: "You are made for this work."

I moved to sit down, still feeling the energy of the performance. I noticed the difference between "You know this work" and "You are made for this work." I felt I was being given the gift of ownership. I could own this work and be in the world to use it in transforming lives and bodies.

We had our graduation ceremony in December of 2005. As we celebrated in the California sunshine, reminiscing about our days in the dojo and our work together, I felt as though I was on the precipice of a whole new way of coaching.

What did working with Richard teach me? One of the most profound things I learned is that our conditioning lives in our bodies, and we can move and act beyond our conditioning through embodied practice. The things we learn—the automatic responses, our "truths" about how the world works, our perspective on ourselves—exist not just in our minds but in our bodies. We may think success is simply mind over matter, but unreconciled stories remain in our bodies, buried deep, and they come through in how we stand and sit and walk and run.

Yet by changing the way we move, we can get past these conditioned responses. If we believe, at some deep level, that we're not good enough for success, for example, targeting where in our bodies that feeling resides allows us to make changes to our movements and posture to help us alter that way of thinking in a much deeper way than simply talking about it. Later, I became an associate for the Strozzi Institute, and I also obtained a license, which meant I could use its models and worksheets in my own trainings.

You're probably detecting a pattern here—as was I!

The training systems I studied help coaches learn to teach others to use their bodies, as both a barometer for the emotional experience and as a place to unpack language. Our bodies are significantly more than a vehicle to exercise or perform daily tasks. The body is actually our vehicle for communication, action, and connecting powerfully with ourselves and others. It helps us achieve all kinds of goals. The first step is connecting with the physical self. Imagine beginning a leadership training by first simply walking around a room and noticing how you walk. Notice what part of your body is leading you. Is it your head? Your hips? Your belly? Do you fill out the length of your body or do you collapse into yourself? Are your shoulders all locked up into your neck, or are you balanced, walking without the herky-jerky motions of someone out of sync with their own physicality?

Once you can see where your body is leading you, you can consciously choose to lead with something else. If you find you walk slouched, for example, you can create power by filling out the length of your body to embrace your full self. If you find you lead with your belly, you can consider how leading with your head or hips might change your approach. If you led with your hips, what would that bring? If you led with open arms, how might that transform your day-to-day life?

The aikido training and Strozzi training resonated so deeply with me that I could feel my ribs strumming. Here were people doing work with bodies—and with spirit, soul, and the whole self—and not just having clients create endless lists or relying solely on words. I had spent my whole life dancing and moving, creating new realities and various moods through movement, and the possibility of using these lessons to support others was heady. Finally, I had a bridge between my dancing and my desire to guide.

My training also changed *me*, not just the way I would approach clients. For an entire year I looked at the body as not only a metaphor, but also a delivery system for living life full-out—committed, engaged, and equipped to lead. I learned how to calm my own high-strung nature when I couldn't dance it out. My training also signified a bridge of awareness between the body's wisdom and the linguistic structures of the coaching work in which I was already invested. I often focused on communication, but the frameworks I'd been exploring opened a new possibility: I could help more people by using the body as well as words as a communication and breakthrough tool. Previously, I'd asked questions of myself or my clients, made lists of blocks, have clients talk through hypothetical scenarios; but now I could also ask questions of the body, uncover blocks in the mind, lead clients in enacting different outcomes. Looking at coaching this way led to some interesting discoveries, both with clients and myself. Maybe I was saying I was fully present at an event, but my body showed I was literally shrinking away from the experience? Well, then the truth was plain: the body doesn't lie.

• • •

Training was one thing, but hanging up my shingle as a coach would still sometimes bring up stage fright. I had been coaching since the Transitions program, meeting clients through networking and word of mouth, but in many ways I was still on new ground (at least compared to my years as a dancer). Even though I was moving in the direction of my dreams, doubts would float up to the surface from time to time.

Those doubts often manifested themselves as clinging to the learning stage of the process, thereby postponing actually putting my new knowledge into practice. I talked to David all the time and jumped at any opportunity to discover more about coaching methods. I trained with David, with Landmark, with Strozzi. I read stacks of books on coaching and self-development and philosophy. I co-led with David and worked with him to develop a Partner's Course, which was designed for couples who were committed to taking their relationships to the next level. Whenever I could, I would sign up for yet another "fly by the seat of my pants," boots-on-the-ground, on-the-job training experience.

Eventually, David sat me down and told me that it was time to look at why I was rushing out to try everything. As I described the latest book I'd read and the newest coaching technique I had unearthed, David looked at me with that little ironic smile.

"You know, Lori, at some point you'll want to see that you already have what you need."

David was obviously well educated, but he also modestly described himself as a one-trick pony. What he meant is that he stuck to his one process, not because he couldn't learn a new one, but because the one he used worked. Often, nuggets of timeless wisdom got revealed through his inquiry even after the client had been through the process several times; each time, they were able to use the same tools to dive deeper. David didn't try lots of Transitions techniques—he determinedly shined a light on what was already there to support his clients as they uncovered their own insights.

In time, I would also streamline what I taught and what I brought into my practice. At first, I was so entranced with the new world I was entering that I wanted a taste of it all. It was like being a young dancer again and watching everyone else—the ballerinas on their toe shoes, Amy's modern dance pieces, the jazz dance next door.

As I defined and tweaked what I wanted to support and bring into my coaching world, David was always there. He has shaped me perhaps more than anyone except my parents.

Over time, I was able to put down the books, look up from the screen, and begin my practice. All of that learning was like potential energy just waiting to become kinetic, bunched muscles prepared to spring; now I was ready to move.

Of course, just because I'd faced my apprehensions about being a coach didn't mean everything was easy from then on out. Internal doubts might be the hardest to overcome, but persevering despite doubt from others is no picnic, either. I soon discovered that like any other profession, the world of coaching can be quite political. The connections and pedigrees that led to power—or lack of it—in this world were based on a handful of surface details: What's your background? Where did you go to school? Who do you know? Since my story didn't match the accepted narrative for an executive coach, there were hurdles in my path: assumptions, judgments, biases. But though I was transitioning to a new career, I was still a dancer at heart; if there were hurdles in front of me, I'd clear them with one giant leap after another.

I met one of my clients, Alice, at an event through a local women's networking group. She and her husband were starting a courier business and were looking for an executive coach. We talked at the event and hit it off, both of us concluding we'd work well together. We exchanged information, and I looked forward to helping Alice create the company she wanted. She would later tell me what happened when she got home that evening.

"There's an executive coach I'm interested in hiring," Alice told her husband while they relaxed on their deck after a long day of trying to get their business up and running.

At first, Rod, Alice's husband, seemed excited. "Oh, yeah?" he asked. "Who is it?"

She rotated her laptop toward him, showing him my online profile.

Rod read over all the details and huffed. "Her? She has a degree in dance from SMU, for crying out loud! She's a dancer and has only been coaching a few years. I'll look for someone else tomorrow."

He shook his head and turned back to the spreadsheets on his own computer. Alice couldn't quite hide her blush.

"But I've already hired her."

Six months later, Alice and Rod had a war room meeting in their company's bustling offices to review quarterly goals. It had been long enough that we could laugh about what Rod had said. He certainly didn't see me as a lightweight anymore. In fact, that day he even handed me a business card. "My friend Roger is a Marine, and he's trying to get his education media business off the ground. I gave him your name."

It wouldn't be the only time someone would assume that I couldn't get the job done. It made me realize I needed to step into my role more fully. It wasn't just a question of semantics or about calling myself this or that. To really empower people, I'd have to present an image and persona clients could trust implicitly. When my clients were able to see me as an executive coach who could transform their lives, they were better able to put themselves in the position of moving forward and receiving that support. Changing how they saw me would allow me to make a bigger impact in their lives because they could invest more in the process.

But first I had to change how I saw myself.

How did I do it? I turned to my journal. I wrote out all the thoughts scurrying through my mind like demented mice, and noticed the stories I was telling myself—or letting others tell about me. I discovered I was telling myself I was a dancer-turned-coach, instead of a coach. I was telling myself other coaches had more experience and credentials than I did. That may have been true, but why was I so hung up on what other people were doing? I meditated and tried to catch myself telling myself stories about what I could and couldn't do. Then, I practiced consciously setting those stories aside. I wrote out new stories for myself, opened myself to new possibilities.

The real world wasn't done with me yet, though. One of my early experiences in coaching forced me to use every tool in my arsenal to make different choices about my reactions.

It all started when a friend of mine introduced me to someone at a major airline, which was having an open call for coaches. The company had an organizational and training initiative that included yearly company-wide retreats so employees at all levels could meet each other and learn about leadership. Many of the frontline supervisors and other important players had offices all over the state, so there was also a push to get everyone working together as a cohesive whole.

I was intimidated as I pulled up to the office buildings they'd rented for the retreat. This was a big event with powerful business leaders and coaches who had been in the business for years. Higher-ups in power suits were driving up in sleek black sedans, and blue-collar types in jeans and plaid shirts arrived in their pickup trucks.

Inside was equally daunting. In each large room, a head facilitator directed the group through workshops and sessions. Tables were scattered throughout the rooms, each one seating five or six supervisors, operations managers, and other company employees. Each table also had one coach to keep things on track and to launch discussion.

My first year, I was seated at one of the tables as a coach. The managers in their crisp suits peered at me over their workshop papers, eyeing my own modest attire, homing in on any weaknesses (or so I imagined).

There were six of us at the table. Beside me was Jackson. With a shock of gray hair and an expensive navy suit, he narrowed his eyes whenever anyone spoke and twisted his mouth in exasperation every time I suggested we try an exercise. Edward was another employee, much younger. His wire-rimmed glasses forever tilted downward, he fiddled with his phone, every once in a while craning his neck up in annoyance when our session interrupted him. Jane was the only woman at the table, sitting ramrod straight in a red suit. When we were first introduced, she had surveyed me carefully. Ben and Alec worked at a different office and spent much of the time talking to each other about suppliers they were dealing with, ignoring everything the rest of the participants said.

For the first few hours, I led them through a set of communication exercises, all the while trying to ignore the prickling sense of judgment radiating from the members of my table. On breaks, I spoke with the other coaches. Three had PhDs and several had advanced degrees in coaching. Of course, the dreaded question came: "Where did you study, Lori?" I stammered my way through an answer. I felt confident in my abilities, but I was only four years into my new career, still more used to dance than coaching.

Throughout the morning sessions, a voice kept piping up in the back of my mind, some tiny but insistent part of me telling me I was a fraud. I felt as though I were on the witness stand, and I could imagine only too well how the questioning would go: Arms folded, gaze steely and cold, the red-faced prosecutor with vibrating cheeks thunders, "Ms. Darley, is it true that your training is in the art of *dance*? Do you even *have* a coaching certification?" A gasp goes up from the spectators, and suspicious murmurs drown my protests.

But that was fear talking, my own worries about what I could do, who I was. *Remember*, I told myself, taking deep breaths, *you have to see yourself as you want to be seen.* I had to actually embody my commitment to contribute to this small group. I reminded myself I wasn't being paid to be nice—I was paid to tell truth to power. This was *not* about me—it was about being a stand for these employees' own self-awareness and growth.

At the table again after a break, I squared my shoulders and sat tall.

One of the worksheets asked us to play out a scenario with a difficult client. Ben and Alec pulled themselves away from their discussion long enough to sneer their way through the exercise.

"Are you aware you're squinting the entire time?" I asked Ben when they were done.

His pale eyebrows shot up to his hairline. "Pardon me?"

"Your eyes," I told him. "The entire time you were interacting with that 'client,' you were squinting. Is that on purpose? Do you do that with your clients?"

Ben glanced around the table. "I haven't thought about it."

I turned to Alec. "How does it make you feel listening to him when he's looking at you that way? How would the client feel?"

Alec didn't make eye contact. "Maybe scared. Intimidated."

I nodded. "Right. It's one thing to create that reaction on purpose. But what happens when you're not aware?"

I knew I had them. For the rest of the session even Edward put away his phone, and after the day was done, Jane asked me for my business card. I collapsed into bed that night exhausted but elated about what I had accomplished. I was taking somatic coaching training at the Strozzi Institute at the time, and I felt a sense of triumph that I had managed to incorporate some of the teaching about body awareness into my work. Working with those corporate employees—men and women who spent their time dealing with millions of passengers and countless moving parts as they tried to fulfill their obligations—I was reminded again how little self-awareness most people have and of the importance in engaging in this kind of work.

The next year, I wanted to colead the facilitators in the mini training program for the workshop leaders that was always held before the retreat. I planned to work with another coach from the Strozzi group, and together I knew we had the tools to teach employees how to help their clients and other stakeholders. The airline agreed, and we were each given $20,000 to develop a module on embodied intelligence and lead the trainers in supporting the program.

When I arrived at the training center that year, I was full of excitement and energy. I had been studying aikido-based techniques that I was confident would help clients become more aware of their bodies and thoughts.

The setup was essential; so, smiling at the group assembled in front of me, I began by giving context for the exercise. I discussed how we are conditioned to have certain responses, which are encoded in us at the physical level. I talked about the flight-or-fight response and how we tend to think of it as an unavoidable instinct, when in fact we can choose how to react. Once I had laid the groundwork, I happily moved into the exercise, eager for the audience to see it in action.

"We call this the grab technique," I said with focused intent, "and it's based on aikido. I need a volunteer to come up here. The way this works is that I will stand behind you, grab your wrist, and emphatically state your name. The idea is that your body and mind will still react as though there's a threat, even though you rationally know there's none."

I glanced around the quiet audience. "Our goal is to work through that instinctive fear, learn to identify it as irrational, and set it aside. I'll repeat the move a few times, and each time I grab your wrist, I'm going to ask you to describe what you feel—what emotions and physical reactions you have. Once we learn to notice them, we can get past them. Now, who would like to come up and try?"

Silence.

I glanced around the blank faces of my audience and felt the blood drain from my face. Despite my best intentions to stay relaxed, my body began to freeze up, my shoulders stiffening, my knees locking. As a performance artist I knew when an audience was with me, and on that day they were not with me. Some had carefully blank faces, while others smirked openly or stared, affecting boredom, at anything but me. I could hear a single titter in the back. I watched a silent revolt happen before my very eyes.

"Well, look who's being grabbed now? Me!" I joked. There were a few sympathetic chuckles.

My coaching partner and I limped through the rest of the session, performing the exercise with each other and continuing our energetic patter. I put on my bravest face, but beneath the surface, I was deeply shaken. I'd had rough performances in my life, but as a dancer, I'd never actually felt bad on stage. I did today. The entire time, no one said anything. When we were done, a cavernous silence filled the room more completely than any applause I have ever heard.

I walked jerkily to the bathroom to splash water on my face, determined to keep my composure. In the corridor on my way back to the room, two of the coaches who'd been in the audience were walking ahead of me. They were unaware of my presence, but I heard their conversation perfectly.

"I can see us bringing in someone who is an *actual* aikido instructor to do this, but . . ."

Their voices trailed off as they rounded the corner and disappeared from sight. But I didn't need to hear the conclusion of that sentence to understand what they meant. To them, we weren't *real* coaches. We were imposters, cheap imitations. A joke.

I held my tears until I got to the parking lot and in my car. But once there, I broke down, the feeling of betrayal like a brick in my gut. I didn't know then that I would be invited back as the facilitator the following year and would continue working with this client for twelve years, while participating in the piloting and design process for six of those. At the time, I just felt the crushing defeat of that silent, disapproving audience.

I will never forget the ride home. My bawling had subsided to short bursts of sobs, and I drove slowly, feeling as though I had just been kicked out of the tribe. Struggling to win the trust of CEOs or entrepreneurs was one thing, but outright rejection from my peers, those who were traveling the path I'd chosen, those I'd hoped would guide and support me along the way—that was something completely different.

When I finally ran out of tears, I got out of the car and walked up the driveway. My breathing was evening out now, my heart rate slowing. The humiliation of the day still burned, but the crying had soothed it to a bearable throb. Sitting in the car, I'd let myself see all my fears about this path I'd chosen, fears I hadn't known I had, though I'd been walking the path for several years. Now it was time to let them go, make choices, and find my strength.

Inside the house, I picked up the framed picture of my mother I kept on a bookshelf and looked at her familiar smile and dark hair. I thought again how my mother, a smart, complex, beautiful woman, had lived most of her life stuck in the story she told herself about who she was. She had eventually died with the music still inside her. She'd never found the words to sing it; no one had taught her the instruments on which to play it. That wasn't the life I wanted. Despite the pain of the day, I was determined to honor my own music. I put down the framed photo and walked toward my office, ready to try all over again.

part 2

claiming your power

Chapter 9 *the clearing*

did try again. As I got distance from that presentation, I realized that while I absolutely knew my stuff, I had lost sight of some of my training as a dancer. When performing, it doesn't matter how technically competent you are if you can't connect with your audience. As a dancer, I had focused on sending love out to my audience, on making eye contact, on dancing for others. That principle held true in coaching, too; I had to form a bond with my audience, whether it was a roomful of high-powered corporate trainers or a single client. But I saw now that the strategies that had allowed me to create that bond as a dancer wouldn't work in exactly the same way when I needed to reach audiences as a coach. It was simply a matter of developing the tools that worked for the situation and for me. I was confident I could do this; I just needed to figure out the right steps.

I spent time thinking about the aikido techniques I had tried to teach, and the more I thought about it and journaled about it, the more I realized I needed to find a way of communicating that was uniquely mine. The direct route to my audience wasn't the training I had gotten; it was to create something entirely of me and to share that authenticity and vulnerability with them. By journaling, I had realized that the connection I felt to performances I had choreographed myself was very different from the link I felt to someone else's vision. I was enthusiastic about trying to come up with my own vision for coaching, just as I had once instilled creativity in the productions I had helped create.

I had to embrace my own voice again. I had to reconnect to the girl whose college performance of a Shakespeare scene had commanded the attention of an entire class, and I had to use *that* part of me to develop my own materials, my own training systems, and my own completely unique vision. It was time to go back to step one and create.

The idea of creation has transfixed me since I was a girl. At a moment's notice and out of seemingly thin air, I watched my mother create magic around a dinner party. Standing at the front of a studio when I was twelve, I would hear music in my head, and out of the scrap of an idea—a hint of a step, a mood—I would start to craft an entire performance. The blank pages of my journal filled steadily with words, new ideas forming seemingly out of nowhere.

Every so often, I wonder about where ideas come from and wish I had direct access to whatever font of inspiration leads to something novel. I think of Carl Jung and his idea of the collective unconscious, or a story

Elizabeth Gilbert once shared about American poet Ruth Stone standing in a field outside her home, seeing a poem rushing at her over the horizon, like a wild mustang. Stone would race inside to try to capture the whole poem on paper before it galloped past.

My own creation process is not usually so dramatic. Instead, I'm aware that I stand on the shoulders of great teachers, and from this elevation I'm able to reach up and touch something new. On sweet, rare occasions, however, the process does resemble that inspired bolt of creation. Lighting has struck twice for me: once in 2013 and again a year later. In both moments, the white heat of inspiration burned away past ideas and allowed me to step into something new.

In 2013, I was reading about Ken Wilber's Integral Theory—work I had long admired. Wilber talks about classifying all ideas into four quadrants. The upper-left quadrant is called "interior individual accounts," and it is all about the "I" and our individual, internal experiences. The lower-left quadrant is where the interior plural accounts go, and includes thoughts about the "we." Jung's collective unconscious is an idea that belongs in this space. The upper-right quadrant is for exterior individual accounts, or our ideas about external objects and experiences. The lower-right is for exterior plural accounts, where we look at societies from the outside, focusing on the "other" or "them." Marxist ideas about the external forces of capitalism or the bourgeoisie are one example of the lower-right quadrant.

I spent a long time looking at Wilber's elegant square, which contained the entirety of modern Western civilization's thought in one nonlinear and compact image. I was viscerally attracted to the simple sleekness of that image.

At the same time, I was working with clients and, as always, thinking of better ways to serve and support. I had come a long way in my career and in my coaching. I had taken classes, led seminars and workshops. Beneath my skin, though, was an itch to do more and to develop something to help clients even further expand into their possible futures.

But how? I had only a nebulous idea that I wanted to build on the Transitions work I had learned under David Zelman and also include the deep work I had done in embodied intelligence and emotional intelligence. Part of me imagined an exciting method of using the body and emotions to support others in creating expanded futures. But how to do that? What did that look like?

I realized I would have to start with clients. I needed to work on attracting conscious clients ready to dive in and do the work. I became enthralled with the questions—who my ideal clients would be and how I would attract them—and spent hours thinking about the issue and talking it over with Larry. I thought about it as I drove to and from meetings and workshops, as I journaled, as I readied for bed after long days of work.

Gradually, an image appeared—a new business, building on the Transitions work but creating something new, too. From these ideas, an idea for a company—Conscious Leaders—slowly emerged.

But what would this new company do? How would it be different? I needed a way of cracking open people's minds and their ideas about possibility. I needed a framework where people could hang their dreams and goals as they stitched their futures. Would it be a system, a program, a metaphor?

The answer didn't appear right away. For a long time, a clear strategy for organizing and communicating my ideas was elusive, and I spent much of 2013 and part of 2014 chasing it down. I had lots of scraps of ideas, like wisps of smoke. They floated through my mind and I plucked at them and tucked them into my journal. I brainstormed various platforms and coaching models and ways to make Conscious Leaders unique. Over coffee, over lunch, and at random times throughout our day, Larry and I would lob names and concepts back and forth in an ongoing cosmic tennis match.

"The Darley Principle."

"The Path." Hmm. That one had possibilities, even if it sounded like a horror movie.

"What about Lovable Lori's Life Lessons?" Larry asked with a wiggle of his eyebrows.

"I could always call myself the Darley Lama."

In the end, The Clearing showed up out of the blue one bright winter morning in December 2014. The conditions couldn't have been further from a Clearing. I was confused and overwhelmed and on the verge of giving up. Larry and I had been tossing around ideas for what felt like a very long time, and though we'd come up with some interesting options, we couldn't gel all my concepts into one cohesive whole.

I was stirring my coffee when suddenly years of reading, coaching, and studying somehow snapped together into one moment of clarity. I felt as though I had swallowed the sun, the idea a bright yellow ball in the center of me.

I dropped the coffee spoon.

"It's a Clearing, Larry!" I shouted.

Larry looked up from his breakfast. "Does it work? With all the ideas you have?"

My mind raced, thinking of the paradigm shifting exercises I'd used for years.

"Yes! To create something, to create an expanded future, you need to have clarity. A Clearing comes when you have Clarity!"

I laughed out loud when I realized I was actually stepping into a Clearing by naming my idea. What had been fuzzy and indistinct for months suddenly snapped into focus, as though I had locked the right lens onto a camera and looked through the viewfinder.

I thought about the ways The Clearing could work, and the words poured out of me, my spirits soaring higher and higher. "When you own your own stuff and then act in unrecognizably powerful ways, that's a Clearing. People experience a Clearing when they see how their worldviews have shaped more than just how they see the world—a Clearing is when you also realize that those worldviews are a bias that can limit what is possible for you."

I forgot about my coffee and food as I scrambled for a piece of paper and a pen. Inspired by Wilber's work, I wanted to create something that wasn't step by step or a checklist. Instead, I envisioned The Clearing as a holographic experience, one that was 3-D rather than a flat line. I drew spirals in my journal as I pictured how clients could enter The Clearing from any point, not just at a predetermined starting line, and how they'd be able to tailor the experience to fit their specific needs. I pictured clients (and myself) climbing the spiral, returning to the parts of The Clearing again and again but at different elevations, with new views. I drew pictures of spiral staircases heading up and up.

It was a huge weight off my mind. I suddenly had an opening into the work I'd be doing in the future, a way of communicating it, of sharing it.

But the work wasn't over yet. I had to create the parts of The Clearing—the pieces that would fit together to form a cohesive whole. I didn't want something rigid, but I needed to organize my ideas and experiences into categories or themes—not steps but areas. Talking it over with Larry, it became obvious that each individual area was its own Clearing.

Now I just needed to name and define those areas. Piece of cake, right—distilling a lifetime of work into a handful of areas? At first, my list of specific areas spanned pages, but eventually I whittled it down to five:

I. Clarity

II. Completion – Closure with the past

III. Connect to what's most important.

IV. Create a context for the future.

V. Commit to the set of agreements/promises that you made to yourself and others.

Not perfect by any stretch, but I could picture supporting people as they entered each Clearing. Each was not a step, but a space people could enter physically, emotionally, and in conversation as part of their journey.

One thing kept bothering me, though. The five areas didn't feel defined enough, as though their edges were muted by a fog. The moving parts were clunky where I needed them to be aerodynamic. I realized I needed to get some clarity myself first. Even though I was close, I had to go back to the drawing board.

I worried about the process. Was I trying too hard? Overthinking it? Would anyone even get this stuff? What was the simplest way to unlock someone's sense of possibility and crack it open?

I set aside some time to call The Clearing to me more fully. I sat on the floor of my office, with large pieces of paper all around me. My legs were stretched out so I could write, my body unconsciously replicating the deep stretches I had practiced for years in the studio. In many ways, this was the same thing: I was practicing and stretching my mind to help create something new, and I knew instinctively that my body would be part of the process. It felt right to start the building of these ideas on the floor instead of at a desk, my whole body leaning forward as I worked.

Sunlight hit the rectangles of white paper before me. The minute I opened the blue marker, before I had even made a mark, the smell hit me, and I was transported back in time. In my mind's eye, I could see my father when he disappeared into his study in Schenectady. He too would create materials for his work with Magic Marker, and I remembered that heady scent now, remembered the hush of his office and his neat hand.

As I looked at the paper on my office floor, I thought of my father and of me as a child. I thought of how I had dreamed of creating meaning with my dance. I had wanted to impress him, sitting next to him in the kitchen while he talked about work. And I was impressed with his dedication to his career. The smell of the marker ink brought it back; I tapped into that basic childhood need for connection and that early lesson in hard work as I bent over my task.

Three hours later, I had filled my pieces of paper. I had whittled down The Clearing to four balanced parts. It wasn't yet perfect, but I had captured the heart of what I felt each step of The Clearing was:

Clarity. At this stage of the journey, the focus is on exploring, on finding out as much as we can about where we are and where we want to be. This is the space where we ask questions that help us understand the lay of the land: What has gotten us to this point? What are the goals for the next stage of our business? Where might that product launch lead? Who else is involved in our team? This is also the space to look for assumptions and rules we have: "If I do this, then that happens" or "Because this thing happened to me, every time I try, the result will be the same." We tend to treat statements as facts when they're really ideas we've created that may or may not be true. This is where our self-perception meets our reputation and others' perceptions. It's about building awareness and recognizing habitual patterns in the body that might be keeping emotions in a recurrent triggering pattern.

Completion. Completion is the step where we move beyond obstacles from our past. After you recognize those stories as your own creation, we then have the opportunity to let them go. Most of us have issues that feel like albatrosses—mistakes or failures that continue to haunt us. For some of us, those past failings can lead to the creation of stories about why we can't live the way we want. In a lot of cases, we make these problems a lot worse than they are and magnify issues that aren't really as crucial as we think. In this stage, I encourage us to ask ourselves whether the stories match reality and, if they don't, to set them aside. Is there really a dragon standing in my path breathing fire, or is it an iguana I've magnified until it is so overwhelming that I have the perfect excuse to avoid starting? If it's just an iguana, we can look it in the eye and keep walking, no longer making that story an obstacle. Instead of trying to find a way around our past blocks, we can simply set some of them down. Once we see that our past relationships and ideas are choices, we can create a new, larger context, and set ourselves free.

Creation. When we are fully present and free from old baggage, we are able to understand that every moment is a choice. The past is over and the future is yet to be, so the only moment we are responsible for is the present moment. We create each new moment with our words and actions; creation is a series of intentional choices and embodied commitments. It's like each of us has a big pot of paint attached to our backs, and we have no idea that we are creating a messy, Jackson Pollock wake in our path as we walk, the paint spilling in all directions. We are also all born with a paintbrush in our hands and can use the brush to paint carefully planned images. Either way, we are making a mark; the only question is whether that mark will be the product of random turns and jolts or one that was painted with the fine brush of intention. We use this brush when we create a better relationship with a parent by choosing to see them as a fellow flawed human—as someone to be gently investigated instead of as a malicious force. We use this brush when we decide to put down past conflicts with a colleague and move forward with today's conversations in a gentler way. That is how we release ourselves from the prison of emotional triggers. It's a process and a continual commitment to creation every day.

Capacity. Capacity is a set of conversational structures that support our commitments—it means the power to do something. For example, we might talk about our capacity for success or our capacity to tolerate stress. How do we get that power? There are a few steps. First, we build systems and processes for accountability so that we follow through. We all know that simply making a choice is not enough. Accountability needs to be concrete—it is something we generate by taking 100 percent responsibility for our words and actions. If a company wants to launch a new product and is dithering, for instance, they might want to designate milestones and a deadline and then organize a party well in advance to advertise the launch. There's suddenly a very real but positive pressure to get everything in place by a determined time. Once we have accountability, we create partnerships and align those we work with around the future we are committed to. When we are building capacity, we come from a place of contribution. Our actions are on behalf of that purpose larger than self, and we are rooted in our commitment to contribute and create partnerships with others who share similar commitments and visions. As we go to scale, maintaining internal values—beyond just our assumed values or whatever we've written in our "official" mission statement—is paramount.

I sat back and surveyed my work. By now, the day was waning, and the white squares had turned pink with the setting of the sun. Yet this was a start and not an end. In a few minutes, I would call Larry in to tell him what I had unearthed about The Clearing. Because that's what it felt like—like The Clearing was a complete entity that had been there all along, waiting for me to excavate it and bring it up into the light. But in that first quiet moment after I stopped writing, I looked around and let the scent of Magic Markers surround me. I sent up a little hope that this material would support many people in the future, would let many possibilities unfold.

I stood up, brushed the stray pieces of paper from my jeans, and opened the office door, stepping into my future.

clarity

When I started coaching, I thought I knew instinctively how to get clear. I had been doing it my whole life, after all. I had been a young ballerina and had become involved in modern dance, where I had to brush away hesitation and stage fright to step into a role. In performance, I had to tap into as-yet-unexplored facets of myself to become new characters. As an adult, I cocreated a dance company, which pushed me to get clear about my priorities and set realistic goals. When something frightening happened to me, like walking around by myself in Moscow or being threatened by Danny, I was able to dip into the clear pools of my thoughts and then go deeper, moving even beyond thoughts, to refocus and reach a clear space for action.

When I started coaching, I needed to develop a system for supporting clients, but I also had to find my own way. Before I ever developed The Clearing Process, I had to go through it myself—and I started with what I would later call the "Clarity Step." In the early days, as DURC was breathing its last gasps, I read books on self-actualization and attended many conferences. I wanted to learn what was out there so I could develop my own ideas.

In a way, it was a little like dancing. Just as I always had to learn the specific steps of a performance before I could infuse them with my own passion and ideas, and just as I had to learn other people's choreography and ideas before I developed my first performances, as a coach I needed to learn the language and concepts of self-actualizing before articulating my own process.

I spent a lot of time talking to Larry about it all, and I journaled about the concepts. One thing that emerged again and again was the importance of clarity. I needed to become clear about who I was, who my clients were, and what I could bring to them. I had to develop tools for achieving that clarity that were quickly graspable and easy to apply. On a basic level, clarity in a business's planning stages relies on getting everything worked out and understandable. But on a deeper level, clarity is not necessarily about understanding—the core concept is about developing access to what you don't know you don't know.

How did I get clear? In part by teaching myself new ways of looking inward to see what was really there. Once again, I turned to my mentors in books, especially Julia Cameron, Natalie Goldberg, Robert Johnson, and Gabrielle Roth. Larry introduced me to Julia Cameron's book *The Artist's Way*. For Cameron, clarity comes from "morning pages," which she describes as "three pages of longhand, stream-of-consciousness writing, done first thing in the morning." She is careful to explain that this is not writing, but rather a sort of "brain dump" of everything that flits across the mind. These are not pages to be shared with anyone—just a way to get out the millions of thoughts and ideas and emotions that take up our spiritual and emotional bandwidth. I found them useful in creating a Clearing for myself; when I was able to set my little worries down on the page, it was easier to move on to the important stuff. I still do morning pages today.

Robert Johnson is another author I encountered in Larry's library. Johnson is a Jungian analyst who writes about dreams and the myths that surround us. To Johnson, as for many Jungians, dreams offer insight into the subconscious. He describes a method of active imagination to harness that power. The idea is simple: you become aware of your dream world by focusing on it, especially in the mornings. You notice the difference between your everyday consciousness and the dream world, and then in your waking life you try to move back and forth between the dream world and waking consciousness, using relaxation techniques, focus, and even music.

Around the same time that I was delving into my dream life, I started exploring my writing life and mind. I had stumbled across Natalie Goldberg's *Wild Mind*, a book that explored the idea that writing (rather than dreams) is the path to uncovering our inner worlds. Goldberg wrote: "Writing practice brings us back to the uniqueness of our own minds and an acceptance of it. We all have wild dreams, fantasies, and ordinary thoughts. Let us feel the texture of them and not be afraid of them. Writing is still the wildest thing I know."

I had been a journal writer for years, but I found it impossible to read Goldberg without wanting to write a lot more. *Wild Mind* was big on free-writing. The rules were simple: choose a topic and write without stopping for a few pages or a specific length of time. Beyond that, you had to be specific about details and stop thinking (about grammar, about whether what you were writing was "good").

Wild Mind gave focus to my writing, and the focus emerged through the process of letting the mind go. I know that seems counterintuitive, but that is exactly what happened. Letting go and giving myself the freedom to write about anything, without worrying about what I was writing, tricked my mind into a clarity I had never experienced before.

Wild Mind taught me how to simply observe the pen on the paper. Follow it. Trust the impulses. I would go to the laundromat on some days and just write short little pieces based on the behaviors and conversations I witnessed there. Sometimes, I'd get creative and turn them into fuller characters, but I loved the idea of simply observing what came up. And it also freed me up to write more stories of my life, many of which have landed in this book.

Then one Saturday, as I was casually running my hand over the spines of several books in Larry's esoteric library, my fingers stopped on *Maps to Ecstasy* by Gabrielle Roth. Roth called herself an urban shaman, and she worked on giving people access to their innermost selves through dance.

The book is Roth's first exploration of her seminal work, the philosophy she called 5Rhythms. It is a map to consciousness that mirrors all kinds of natural cycles, such as the life cycle or the sexual cycle. In the book, Roth reaffirms the idea that the body is a lot more than something to move or live in—an idea I had been playing around with myself. She writes: "Your body is the ground metaphor of your life, the expression of your existence. It is your Bible, your encyclopedia, your life story. Everything that happens to you is stored and reflected in your body. Your body knows, your body tells. The relationship of your self to your body is indivisible, inescapable, unavoidable."

Roth sees movement as a type of meditation practice that can lead to healing and a greater connection to the soul. The basis of this meditation is the five rhythms (flowing, staccato, chaos, lyrical, and stillness). When they are danced in order, they are known as a Wave.

Needless to say, I fell in love with Roth's work. Here was another dancer speaking my language, putting into words something I was still trying to express for myself. The work was also a variation on and validation of Martha Graham's famous quote, "The body doesn't lie." When you see how people move, you can read their conditioning and also what they are committed to. I have watched so many people be transformed by this work, and I know there are thousands more.

These four writers, who came into my life at different times, helped me get clear in different ways. Julia Cameron taught me to use stream-of-consciousness morning writing to clear out what was in my mind so I could focus on new thoughts, while Natalie Goldberg taught me to reach deep and uncover thoughts I didn't know I had. Through dream analysis, Robert Johnson taught me to get clear about the things I wasn't aware of in my waking life, and Gabrielle Roth helped me to get to know the emotions and ideas that were preverbal and lived only in my sinews and bones. While I wasn't religious in a traditional sense, my deep love of these works reflected a perception of the world that went beyond the physical plane. My spirituality was based more on ideas than faith, but I believed, as my mother did, that everything was connected.

. . .

The word "clarity" itself is interesting, with a rich history dating back to fourteenth-century English. The word "clear" comes from French and Latin words meaning "bright." Today, it suggests a sense of purity. Think of the word "clear" as an adjective, and images of shining pools of water or cloudless skies might come to mind. Look up the verb, though, and you'll see that the word is all about removal. To "get clear" or "to clear" means doing away with obstructions and impurities.

So to get to the bright purity of Clarity, you need to be willing to put down some baggage and do away with some of the obstacles in your path.

One of my early clients was someone who made me see Clarity differently. Sheryl had founded a midsize film company and was now the CEO. She was in her late thirties and traveled almost every month—the picture of modern success in her monotone urban gear with a single silver bracelet.

The outside image told only part of the story. Sheryl wanted to create a family in her business. Her grandmother had been the ultimate survivor—she had emigrated alone as a young teenager from war-torn Italy in 1945—and she had largely raised Sheryl. Some of the fear from her early days would touch Sheryl deeply, would make her yearn for something at work the way I had once longed for connectedness and peace at home.

"I want my team to feel connected to each other, to work together," Sheryl told me over coffee in one of our early meetings. We had been going over the tensions between the creative departments, who were in charge of putting together storyboards, and the departments handling casting, marketing, and postproduction.

Sheryl told me stories about the squabbles, which reminded me of my childhood fights with Amy.

"When we all work on a tight deadline, we pull together," she explained, sounding tired. "But otherwise, there are so many arguments. Last week, someone from the writing team told me that postproduction 'butchered' their vision. Jim from postprod heard about it and ended up yelling 'I saved that ridiculous script' at the weekly meeting. It was horrible; I should have been there to talk to them or to help with edits. Things are still tense after that."

I nodded as she let her head droop over her coffee cup. Sheryl was certainly taking responsibility here—too much. It was clear to me that the team was hamstrung by Sheryl's inability to be everywhere at once. I could also see that her leadership team needed new tools to allow them to scale the success they had enjoyed until now to a bigger level.

"What would it take to make you feel as though everyone is working together toward the greater goal you see for your business?"

The question made Sheryl pause, her cup halfway to her mouth. To Sheryl, her business was so much more than just a place to create products, serve clients, and make profits. Her business was a deep spiritual undertaking—it was a reflection of her deepest sense of self, and its success was tied to her feelings of self-worth. I understood that completely; I had founded DURC for many of the same reasons. While our stories were different, our human impulse was the same.

Travel kept her away from the company, and she felt her team resented that.

"If they could remain motivated, growing revenues and delivering storyboards and films on time, even when I'm not there, that would be a huge step in the right direction," she said. Then she sighed. "They're acting out their frustration that I'm gone all the time."

It was true that the company had had three high-level resignations in the last four weeks. She felt like a momma bear who had abandoned her cubs, and upon her return, the cubs were turning on her with teeth bared. Revenues had dropped, and they had lost a big project with an up-and-coming director.

"I know they're loyal to this company, but I have to do something to change the culture, to have them connect with each other and with me in a way that will allow us to thrive in these circumstances."

I met with Sheryl's team individually to get their perspective and to dig deeper into what might be happening. Part of finding Clarity can sometimes mean looking at the same issue from different perspectives. Everyone at Sheryl's company talked about her frequent trips, but no one could explain to me why she traveled so often. Finally, I went ahead and asked her.

"I make documentaries. These are real passion projects for me," she told me with characteristic modesty.

When I dug a little deeper, though, I was blown away. She wasn't "just" making documentaries. Sheryl was traveling to some of the most war-torn areas of the world and some of the most impoverished places on earth to film conditions there. She risked her life, often taking only the smallest crews, to shed light on what most of the media kept hidden.

"These stories are so amazing, Lori," she explained to me. "They could help create understanding between people. They could help heal untenable conditions, make a real difference. If people saw these films, more resources would pour in and lives could be changed."

The passion in her voice was palpable, and it certainly gave me a whole new perspective on her staff's complaints that "she's never here." This wasn't someone who was gallivanting around the world living the life of a high-powered executive. This was someone trying to bring healing change to the world.

Sheryl had big dreams—both for her documentaries and for her business at home—but how could she make both of those visions work? Sheryl was extraordinarily self-aware—a voracious consumer of the literature on leadership and self-actualization—and she'd hired coaches in the past, workshopped with the best and brightest.

At first I was afraid I'd be just another ontological notch on her belt, but soon I realized that like most of us, she still needed help realizing that she was not her thoughts. That the stories she told herself about what her employees did or didn't need, that the labels she used to describe what kind of leader she was or wasn't, became a kind of self-fulfilling prophecy. That with a change of language—a shift in perception—she could radically alter the culture of the company she loved and maybe her world. Coming to these realizations is much easier said than done.

I had been trained to listen for unconscious assumptions—the assessments and judgments that have defined a personality sitting in front of me, usually without their knowledge. So a few weeks into our sessions, I asked Sheryl how she defined herself in her company.

"They see me as their mother and the leader of this team. I take care of the people here," she replied.

"That's interesting," I told her. "How are you the mother and leader? Are those connected?"

Sheryl took a few moments to answer. "I guess I want to be in charge, the way a mother would be, but also lead, guide, and nurture. I don't want to be a faceless leader or a heartless executive in charge. I want people to be connected through me and to me. I think mothers are leaders, but in a way that isn't a dictatorship."

"When were you first a leader and a mother?"

"I guess . . ." She shifted in her chair and looked out the window, pausing. "I guess it was when I was taking care of my brother. I was six, and we were still living with my mother. My father had died two years before and my aunt hadn't taken us in yet. My mother would go out at all hours, leaving us alone, and my brother would get scared. He'd cry for Mom, and I'd sit with him in the living room, making up stories and songs so he wouldn't be scared."

I thought for a moment, then tried to word my response as gently as I could. "It sounds like you were brave, filling in where the adults around you were not fulfilling their obligations to you," I said. "When you're a young child, you're imprinted with an identity from your parents, school, your friends. You get rewarded for being a certain way."

I could hear Sheryl's quiet breathing filling up the room, and I hoped she understood what I was saying. "You sentence yourself to certain things, and you are being sentenced, but you don't have the language to understand why when you are young. When you're an adult, though, you get to choose. You can choose to be a leader and not a mother. You said that the team sees you as mother and leader—but you can choose something else. You can actually choose anything you want."

Sheryl was quiet with that last sentence for a bit.

"Thank you," she finally said. "Thank you."

"Let's try something," I told Sheryl. "Think about when you feel like a mother and a leader at work. Think about a time when you feel like you should have been there for your team as mother and leader."

I gave her a moment.

"Now, notice what your body is doing. What are your muscles doing? What is your posture like? Is there tension anywhere? Stand up and walk around and tell me what you feel physically in your body."

She stood up from her chair with a bit of hesitation and walked around the room. "I feel tense, and my shoulders are curved forward. My hands feel shaky. My legs are jiggling, like a runner's."

"Good," I told her. "What else? Stay with that feeling. Keep walking and examining what your body is sending you."

"I feel the weight of the world on my shoulders. I feel that everything is up to me. I'm terrified of letting them down. I feel so heavy." She paused and looked up at me with deep realization in her eyes.

"Good," I said. "Let's shift gears now—let's shake it out."

She raised an eyebrow at me but shook herself, her body losing some tension.

"Now picture the same situation," I went on. "But instead, picture yourself as just the leader. Think of the mothering part of yourself, and take that part out. Put it down for a little bit. All that caring and compassion is still there. We're just calling on the leader. Put yourself in the moment. How do you feel now? What is your body doing now? What do you notice?"

She paused. "I feel lighter. But also stronger. I am standing up taller, and I picture myself looking my team right in the eye. 'You're all professionals, and I trust you to make this film work. I trust you to show up and do the work.'"

"How does that feel?"

I could hear the smile in Sheryl's voice when she replied. "It feels great. I think leader Sheryl needs to come out more."

It still left one big problem: there was a fundamental conflict between Sheryl's two passions. She loved her production company, but in a very different way than she loved her documentary work. One was deeply commercial, and one was deeply tied to Sheryl's personal purpose. I had to address these issues with her in our work together.

But first, I needed to get some insight about Clarity. Sheryl's story made me think about my own U-turn in business—when I moved from leading DURC to becoming an executive coach. The transition, in many ways, was not an easy one.

At DURC, I had done it all. As cofounder and director, I danced, choreographed, directed, produced, trained dancers, wrote grants, begged for money, fought for performance space. DURC was like my own child. Everything I thought I was, as a human being and an artist, my entire identity, was wrapped up in this company.

What else was I supposed to do with my life? I was a dancer! So I turned inward and explored. I journaled about the transition, and slowly a picture emerged.

Because my life's work had so far been based in the body, I'd felt a desire to connect to truth and authenticity in every moment for nearly as long as I could remember. Looking back on it now, all those early experiences with dance set me up to be able to open my mind, and eventually to help others do the same. With Sheryl and others, what was going on in their minds flowed through their bodies. Making them stand up straighter and pay attention was the first step in helping them think and act differently.

In supporting Sheryl on her journey to Clarity, I suspected that her years of work on documentaries would be the clue that would lead to insight. I wanted to sit down with her and help her cut through her internal dialogue and the not-so-quiet feedback she was getting from her team so she could find that Clarity for herself.

I got my chance when we were both at the same conference in La Jolla. It was a typical California summer day—warm and sunny. The resort hotel hosting the conference was full of entrepreneurs, some of whom were also filmmakers who had arrived at the conference to talk about building conscious businesses. I had invited Sheryl to come because I thought it might be a chance for her to explore with like-minded people.

These, too, were people passionate about peace and about exposing injustice. I was at the conference as a one-on-one adviser, which meant attendees who had signed up for coaching and mentoring were paired with me so I could offer business advice and support. I received a list of clients and times when I could meet with those attendees. After a few hours of talking to people in different industries, I was scheduled for a break, and I happily met up with Sheryl.

The hotel was full enough that the air hummed with a thousand networking conversations. The air conditioners were on overdrive, but the heat of people crowded together ensured the cool air didn't quite reach me. My clothes clung to my back. People walked by in suits and in modern tie-dyed t-shirts with jeans. Most were either clutching stacks of notes or talking animatedly to each other, arms waving around.

Sheryl looked around the crowded hallways. She turned to me. "Hey, you know, I'm feeling so full and overwhelmed right now. Can we catch some girl time? I'm not ready to go back into the fray right now."

I didn't need an excuse to sit down with someone who was quickly becoming a friend. "Sure, we can just call this a one-on-one advisory session!"

We left the building and stepped into the sunshine. A gentle breeze wafted over us as we found a bench outside. It was more refreshing than the hotel's high-powered air conditioner. I took a deep breath, focusing on the hills around us and the sounds of the ocean nearby.

We had been still for a few minutes when Sheryl spoke. "There is so much going on with my business right now, and I'm becoming more and more involved with these documentary film groups. I'm feeling this incredible energy around how I might be able to make a difference."

As soon as Sheryl said that, my ears perked up. I can smell change coming on the air, and I sensed that Sheryl was going to walk away from this conference forever transformed. I waited for her to continue, but curiosity got the better of me, and I had to ask. "Sheryl, something seems different about you now. I'm hearing that you might be ready to make a big change. Am I reading you right?"

"I'm not sure, but I think I'm seeing all the networks I'm a part of somehow melding into a future that I never saw as clearly as I see now. I don't know how it's going to work, but I am so fired up that I can't *not* do this!"

I could feel her energy crackle like lightning on the desert sands, but I knew she needed to focus that energy with precision.

"What's 'this'?" I asked her, and waited.

There was a long, long pause.

"I want to shift my company from making commercials to becoming a force for positive change. I want the films we produce to pull communities together to support peace on the planet." Sheryl's eyes were shining.

"Is that all?" I joked. "That's beautiful, Sheryl. And why the heck wouldn't you want to do that?"

Suddenly, Sheryl was talking a mile a minute. Her visionary gifts just poured out of her. What I sensed was that right then, in the middle of the afternoon of this conference, sitting outside on a bench in the desert, Sheryl was outlining for herself and me the blueprint to her future. To the outside, we looked like two women taking a break and talking; a closer look would have revealed the revolution sparking all around us.

Sheryl navigated the transition, but it was not without speedbumps. When Sheryl first went to her team, glowing with excitement about her new plan and vision for the company, no one wanted anything to do with it.

"But I don't understand," her business partner said. "We're doing good work. We're doing well. Where is this coming from?"

The other people in the room didn't want to meet her eye. Everyone in the meeting knew the truth: once Sheryl was committed and passionate, she tended to shut down anything standing in her way. But at the same time, no one really understood what their roles would become or what the company would look like going forward. It was Sheryl's excitement and passion, not theirs, driving the change.

But Sheryl had a weapon. Coaching with me, she told me, made her realize her love of documentaries wasn't going away. This was it for her. In the end, Sheryl had to decide how much it meant to her. In a word: almost everything.

At first, she had tried to make the new plan work with her team. She made her documentaries and supported the company. The company suffered financially. Team members left. Arguments continued.

We had a phone call in which Sheryl updated me on how the transition was going. "At one point," she told me, "my business partner said I was selfish—not in so many words, but the hint was definitely there. After that meeting I just sat down and cried. It was a dark moment, and I asked myself if it was all worth it. I got the answer back from within me almost right away: I have to be who I am, and if it means the company falls apart, that would be okay. I cleaned up my face and went back into battle."

It took Sheryl two years to make the shift and another year before her company recovered financially. First, she teetered on the edge of bankruptcy, going so far as to start the filing process. The next day, though, she got an offer to merge with another company.

She prepared for the meeting by giving herself a pep talk, trying to drum up some optimism. The long months of dropping profits and letters of resignation were starting to wear on her.

The greeting from the CEO of the company floored her. "Hi, I'm Austin. I saw one of your documentaries, and I'm thrilled we're talking about working together."

Austin wanted to talk about not just the company's mainstream work but also the documentaries that Sheryl's partners had feared would drive them out of business. He listened when she talked about her commitment to changing the world one film at a time. Then he made her an offer:

"Let me create an environment so you can be who you are."

Simple. Revolutionary.

There was a gap between the current way of doing business and the tools Sheryl needed to support her art. With Austin's help, though, closing that gap took just a year. His company merged with hers, and he was true to his word about making space for her to follow her passion.

Today, Sheryl continues to travel widely and works with people who can see the power in coming together through business and shared values.

Back in the office, Austin and other team members assume leadership roles when Sheryl travels, while others enjoy more flexible work arrangements so they can pursue their own passions. Far from feeling abandoned, Sheryl's team is thriving and finding new opportunities of their own.

When I walked away from Sheryl that day in California, our conversation was complete, but much of Sheryl's work was just starting. She had thought she was clear on her ideas and her business—she had been running a successful company for years, after all—but some digging showed her she needed to get in touch with new clarities. As soon as she did that, it was as though she were looking through an entirely new camera lens. Getting clear about what she wanted and what her choices were allowed her to step into a new possibility and embrace a new way of being. And it all started with getting clear about what was going on in her body and her life.

Like me and everyone else, Sheryl might need to return to Clarity one day, but now she has the tools for the multistep process. Just like I need to return to morning pages or check in with my dreams, even though I've worked with the tools before, Sheryl might find that once she gains clarity about one subject, new issues will emerge on which she needs to get clear—how to run her new business, how to make the most impact with her documentaries. I was proud of her for looking through a new lens and stepping into the new opportunity. It was an adventure of a lifetime.

Chapter 11

completion

O nce we get clear about where we are and where we want to be, we often have to work on putting down any baggage. In Sheryl's case, her upbringing made her feel as though she had to be a mother figure to her employees.

In other situations, the baggage has to do with past failures or with stories told internally, often unconsciously—stories that prevent people from finding the freedom to create the life they deeply desire. I learned firsthand about this type of storytelling when I worked with a company that had two groups of employees, each of which was telling itself stories about what the other group was supposedly like and how they "couldn't" work together. I'm not just talking about different personalities, but a corporate structure that itself created divisions. It's more common than most business owners think, and in many cases organizations set up business structures that encourage these kinds of disunions—often without realizing it. Whether it's staff and freelancers, tech teams and creatives, or temp and permanent workers, structural divisions can create an "us versus them" mentality that's tough to overcome.

Javo was a $300 million, ten-thousand-person company that manufactured drywall and other products used in the construction industry. On a spring day, I was contacted by Benny Gamon, who ran one of their subsidiaries dedicated to making chemical-based building components. Benny had been a longtime employee and was now in charge of marketing and attracting new clients. But he had bigger concerns, too.

"I know what the problem is," he told me. "We have hourly workers and salaried workers. Some of the men—excuse me, but most of our unionized workers are men—are on the floors and in the factories, working at hourly wages. Then there are the salaried workers, who are 'management' according to the unionized workers. There's a lot of grumbling."

"What kind of grumbling?" I asked.

"The unionized workers think management is out of touch and isn't doing the 'real' work. Our salaried staff is worried the workers on the floor are not taking their tasks seriously—some projects are ongoing and not getting done and we have some safety issues, too. We need full compliance with safety training, wearing of safety equipment, and so on. But we're running up against some resistance on those fronts."

Color me impressed. It was obvious Benny had done some work up front. He even sent me some files, outlining some of the problems he saw.

While with many clients I have to start by clarifying the problems, Benny had already gotten a good grasp on clarity. He knew what the stories were. Now he needed help getting both sides to let them go and step into new possibilities.

One of the advantages of The Clearing is that it's possible to enter the process through any of the Four Cs. In plenty of situations, I start with Clarity because clients are unsure about what they're seeking or what the issues are. With Benny, he had some clarity, but we needed to gain more insight around his emotional responses, so that he could *choose* how to respond rather than react unconsciously.

So while we did some preliminary work in Clarity, the majority of our efforts focused on Completion. That didn't mean that we had missed a step or that the solutions were easy, though. It would take a year for Benny to be proud to call Javo his baby again.

In addition to helping the team let go of their stories about each other, and their assumptions about workers on the floor or unionized workers, we focused on Creation, or building something new. As I have often found, when we work on one area of a business or a life, other areas also inevitably get support. Clarity naturally leads to letting go, which creates a Clearing for something new, often an opportunity to branch out toward new allies.

A month after that first call, I was doing my own recon with Javo. I started by meeting Phil, who worked with Benny and was technically in charge of the safety division. I took a tour of a factory and went to some training sessions with Phil to get a sense of what safety issues the company faced.

I also talked to Benny more to get more insight into his personal and work goals. We met in his office, which was in an industrial trailer. Benny was a former Marine, and it was clear from the décor—or lack thereof—that he didn't waste time on aesthetics. There were old aluminum chairs and a few leather ones with cracked cushions. There was no artwork, and in fact, the only items that didn't serve an express function were the athletic trophies that lined his walls.

Benny himself looked the part of an ex-football player. He was wearing cowboy boots with his khakis and button-down shirt, and his body seemed all shoulder and muscle with a soft belly.

"We definitely need to improve communication skills," he told me after politely offering me something to drink. "Can you do something about listening? I feel like getting anyone to listen around here is a lost cause."

"Can you give me an example of that?"

"It's like no one is motivated to get anything done. We were going to develop a prototype for a new kind of joint, and I mentioned months ago that it's important, but it's still in the works. I don't have a prototype. And it's not like that's an isolated incident—we have a bunch of projects that are forever in limbo rather than getting completed. At every meeting I go over how important it is to commit to the safety training, but people don't show up for their training. And that's after two injuries in the past six months at our San Antonio plant."

"Got it." I made a mental note to ask the employees about the safety training, too. "What else do we need to work on?"

"Definitely getting everyone working together to meet goals. Right now, we have management and union employees—salary and hourly employees—on different tracks. It's leading to problems and low morale, not to mention problems with the union. We need to improve all those points. And better planning to make strategic improvements."

"And you? What are your goals?"

He paused at that, as though not expecting the question. "I'd like to work on my leadership skills. Become a better leader."

Once I could see Benny's evaluation of the problem and his goals, it was time to interview both the salaried and hourly staff. It quickly became apparent that the divide between the two was every bit as wide as Benny had suggested.

"Why are you here?" I asked again and again. "What would you like to get out of this training?"

Some of the salaried workers had gotten training before and were at least able to articulate what they wanted, but a lot of it came down to passing the buck.

"We need to get more done, complete more projects, and we need to get the workers in factories and plants listening. When we implement quotas and communicate what we need, we don't always get it. The workers complain to the union, but they don't always even show up for meetings."

From the other side, I heard similar tales of woe about management and "higher-ups" not listening. At one point, I interviewed Marv, who had been with the company for twenty years—since the doors opened. He was a silver-haired man who spent his days at the plant, and when I met him, he was still in his work overalls. When I looked closer, I could see that he took pride in his appearance and his work. His work boots were in pristine condition, each one tied in a precise bow. When I walked into the interview room to speak with him, he stood up from his chair politely, his back straight. His handshake could crunch bones.

Marv also pulled no punches. "You talk to management. They're always telling me that we're not doing enough, not getting deliveries completed. Well, I send in word if we're understaffed or when we need more workers. I tell them we're losing men to factories that can pay more or losing time on older machines that don't work right anymore. They don't listen. We tell the union, because at least they hear us, but management just sends us to these safety seminars to sit around. If they want safety, they should buy new machines, not old machines they've made over. The conveyor belt on the gypsum board–forming machine we use is from 1996—1996! And it's in terrible shape. The shoes I have are in better condition, and I'm not asking them to carry dozens of tons of gypsum."

Marv took a break, shaking his head, but he had warmed to his topic fast and still had plenty more to say about the communication barrier between the different sectors in the company. And Marv wasn't the only one to talk that way. Lots of people pointed out that daily tasks weren't getting done and products weren't moving to completion, but everyone had a different idea of why that was.

I started meeting with Benny regularly, too, to coach him. After about five months together, it was time for training sessions with both the salaried and hourly workers. Since part of the goal was to get everyone working as a team, I combined both types of workers in one three-day session. We got off to an encouraging start—though I'd worried that there would be resistance, almost the entire team showed up.

We met in one of the larger multiuse conference rooms, and I stood at the head of the table. I noticed that the fifteen people there were not used to sitting down together; some of the men from the floor had obviously not spent much time in the offices. They shifted around, looking out of place. Marv sat in the far corner, wearing what was probably his version of formal wear—khakis and a worn but immaculately pressed plaid button-down.

I introduced myself, reviewed what we'd talked about in our individual sessions, and then got to the heart of the problem: the stories people were telling themselves about the past, present, and future that were keeping them from reaching their goals.

I clicked to the first slide, which highlighted several of the key items uncovered in the interviews. "When I spoke with each of you, I heard the same things from both sides. Problems with communication. Lack of teamwork. Projects not getting done."

Silence.

"I want to talk to you about listening, because many of you don't feel heard. I'd like you to differentiate between conditioned and creative listening. Think of it this way." I clicked to a slide showing two columns—one for creative listening and one for conventional listening. "If you are listening from a creative place, you are listening from a space you create for yourself; it's actually a mindset you choose, rather than one that comes from hoping that someone will listen to you in a particular way. You can alter your own listening rather than try and change someone else's listening. No one owes you listening—or happiness. I want to give you the tools so that you can create the kind of relationships here that work, and one of those tools is changing the way you listen to your own internal conversations."

I continued to talk about communication, until I felt everyone understood the basics—that listening comes from within. Then I moved on.

"I want each of you to write down a goal you have in your department or area of your work. One goal."

I walked around the front of the room, aware that all eyes were on me. I needed my audience to understand the next part, because many of them (like so many of us) spent their time looking into the future or the past rather than focusing on the now.

"The thing about goals is that they're in the future, where you're not," I said. "And they're often based on the past baggage and stories you're bringing with you. Guess what? You're not in the past, either. Your goal, whatever you wrote on that paper a few minutes ago, belongs in the future. I want you to put it there. It may happen or it may not. Both are possibilities. What we want to do with that goal is to shift the probability of it happening. How do we make it more probable? We need to think about what affects your actions in the present. Your present is already leading you to that future, where your goal will either happen or won't. So how would you describe the present moment? What's happening now?"

I could hear the wheels turning as they struggled with the question.

Finally one man in the back quietly offered, "Well, we are sitting. You are talking, and we are either listening or not."

"Great!" I exclaimed, thankful that at least one person was with me. "Now what do you notice is going on in you?"

The man shrugged. "I mean, we're thinking, right?" He looked around at his colleagues uncertainly and then back at me.

"Yes!" I said, smiling in encouragement. "That's right. Some of you might be trying to figure out if what I'm talking about is going to offer you any kind of value at all. Others might just be thinking about lunch. And some of you would rather be getting a root canal than have to sit in an office and talk about thoughts and feelings!"

I flipped to another slide, which showed one way of taking actions that produce results. I paused to sip some water. Fifteen pairs of eyes intently focused on the front of the room.

"Your beliefs and feelings change. Do you have the same beliefs you had when you were four and believed in Santa Claus? Unlikely. Because they shift and change, beliefs and feelings are not the strongest basis for action. The strongest foundation for taking actual measurable steps toward a goal is commitment. When you commit, you decide for yourself, and you can and will hold on to a commitment until you decide it no longer serves you. It's not as changeable as beliefs, so you're more likely to act on it. And most importantly, your commitment is tied to your word. Integrity is all about keeping your word, especially when no one else is looking."

I flipped to another slide and turned to face my audience. I felt a buzzing in my fingertips because I knew how powerful this exercise could be—imagining a new possibility and stepping into it. "I want you to write down the answer to this question: What is the future of Javo, and what is everyone's role in it?"

I waited until everyone stopped scribbling.

I divided the room into two groups and had them talk about their ideas. While they discussed, I circulated around the room, listening to each group and offering advice if anyone seemed especially stuck. I wanted each person to think about what they were doing individually to bring about success. More than that, I wanted them to dig at the stories we tell ourselves—the tales that lurk deep in our consciousness that we often don't even think about. I had to get everyone thinking about those stories.

I hadn't at that time developed The Clearing, but what I was talking about was Completion. Once the team was able to put down their stories about what they could and couldn't do, once they stopped seeing each other as two sides and started embracing the "us" in their company, they could create new results.

The group didn't disappoint. Not surprisingly, from the union workers I heard that floor workers would be the backbone of Javo's success—they were the ones laying the groundwork, the "real" work.

"It's our work companies hold in their hands. Without us, there would be no deliverables. Ever," Marv said, looking around and obviously proud of his work.

"Absolutely," I agreed. "Your work is vital to this company. Now, what role does management have?"

"To support us and to listen when we need more support."

I turned to Gen, a tall blonde woman who had been scribbling notes the entire time I spoke. "And what's your role in Javo's success?"

"To bring in customers and to ensure deliverables get made and find a home."

"Fascinating." I looked between Marv and Gen for a moment. "And what role do the floor workers have in the future success of this company?"

"To offer their best work and to follow our leadership. To make the deliverables." Gen spoke up, and Marv nodded along.

"Outstanding." I paused for a moment, letting everyone think about what had just been said. "So if the floor workers are letting leaders know about what's needed, and management is telling union workers what they need to do, who is doing the deep listening?"

Both Gen and Marv looked ready to speak, but in the end both just looked at me. I went on: "Okay, let me ask you something else. What stories would each of you have to let go—what assumptions and beliefs would you have to relinquish—to make this company a success?"

More silence. I decided to work backward, to have them imagine a future success and then trace what baggage they needed to leave behind to make that vision succeed. "Picture yourselves five years into the future, reading the *Wall Street Journal*. Imagine there's a headline on the front page about Javo. What does the headline say?"

Without any prompting from me, everyone worked together to come up with one headline: "Javo Wins Award for Safety, Announces Record Sales."

I pointed to the headline. I wanted to get the group fired up and stepping into the picture. This wasn't an intellectual experiment—for this exercise to work as I hoped it would, I'd have to help the group *feel* the power of the headline the way I felt a character or dance in my marrow, joints, and cells before I ever stepped on a stage. "Okay, does that kind of headline show up without conscious intention? I think we all know that the answer is no. It takes guts and hard work, and there's no one at this table who's afraid of either. But this headline also takes commitment."

I opened up my posture, throwing my hands wide. "Here's the thing. We need to pay attention to how people relate to commitments. Some people experience lots of resistance. This is especially the case if they put their goals in the future. 'I'm going to start losing weight' or 'I will start looking for a new job' or 'We're going to become leaders in our industry for safety.' That's all in the future, but what about now? You have to make commitments now, because the present is where we live. Let me ask you all a question. Have any of you accomplished something big? Has anyone here ever committed to raising money for research, for example, or learning how to rock climb, and achieved their goal?"

A few people raised their hands, and I pointed to Gen. "I took up rock climbing last year as a way to get in shape."

"Did it happen right away?"

Gen shook her head. "I trained with an instructor at a climbing gym for months, then signed up for climbing tours. I spent a few weekends traveling to try out spots where I wanted to climb."

"And did you start scaling the walls on your first try?"

"No way," Gen laughed. "It was a New Year's resolution for years. I told myself I was going to do it, and it wasn't happening. I was nervous about falling. When I eventually got started, I had to build up strength in my hands, arms, and legs to really go for it."

"That happens to all of us. You were *going to*, sometime in the future, so it never showed up. If I were to guess, something happened to make you commit—really commit. And when you did, you probably said 'I am going to really try this rock climbing thing.' Does that sound about right?"

"I said something like that to my husband just before I started going to the climbing gym. And then one of my best friends signed up first, so that made it easier to show up."

"Exactly." I turned to the rest of the group. "There is only the present, right now. You become powerful by committing to the future you want. Here's the issue: the only place you can be committed is in the present. So when we commit, we are essentially standing in the now but making statements about the future. And we don't know what's coming in the future. On top of that, many of us have stories we tell ourselves about the future. We tell ourselves we've failed to commit to goals in the past, or we let ourselves feel stuck. These conversations we have with ourselves about commitment keep us from moving forward.

"Gen, not to pick on you again, but were there stories or beliefs you were telling yourself that for years kept you from going to the climbing gym?"

Gen paused, her pen halfway in the air. "I guess I kept picturing falling and being out of work for weeks."

"And when you started going to the gym?"

"Well, my friend Alicia kept telling me how exciting it was going to be."

I nodded. "Exactly. In the moment, you changed your story. You let go of the old image because a new possibility opened—having fun. I'd like to invite you to do the same here, but intentionally. Rather than telling yourself a story about someone else in the company listening or not listening, I want you to be aware of the stories you're telling yourselves and the ones you need to let go of to move forward. What's holding you back? Let go of it, or you really might fall."

We brainstormed ideas about what was holding the company back. What stories were people telling themselves? Where were the blocks? Although the team had good ideas on the big picture—lack of cohesion, no forward momentum—we had a hard time coming up with specifics. Every other suggestion started with that old idea: "They." They don't listen. They don't value us. We needed to do more work before we got to the heart of what was holding this team back.

After the third day of sessions, Gen came up to me. Her notebook was tucked under her arm and her hair was piled high up on her head. "Thank you," she told me. She held up her notebook and winked, then walked out of the room.

I smiled as I packed up my laptop and books. I had a good feeling about those sessions, and time would prove me right.

I worked with Javo for months, and the challenge was that there were two groups in that workplace—groups with their own stories about themselves and each other. I couldn't change the facts or the structure of the company, but I could get people talking and thinking about their dialogues about themselves and each other. Shining a light on these hidden discourses created an opportunity for setting them in the past, where they belonged.

Instead of focusing on the differences, I could get each group committing to the conscious choices they could make now. Instead of living in that older pattern of salaried and management workers, what was the new narrative glimmering on the horizon? Having the team look forward helped put that old baggage to rest. Coming up with new stories meant picturing headlines about Javo in the future and practicing how bodies would feel and move when involved in teamwork. The process took months, but it was worth it as the workers started living what they learned, their bodies more relaxed around each other. By the time the sessions drew to a close, floor and management workers were sitting side by side, trading jokes and comments before and after the exercises.

By the time I was done, Javo's on-time and full shipment deliveries were at 98 percent and participation in safety training was at 100 percent. As the team started acting like a group to get these results, they let go of some of the blame they were casting at each other, and that in turn let them get the results they were after.

· · ·

Years later, I met Benny again. He had called my office out of the blue and asked to meet for dinner. Larry and I made plans to meet Benny and his wife at Chamberlain's Steak House in Dallas.

Benny showed up at eight with a tiny, graying woman who was about half his size. She smiled wide and almost crushed my hand in her pearl-ringed fingers. "I'm Ellen. It's so wonderful to meet you. You made such an impact on Benny and on us."

Benny smiled, looking around at the elegant wood tables and brick walls. "Life's been good, and she's right—that work we did together left its mark."

"Are you still with the company?" I asked as I arranged a linen napkin in my lap.

"Oh, I left about two years after you talked to us. We landed a few contracts and then merged with another aerospace provider. The funny thing is, I kept thinking about how you'd ask us 'What's possible?' I started talking to Ellen about it, and we'd ask ourselves the same thing. I ended up finding out that what I really wanted to do was make a change. I ended up buying a ranch up in Colorado. Best thing I ever did."

I had to smile. It's something I've seen again and again: when you start doing the work to get clear, where you end up is not always where your original goals suggested. But the results are always powerful.

Hours later, still laughing at Benny and Ellen's anecdote and feeling pleasantly full of halibut, Larry and I drove home under a starry Dallas sky. Getting ready for bed that night, I thought about what I had learned from working with Benny. After working with Javo, I had carefully reviewed my slides and the video I had taken (with Javo's permission) of the workshops. Like any football coach, I had gone through the play-by-play, looking for ways to improve. I had noticed that my confidence had grown as I worked with the company. At that first meeting with Benny in his barren office, I felt as though I had something to prove. I felt I had to show I belonged there and could help. But that was a story I was telling myself; Benny was accepting of my credentials and abilities. As I focused on the Javo story rather than my own and as I got to know Phil, Marv, and the others, I was able to put my own story away so I could help with theirs.

Clients often ask me about the secret of success. After all, I teach success, in a manner of speaking, and most want a simple answer—a list, one path. When I first started working with Benny, he was certainly a "results man," and what he wanted—or thought he wanted—was to get people listening and doing their job. Instead, he got a team committed to each other and, eventually, his own ranch in Colorado. The thing is, his entire definition of success changed over the years, and his path to it was winding—but he made it.

So to answer that frequent question, I tell clients that success comes down to our capacity to take action on behalf of something larger than ourselves. But to do that, we have to allow ourselves to let go of everything that's keeping us from taking action. Most of us know what we need to do to move forward. Javo employees—all of them—knew they needed to increase safety training participation and to start delivering products clients would be happy with. But what they were telling themselves about the company bred resentment and caused everyone to act out. Everybody was saying it was someone else's responsibility to listen. Once they started different dialogues—what sort of success do we want and what's *my* role and *my* responsibility in that—everything changed.

And it wasn't just the great people at Javo learning these lessons. I had to let go of some stories myself. I came in with a chip on my shoulder, no matter how much I denied it. I felt so worried about not having a PhD, like David, or years of coaching experience, like my peers, that I felt I had something to prove.

When I put down the story about having to command respect, I was able to step into my role of supporting Marv, Benny, and the others more fully. When Benny and his company put down the stories they had about management and union workers and were able to pull together for a bigger vision—a vision that started with a fictional *Wall Street Journal* headline—they were able to reach a level of success that seemed impossible before. It opened the door to an entirely new path and direction.

When we can move beyond our egos and yield to the larger dance, we tap into something much greater than the dreams and goals we think we have for ourselves. And when you finally figure out what that something is—that's a ride and a half!

Chapter 12

completion with an aching heart

It's one thing when Completion is about a workplace scenario. In those cases, it can be emotional enough. But what happens when it involves something more personal and painful? In many cases, the stories we tell ourselves and the baggage we carry come from deeply traumatic situations. Completion is a simple concept on the surface, but how do we find completion with instances of abuse and betrayal? How do we move ahead when we're breathless with hurt?

Completion isn't just a technique I use with my clients; like all of the steps in The Clearing, it's also part of my own practice of self-development, my own journey of lifelong growth. Sometimes it comes up in small ways—letting go of an argument with Larry from months before or taking a physical relic of childhood to Goodwill, accepting I no longer need it—and sometimes I work through a big Completion, around my parents' marriage or the expectations I had for my life when I was young. And every now and then, a process of Completion starts out small and ends up shifting the landscape of my world.

It all started with a movie. In late 2015, Larry and I decided to join a friend for a movie. As I scanned the listings, I got a jolt when I saw the details of *Creed*. Rocky was back, this time not only with Sylvester Stallone but also an actor playing Apollo's son.

With trepidation, I read the reviews. The last time I'd seen a *Rocky* movie I had been married to Danny. The violence of the movies had been a backdrop for our tumultuous marriage. We chose another film. The decision was partly motivated by the simple fact that I don't usually enjoy violent films. But I also wanted to avoid it because I thought I was unready or unwilling to revisit that chapter of my life, even in the anonymous dark of the movie theater.

Perhaps learning about the movie stirred up old memories; perhaps they'd simply been waiting for a chance to come to the surface. Whatever the reason, a few weeks after the movie came out, I was running some errands and parked my car at the grocery store. As I sat in my car, reviewing my shopping list in my head, I was suddenly struck with the overwhelming conviction Danny was dead. I hadn't been consciously thinking of him, and I hadn't heard from anyone in his family in years. There was no reason for my mind to be on my first husband, but like a flash out of the ether came the information that he was dead.

The last time I had seen Danny, he had been shouting curses at me in a parking lot. I had run into his sister sometime around 2005 and she had told me he was still chasing his dreams of being a pro golfer. Now I went online, and it only took a few seconds to find out the truth. I stared at the date on his obituary: he had died on November 11, 2013.

I shut off the computer and returned to my life. I ran meetings, completed my to-do lists, and coached clients. But somewhere in the back of my mind was that obituary. After a few days of letting it sink in, I decided to seek out more information. Danny's death was gnawing at the back of my mind, and I needed to find completion.

With some hesitation, I called his mother. I wasn't quite sure what to expect, but in some ways I wasn't surprised by her generosity.

"Lori!" she exclaimed when she heard my voice. "It's so good to hear from you."

"I just heard about Danny. I know it's been a few years now, but I just needed to call and tell you I'm so sorry for your loss."

I spoke to Danny's mother and sister for some time, and it was a healing conversation. They didn't blame me for leaving Danny, and they understood why I had left. They told me Danny had been diagnosed with congestive heart failure a few years before his death, but, stubborn to the end, he refused treatment. He had spent the last two years of his life on oxygen before passing on.

As we talked, I felt some of the past's grip on my heart ease. I hadn't even realized how much sadness, anger, and pain I was still carrying around from my first marriage, but now I felt those old stories rising up and then bursting into nothingness, as insubstantial as soap bubbles.

That night, though, I had a lucid dream. Danny was in it, and he was angry, restless. When I woke, I could only remember disjointed images, but I was left with the feeling that Danny hadn't found peace. Still, I put my feet on the floor and moved forward, my schedule full, my time already dedicated to various projects. I tried to put it out of my mind.

The final piece of the puzzle didn't fall into place until I went to see *Creed*, giving in to the pull I'd felt when I'd first come across the title, that powerful desire to return to a familiar story. It wasn't until the end of the movie that the tears began. By the time Adonis, Apollo Creed's son, and Rocky make their way up the steps to the Philadelphia Museum of Art, and Rocky gives the speech saying, essentially, that only time remains whereas none of us get out of this life alive, I was crying. Once the immediacy of the pain of that evening had dulled, I turned to Larry and my journal. I realized that not only had I not been able to grieve over Danny's death, but I had also never mourned the other losses that had attended that relationship: Danny's thwarted ambitions, our marriage, my own early dreams. Had I been brave to put on a resolute face and carry on? Maybe. But that choice also robbed me of the chance to get complete and whole about what I had lost or gained, learned or overlooked all those years ago.

Now, I unpacked those old memories, taking out each piece to examine it in the bright light of an open mind. I considered the fact that Danny had died without realizing his dreams or finding peace with his father, with the music still inside him. As deeply as he had identified with Rocky Balboa, he'd only lived a part of that story—an underdog, like so many, who never made it to the top.

At the same time, I allowed myself to experience all the ways he had been supportive. Even though he didn't dance, he supported my dancing and tried to be a good person. He wanted to be a hero.

In looking closer, I realized the ways I had painted Danny in my marriage didn't really serve me. I wasn't a victim who had stayed in a bad relationship for thirteen years. I had chosen to stay because in addition to the conflict and disappointment, there was love and kindness in our relationship. As I let myself feel again the love I had felt for Danny at one time, I realized that our journeys overlapped in many ways. During our marriage, I had been fighting my own underdog story, in a struggling dance studio instead of a boxing ring. We both had dreams of success and overcoming great odds. For a time, we had walked together on the same path. The fact that our roads had diverged didn't make the leg of the journey we'd shared any less meaningful.

When I set down my pen, I took a cleansing breath. I was grateful I had been given the opportunity to find completion around the narratives about my first marriage; I'd been carrying them all this time without even realizing it. I was ready to set that story down, to continue my journey with a lighter and more loving step.

Chapter 13   *creation*

At the root of any self-development approach worth its salt is choice, and The Clearing is no exception. We live our most authentic, most meaningful lives not when we wander wherever circumstance takes us, but when we identify our desires and build our ability to achieve them. Because choice is so central to growth, it's woven into every step in The Clearing. In Clarity we choose to look at where we are and what we want. Completion is about choosing to let go of the obstacles holding us back.

But Creation—that's where the rubber meets the road. It becomes about making something, about shifting from preparation to action. You've already determined the task you want to undertake; you've cleared away the clutter preventing you from getting to the starting line; you've selected the tools you need. At last, it's time to begin. In Creation, choice gets big and bold and utterly beautiful.

Some of us may think of Creation as the domain of the artist. And it's true that artists tend to think about the process of turning the ideas inside their minds into external realities more often than most people. But artists aren't the only ones who create. We are all capable of Creation—that ability is part of what makes us human.

Of course that doesn't mean that it's easy to make the choices needed to begin the work of Creation. In fact, Creation is a step where many of us can get stuck. Think about it: How many times have you worked on a plan, gotten everything in place, assembled the tools you needed, and then not followed through? The moment of Creation has arrived, but instead of leaping into it, we find ourselves stuck. Sometimes we may stall because at that moment there seem to be infinite options, and it can be hard to make a choice and start creating. Or we may be telling ourselves a story that we're caught between two equally appealing (or equally daunting) choices, and so instead of choosing one, we endlessly pinball between them.

I do these things, too, but I've learned that it's possible to hit a big pause button, connect to what matters, and then make a conscious choice. I can choose to return my focus to the Clarity and Completion I've already achieved, and in doing, I remember that I am ready to step into entirely new possibilities.

In my clients' lives, challenges around moving forward with Creation tend to come up when they're facing a transition.

In 2013, for example, I worked with a client who was interested in transitioning in his career. He wanted to create a new life for himself and his family—one that allowed him to make a difference in his community. He had worked with a financial services company but yearned for something more significant, and had been considering a job with a multimillion-dollar nonprofit focused on land development or a career as a consultant. Derrick's wife, Amanda, had a high-level government job in DC, and Derrick wanted to continue to make financial contributions to their family of four. This tension between his desires and his obligations made him stall and stop, unsure how to make a significant social and economic impact in his community while also not turning his back on his obligations to his family. In fact, part of him felt guilty for even worrying about money, because he felt so passionately about the causes and values close to his heart. He also wanted to keep the financial consulting business he had been running on the side and wasn't sure how to juggle two professional paths.

Derrick and I did our work together over the phone. At our first session, I took out a notebook and pen so I could focus on his words. I knew that finances were on his mind, and that it was one of the things Derrick needed to get clear about. Derrick wanted to create a new life and new career, but I suspected his attitudes about money were holding him back.

He started by talking about his father and his attitudes about money.

"We grew up without much, and my dad still believes that money corrupts. I know this comes from a noble place—it's at its root a question of sufficiency and how much is really enough."

"And you?" I asked.

Derrick sounded uncomfortable. "While he wouldn't say it this way, my dad doesn't agree with the way I live my life. I mean, he's of that generation and believes that if you just work hard, you'll have enough. But I think he thinks I spend too much and that I'm always chasing the dollar."

"And what do you think?"

"I've told my dad that I can earn money and raise Isabella and Ben well, so my children grow up with good values. Just because we grew up with limited means doesn't mean we have to stay that way. Does that make sense?"

It did. I certainly understood what it was like to choose a life very different from the one your parents had offered you.

"But you're not just after money," I pressed. "You want to make a difference, too?"

"Yes. I think this position with this development company can do some good. It's all about building relationships and bridges with the community, fostering community projects and businesses—businesses of every size. We could make a difference in people's lives and the community as a whole."

I nodded. I knew that Derrick wanted to transition to a job that was more about supporting social entrepreneurship. He also wanted to create his own consulting agency, offering creative content and PR/marketing services to businesses. He had done some work with businesses, expanding their sense of financial-health consciousness, but he was nervous whether he could make the jump into a nonprofit job with this much reach. And if he did, he might be earning less for a while, which brought up all kinds of money worries for him.

I often see people stuck like Derrick between two choices, and those choices can look suspiciously like an "either/or" paradigm in play. When I notice that kind of thinking, I begin to get curious whether the mental split is camouflaging a more deeply held belief.

"Well," I said. "It sounds like this possibility excites you but that you're hesitating over your ability to give your family enough. So what I want to know is this: How much is enough?"

"Enough to set aside a nest egg and give Isabella and Ben a leg up. Enough to protect us if something goes wrong."

I smiled, knowing that Derrick's nest egg was larger than those most people have put aside. "How big an egg are we talking here? What do you need to feel safe? A goose egg? Ostrich?"

Derrick laughed. "Maybe I'm thinking dinosaur size, just so we always have enough."

"And what would 'enough' be for you? Is it something you can put a dollar amount on? Is it a financial achievement, like paying down a mortgage or saving enough for your children's college educations?" I asked.

There was a pause, and then Derrick sighed. "You know, when you put it that way, I'm realizing it's hard to think about 'enough' as something achievable, something concrete. It's almost like . . ."

He paused again, and though a little impatient voice in my head was dying to finish his sentence, I breathed through the silence, letting Derrick come to his conclusion.

"It's almost like I'm not really thinking about money, per se, but myself," he finished after a few beats.

"Interesting," I said, smiling. "Not a bad insight for our first session. So that idea—what does that bring up for you? What does it make you think?"

Derrick laughed. "That I just opened a big can of worms."

Over the next few weeks, Derrick and I worked through Clarity and Completion. We discussed the stories that Derrick had inherited early on about money—that there wasn't enough at home and that money can corrupt but is still necessary. We'd talked about the life he wanted to create for himself and his family. Derrick allowed himself to sit with the idea that he and his family had enough. They could pay their bills. What Derrick really needed to let go of was the idea that he needed "more."

Once he had determined he had enough and wasn't in financial danger, Derrick had to focus on making choices and creating new possibilities.

Before our fourth meeting, I had asked him to jot down some ideas around how he worked with coworkers. How did he work as a team member? How did he want to work as a team member? How did he think others saw him? How might this impact his ability to create new job possibilities? I didn't want Derrick to just answer a lot of questions. I wanted him to react viscerally on paper, turning off the second-guessing in order to dig at the truth.

"I did the writing assignments you asked me to complete about how I interact with coworkers—the experience was really powerful! I've asked Amanda to do them too," he enthused. "It got me thinking about how I come across in different situations—I think maybe I need to make changes to how I talk to people. I guess when I'm talking to people at work, I'm sometimes rushing through to get to the next thing and not giving them full attention. If I'm going to be developing relationships with community leaders, I need to change that."

"How so?" I asked him.

"Well, if I get the job with this organization, each meeting will probably be in a different place. I might meet an architect in his studio in the morning and a city planning leader in his office in the afternoon. If I'm rushing through, I can't build that connection. I won't be able to serve them."

"You're probably right," I began. "This is about creating a space—allowing spaciousness in your thinking can free you up to connect to your resourcefulness, to your creativity, your higher wisdom. These practices can support you in all the ways you are already successful and help you build on those."

I thought of my own schedule and the calendar on my computer. "Think of how things are when your schedule is full, for example. Your time is so filled with meetings and responsibility that you can't fit in time for yourself or new opportunities. Most people understand the importance of clearing out their timetables, their inbox, their homes. Many of us don't think enough about the importance of clearing out our thinking or our inner lives. But the fact is that it's harder to create when there's a bunch of old stuff lying around reminding you of your old attachments, old visions of the future, and old ways of doing things."

I thought of all the times in my life when I had to create new space in my life. I thought of leaving Danny and leaving Bill. I imagined the moment when I concluded my last performance with DURC. Sometimes letting go feels freeing, and sometimes it hurts like hell.

"If you want to create new possibilities in your life—whether it's a new venture or a new way of running your personal life—you have to have space for that," I went on. "That's why we handle Completion before Creation, and we need to make sure before we start Creation that anything standing in our way has been cleared out, that we have room to create structure and chart an intentional, planned path."

In the pause that followed, I guessed that Derrick was probably looking around his office. "I'm already pretty organized."

I nodded, wanting Derrick to move beyond organizational systems and look inward. I was looking for him to recognize how he had cleared away some of his inner dialogue and was consciously creating new commitments.

"That's true, and I'm sure that's a big help in your work," I conceded. "This isn't exactly about a planner, though. It's not about being organized. It's about having your own back, taking ownership of your choices and being accountable to others, of course, but especially with yourself. The first step of Clearing is making sure you aren't just going through the motions, animated by ghosts of past actions. How will you make sure that you have a real system so that you're moving forward?"

Derrick took a moment, but he couldn't give me an answer right away. "I'll have to think about that."

I could tell from his tone of voice that he meant it; this was something he needed to dive deep with. "That's okay. It's actually great to acknowledge that. We'll pick up with this question in the next session."

When we had ended our time together and I was preparing for a meeting the next day, the question I had posed to Derrick stayed with me. I envisioned Derrick committing on a whole new level and then building systems to support his new life. And I felt confident about this plan of action because back when I was a dancer, the absolute height of my career was a piece that required more of me than I had thought I had to give. At that time in my dancing career, I had to create something new and commit on a whole new level to create the performance the audience deserved. Getting to that level meant I needed to make entirely new choices.

The piece was called "Nonce." The word means the present, or immediate, occasion or purpose (usually used in the phrase "for the nonce"). Dancers Unlimited had the extraordinary opportunity to work with not one but two former members of Pilobolus, a trailblazing group that introduced to the dance world the kind of athletic dance-gymnastics hybrid later emulated by Cirque du Soleil. Pilobolus was famous, even then, for the physicality of its performances, the striking images created by the complex interplay of dancers' bodies working together. "Nonce" certainly had all those hallmarks.

I performed the piece dozens of times, but the first time was during the 1987 season, and we danced it again in 1992. That year the performances took place at the Dallas Museum of Art. Pulling up for the performance the first day, I glanced up at the white, shimmering building, with its modern architecture and sharp curves. Later, as I prepared myself for the stage, I glanced out at the crowds that moved from the cool, green courtyard into the airy lobby, most of them dressed in casual slacks and light sweaters.

"Nonce" was first on the program. Hanging from my partner's wrists in a seated position, arms taut, back straight, I drummed my toes on the floor as we scanned the stage, like diviners searching for water. We settled, finally, the two of us both gazing far into the distance, downstage left, into the same light. In a slow-moving gesture, he reached for my shoulder, gently pulling me into a thigh-burning hinge before we did a quick pivot and he propelled my entire body through his wide open legs as the drum began. We called that move the "masturbation" step: I clung to my partner's waist from behind as he swung me over and over between his thighs, my lean body simulating the thrust of the erect phallus—an image which almost always brought cries of laughter from the audience.

Our sexual cartoon still burning in the minds of the audience, my partner seamlessly took my waist. I was upside down now and hanging in front of him, face first. I hooked the top of my arches over his shoulders, and we both slowly disengaged our hands for a slow-motion, silent shout of "Look, Mom! No hands!" He grabbed my legs, leaned back and back farther, hinging as if under a limbo bar, with my full body weight balanced on his. I arched my head up, my hands cupping my ears, elbows stretched outwards as if to say, "I'm not listening to you!" We balanced both our bodies, mine on top, parallel to the floor. We stretched out our horizontal moment until abruptly he lay flat on the floor, his arms extended and locked over his chest, hands holding me at the waist. I just as abruptly contracted into a tiny ball, curled like a slug defending its life, and dangled helplessly from his hands.

Oh, how I loved performing this piece. Our audiences loved it as well. Among ourselves, we made fun of its slow, Zen-like quality. It's like watching grass grow, I'd say. But I knew this piece had power. When we danced it, I connected to the journey, not only of my soul, but of all the souls who shared a similar path to my own. I'd look at my dance partner, and when I danced with him, I connected at a much deeper level. I saw him as my partner, yes, but I also saw my father, my husband, my lovers, my dance partners, and everyone else who made a difference in my life.

I've heard it said, "The way you do anything is the way you do everything." In dancing "Nonce," in those moments of deep stillness and deeper connection, I realized that the quality of attention I brought to this dance was the quality of attention with which I lived my life: intensely focused, my heart filled with joy, and my mouth poised for laughter. Like a Zen master, the dance made fun of life itself, turning the human form into flying turds, helicopters, and an Egyptian queen riding riverboats on the Nile. We actually used those terms to describe the partnered moves we'd rehearse endlessly in order to create the magic of the message.

For me, the dance was about the journey of relationships, the transcendent path of creating a connection with someone else, with all the wonderful and sometimes messy parts of intimacy and power woven in. But I knew, too, that dance is a paradox. My expression through movement might mean something to me in the depth of my heart, but the meaning of that dance is ultimately up to the viewer.

One part of the dance, though, truly tested my mettle. We called it The Rock. I'd rest on my shins, tucked into a ball, hands grasping my heels, forehead on the floor. My partner placed his head at the base of my spine and on all fours pushed my little rock form across the diagonal length of the stage. Now, on some surfaces this wasn't a problem, but when we performed at summer festivals, our stages often had a roll-out floor covering called a Marley to provide sure footing and protect us from the hard surface underneath. The problem was that it would heat up and become very, very sticky. More than once, I emerged from a section of the dance partially bald, hair literally ripped from my forehead. Taking our final bow, I would proudly display the blood dripping down my forehead as the badge of pain that somehow sweetened the beauty of the dance.

I also realized the first time around that I couldn't perform this piece if I had had too much coffee. Adrenalized energy wasn't what the piece called for. I had to be pure, not only in mind but in body as well. Was I willing to give up my daily jolts of dark roast? Yes. Because "Nonce" dared to ask so much, I was completely devoted to performing this piece at the highest level. That meant creating on a new level and making new choices and commitments—not just to working harder than ever before (although I got my butt into practice more often than ever before out of a profound sense of joy with the music and movement), but to working in different ways. "Nonce" pushed me to think about what the dance meant and to move even more deeply beyond the sum of its individual steps.

This dance asked us to slow down and view art not as a simple narrative, but as a symbolic way to know and appreciate the beauty, humor, and suffering in life. I had to put down the daily rush, the desire to do more. I had to fill each movement with meaning precisely because there was no linear narrative. Instead, I was free to convey grief, evoke laughter, and raise eyebrows. Meaning became more than one thing after another. It became moments in time, each one complete in and of itself.

Dancing "Nonce," I felt I had fulfilled some of my life's purpose, moving people emotionally and sharing fully in that fleeting moment that can only be experienced during live performance. This piece also stepped onto my life's stage at exactly the right moment. It defined and reflected the fact that I was entering into a new way of perceiving life and my way of being in it. I was connecting on a deeper level not only with audiences, but also with people in my life, and a new purpose for my life was on the horizon.

As an executive coach, a big part of my job is helping people with just this feeling—connecting to new purposes.

Thinking about Derrick and "Nonce," I wanted to ask Derrick to connect to his new purpose, to leave behind any other possibility. I was standing for him, for the possibility that he could approach his new life and work with passion, intensity, and joy. So the next time we met, I asked him about the question I had asked before.

"How will you make sure that you have a real system so that you're moving forward as you build a new career? What environment do you need to create? What are the moving parts of your life that need to be in place so you can make this transition?"

Derrick was still struggling. He was thinking along the lines of a mission statement, but though the ideas he'd come up with were useful, they didn't seem to be igniting the kind of excitement that I'd heard from him in other conversations. It was my job to help him keep in his sights those moments in which he'd been most connected to his purpose, to hold for him what I'd seen in those moments—power, fulfillment, delight—and reflect it back to him.

I thought about why Derrick was struggling and thought back to the way I had felt with "Nonce." With "Nonce," I leapt from bed every morning, eager to get started. It allowed me to push past the pain I was feeling in my personal life. "Nonce" made me feel *alive*.

It's easy to feel passion when it comes to creation of any art, but even when we're creating a new business venture or department, we need to tap into the same passion and love that creates ecstatic dance, words that move us to tears, or art that we can't stop looking at. We need to find the fire.

I wanted Derrick to feel a little of that spark. I could hear in his voice that he was excited about the prospect of a new career and new opportunities, but he needed to connect to that at a visceral level.

The next time we talked on the phone, I decided to tackle that issue. "Derrick, when you think about your new career path you're building for yourself, what does it feel like? How do you imagine your life will look when you have created this new opportunity?"

Derrick's enthusiasm radiated through the phone lines. "I guess I'll be able to make a difference. It won't just be about punching the clock and showing up. I'll be able to see communities growing and people thriving because of what I do."

I could picture Derrick sitting up straighter as he peered into his future. He was in his element. "Hopefully, I'll be able to take someone's tiny idea for a business and help them cultivate it. Maybe after a few years, I'll be able to drive by businesses and neighborhoods that I've helped build up. There will be these towns and cities that allow people to thrive and make a difference to other communities—a whole web of support!"

Derrick took a deep breath and laughed. "That would be so great. So how do we make it happen?"

The energy on the phone shifted as Derrick tapped into that source of excitement, and I wanted to support him even more than that. "Do you know that when you talk about your new career, your breathing changes? It becomes deeper."

"I feel calm, like this is something I'm supposed to be doing, but worked up and excited about the possibilities."

He had just described the zone every dancer experiences in performance. We had started to make a Clearing for him out of passion and excitement, rather than an intellectual exercise. When we moved forward, I could remind him to get back to his calm but strong stance when we needed to enter into that space again.

Even though we had done the mental and physical work, there were still some practical systems to work out, too. We needed to dig some more and come up with more ideas as to how Derrick could transition. I asked him to take out a legal pad and brainstorm.

I invited Derrick to let his imagination go and come up with some ideas he could use to get his new career started. I asked him to map out his current working relationships and projects, and look for patterns of strengths and weaknesses. With those in mind, I asked him to set a timer and told him no idea was too silly; he was not to edit at this stage—just come up with ideas. An hour later, Derrick had come up with four ideas:

He would create a software system to keep track of communities and businesses within communities, so he could be aware of whom he had talked to and what needed to happen next.

He would have a weekly and daily personal check-in so that he could plan his next steps and what communications he had to make. A meeting didn't go well? Rather than thinking about it during other meetings, he'd wait until his check-in and use that to reach out to the person or group again.

He would create a weekly report about community matters and conversations with the leaders of those communities. He would send it out to his bosses to let them know how his meetings went and what he would be focusing on next.

He would create a marketing plan for his consultancy business.

A week later, I met Derrick again to see how he was progressing with his transition. He had made business cards for his own business and had met with a marketer about promoting the marketing and PR services. Ultimately, though, he decided he'd be best served by using his own knowledge of PR to promote his marketing firm. At the same time, he had applied for the job at the nonprofit and was nervous about the interview.

"Since my consulting work is about helping businesses succeed, I need to find a way to get my message in front of growing businesses in need of marketing and content. I think I need to network. It's also what I need to do to land this job."

He paused. "And I don't know what I'm doing wrong with my consultancy business, actually. I show up, do the work, and get results. I keep expecting money to flow toward me, but it's just not happening yet."

"Maybe," I told him. "Let's look deeper at your conversations around money."

It was a subject I felt I had lived. In a way, Derrick reminded me of me. Back when DURC first opened, I was an idealist around money and, frankly, didn't think about it much—until, of course, it wasn't there. I quickly learned that money didn't just flow right in. Getting the funding to keep the company running required me to do another dance popular in the '80s—the Hustle. It required grant writing and sometimes working extra jobs. The importance of being aware of money—whether it was a lack of it or opportunities to find it—was a lesson I'd learned the hard way.

"You're already conscious about your clients," I reminded Derrick. "You're thinking of ways to reach them, imagining ways of assisting them. What if you got curious about money, as a dynamic? As an exchange of value and energy? Who do you have to be so that money starts to show up?"

"I have to be confident first and foremost," he mused. "I have to be in hypercommunication with all the people I work beside—and I have to be real. I have to feel free to be myself and share my gifts."

"True," I agreed. "How do you get to that feeling of freedom? And how does that relate to money?"

I could hear Derrick shuffling papers on his end of the call. "You know, it goes back to that conversation we had a while ago, about the nest egg," he said after a moment of silence. "I've heard other people talk about money the way you just suggested—that it's an exchange of value. But I was always thinking about that value as services or products or cash. I wasn't really thinking about my value—or rather about how I see my value."

"So it sounds like you're saying that getting the money right isn't really about other people's perception of you; it's about your perception of yourself."

Derrick laughed. "It sounds simple when you say it. But basically, yes. That to have enough, I have to be enough, and to be enough, I have to embrace that I am enough. When I believe that, I'll be able to ask for and receive the money that corresponds to my value."

I beamed. "Deep stuff, there, Derrick! So what Clearing have you now created for yourself?"

He paused for a fraction of a second and then said in a firm voice, "That I am enough. That because I am enough, I can charge for my value, knowing that my clients are investing in me and themselves. That because I am enough I am more than capable of providing security and ample resources to sustain and expand the well-being of my family."

If I hadn't been holding the phone with one hand, I would have burst into applause.

"Bravo!" I exclaimed. "I think it's time to get that dinosaur nest egg. Now, let's talk about the intersection between the nonprofit job and the consultancy. How do you picture weaving these two positions to create a new career?"

That conversation changed the way Derrick did business. After that discussion, he called me to tell me that he was taking this coaching more seriously. He also dove into the community development position and didn't look back. It took some work, but he developed a career in which he was working at a nonprofit and building his consultancy. Over time, he had a plan to cut back his hours at the community development position to focus more time on his family. He thanked me for guiding him to clear a path to pursuing work that felt meaningful, work to which he felt called, without giving up his family's security. I assured Derrick that it had been a pleasure to support him, and a few moments later we said our goodbyes.

After I'd hung up, I found myself smiling. That wasn't just a polite line I'd used—it had truly been a pleasure working with someone to realize his goals. Showing him how he could make different choices and commitments to create something new—in his case, a new career path—was rewarding to me on a personal level.

Chapter 14　　　　　*capacity*

There's a popular narrative about success that goes something like this: a brilliant person has a brilliant idea, and with hard work, skill, and perseverance, she makes that idea a reality—a restaurant, a software program, a business. Perhaps that brilliant person didn't come from wealth or privilege, and thus he's a self-made man. This common narrative holds these people up as examples of American individualism and self-reliance; they pulled themselves up by their bootstraps!

We've heard the story so many times that we probably hardly give it a second thought. But if we consider it more closely, it becomes glaringly obvious that it's a myth. Are there brilliant people who've realized brilliant ideas? Yes! Did some of those people begin their journeys without privileges or resources and overcome great obstacles? Of course! The mythical element of this tale is in the assertion that any of these people succeeded alone. Just take a moment to think about the "bootstraps" cliché: it describes an impossible task. In fact, until the early twentieth century, people used the phrase to refer to an absurd claim, a feat no one could actually achieve. The truth is that we can't rise using only our own strength; we need structures to climb up on and hands to steady us over slippery rocks.

That's where Capacity comes in; it's the step in The Clearing designed to help us craft possibilities with others. Capacity is about building community, a group of allies, and a legacy that lets us make a greater difference. It's about enrolling others in the vision that we are committed to, and then taking the long view of our lives and our possibilities.

Some of my earliest memories of building community are intertwined with crucible moments, the challenges that hold high-pressure possibilities and have the potential to go terribly right or terribly wrong. One of the first times I reached out to make a difference was when I was still with DURC. I was unhappy with my marriage to Danny and saw no way out, but some part of me was looking beyond that unhappiness for a place I could contribute. I ended up finding myself in grammar schools, using dance to teach not just art or expression but core curriculum subjects like math, science, and reading.

The group was called Young Audiences, and it was exactly that: a program to put arts in front of children and adolescents. The program directors collaborated with arts organizations around Texas to help provide curriculum support. We artists brought our craft, teachers brought education, and students brought their enthusiasm.

Eventually, Young Audiences became Big Thought, a group still active today, and DURC worked with them throughout the 1980s and 1990s. It was so amazing seeing children react to our performances that I sought out new ways to bring dance to young students. DURC applied for a grant to create a special program with the City of Dallas to bus in school children to see us dance; it was at one of those performances that I met Bill. Then, in 1994 and 1995, I was asked to stretch my creativity even further. Lakewood Elementary School invited us to create a huge program for their science curriculum. Our mission? Teach children in grades K–6 about science using dance.

Well, we were nothing if not ambitious, and we created a program that taught students about the human body, the solar system, and the laws of motion. The program was so much fun that we kept adding to it until we developed it into a mini-show called "Blood, Bones, and Breathing." The dancers acted out red and white blood cells and a beating heart. At one point, the program featured us rapping about bones. I was the mad scientist-doctor, complete with bald head, lab coat, and Groucho glasses.

It was freeing to perform in front of kids. We captured their imaginations, and they sat enthralled, laughing as they watched our antics on stage. For them, this was about learning and fun. For me, it was about making a difference. Many of these kids were falling through the cracks, often because they were kinesthetic learners. Seeing blood cells move rather than reading about them in a book allowed many of them to understand concepts they had struggled to grasp before.

Even from the stage, I could see lightbulb moments in the audience as the kids "got it." The experience underscored my passion for arts education and made me determined to do more for the children in our community. I had groups of dancers around me at DURC and in my professional life, but as I built a Clearing for Capacity by giving back to children, I felt an entirely new sense of possibility. I was coming alive to the many ways I could use my skills and knowledge on a larger scale than I had ever before imagined.

However, it wasn't just kids who were hurting, and I began to dive into the opportunities to contribute that were appearing all around me. One such opportunity came in the fall of 2001, when I was just starting out as a coach. My training proved deeply useful in a moment of great need and allowed me to act as a support for others in a time of deep crisis. I had been working for less than a year as an executive coach, and had worked for weeks to promote one client, Jill Williams, to lead women through a program about career transitions. The program was scheduled for October, so I had a month to promote it and invite people who might benefit from it.

One morning, I was in a meeting to network for the October program. I made it into the restaurant and dropped into the seat, putting the linen napkin on my lap and thinking of coffee. I hadn't even picked up my glass of water when I noticed something was wrong. The serving staff and some of the diners were sitting around monitors, and there was an uneasy muttering from nearby tables.

I got up and walked to one of the monitors, aware that the room had become quieter and quieter as people talked to each other in near-whispers. When I got to the TV, it took my mind several seconds to catch up as I watched plumes of smoke coming from two towers that I had visited many times on trips to New York City.

"That is once again a picture of the World Trade Center, in lower Manhattan, on fire," the newscaster intoned. "What is believed to be a commercial airliner has crashed into the south tower."

At a neighboring table, I could hear someone slowly repeating, "Oh my God, oh my God." Suddenly, I was thankful I hadn't had breakfast.

I couldn't think what to do, so I did the one instinctual thing: I went home. I sat on the edge of my bed, still dressed in the suit I had worn to network in, and watched the small bedroom television. By the time I had gotten home, there were images of the second tower battered and broken. I watched in horror as the two towers collapsed. It took me a second to realize that the scream I had heard was mine.

Oh my God, I thought. *We're at war.*

That day, and the days that followed, changed the nation. Like Americans everywhere, I was hammered by a screaming wake-up call for global consciousness, and the truths I had to confront about our place in the world, as a country and as individuals, altered my perception indelibly. But the changes that day made in my life weren't just ideological and abstract. September 11 thrust me, quite literally, onto a new stage.

"You really can't come?" I asked.

Jill and I had connected by phone a week or so after the attacks, and she told me that she wasn't going to do the women's transitions program in October.

"I'm sorry, Lori," Jill replied. She sounded almost as exhausted as I felt. "You're going to have to cancel my presentations." I told Jill I understood, and we hung up. I sat at my desk staring out the window with glazed eyes. Canceling Jill's presentations would probably mean canceling the whole program; she was the lead facilitator, the main event—really the *only* event. If someone had told me on September 10 that we were going to have to cancel, I'd have been devastated. Now my feelings were a mixture of disappointment and relief, both muted by grief. Maybe it was for the best that the event wouldn't go on. Maybe no one had the energy to worry about career transitions right now.

At the same time, I hated the idea of doing nothing, of retreating from the world. I was watching the television and reading the news almost all the time. Story after story emerged about people hurting in the wake of the terrorist attacks. In my core, I felt a deep calling to help. *How can I serve and live passionately in the face of disruptive change? People will need help—how can I do that?* I felt a strong sense of personal responsibility to fulfill my role at this crisis point in our nation's history.

I wanted to lead a conversation about how we could give ourselves permission to contribute. How we as leaders and members of society could be generous of spirit, be compassionate, and avoid making other people wrong. I felt the impulse to stay creative and push out against the natural reactive response in times of stress and trouble, which is to shrink and contain and protect.

I got another powerful reminder of my desire to help around the same time. David was already my mentor the day the planes hit the Twin Towers. He had been in New York that day, and it took him days to get back home. When he arrived, he looked worn and as emotionally ravaged as I felt.

"How can I help?" I asked him. I was loading a lot onto the backs of those words. I was asking what I could do to heal the hurt in the faces of everyone I saw around me and to soothe the ache in my own spirit.

David replied to my simple question with words that still resonate with me today: "Find out what is wanted and needed and provide that."

Such simple words, but they took my breath away. The simplicity and truth of his statement rang through me like a bell. After days of being in shock and feeling called on to help but unsure what to do, I became a woman on a mission. Filled with new purpose, I looked for what was needed and wanted and ways I could serve. Even today, when I'm working on making a change in my community or I want to inspire change, I ask myself, what is wanted and needed and how can I provide that? It has become my soul's battle cry for change.

I had moved from thinking about career transitions, Jill, and my growing coaching practice to much larger questions: How can I make an impact? How can I serve? How can we heal together? On some level, I had been asking these questions already as I supported leaders in their companies, but as I stepped more fully into The Clearing for Capacity, I asked these questions explicitly and committed to them on a whole new level.

I decided I wanted to use my training to make any difference I could in the quality of people's lives. I wanted my existence on the planet and the work I did to make an impact on the way people lived. I wanted to help people lead better lives—lives on their terms.

I had two trains of thought: my desire to help people and my desire to salvage the program for all the women who had already signed up. I worked on the second task first; it was the more specific and concrete of the two. I decided that I would step into the role that Jill had left and lead the program in October. I pulled up a file on my computer and started drafting what I would say. Though I had worked with friends and volunteered in the past, this would be the biggest program I had led.

Once I'd revised the program, I opened a new document and turned my attention to the first goal: helping people in this period of mourning. I decided to create a process to help people transition and lead, even in times of change. The cursor blinked at me from its blank page. I had the tools to do this. I had been training with David, and through his work I knew how to serve others. But now it was my chance to introduce this work to others, and to add my own words.

I took a deep breath and looked out at the autumn sky. Soon, the day would turn into evening, and I could see the leaves curling and turning golden for winter. I leaned closer to the hum of my computer and started typing. It was the start of soulful work, and once again I reached deep into myself, choosing action rather than reacting to pain.

Out of these deeply personal desires, I created a workshop in the fall of 2001. That workshop—Living Passionately in the Face of Disruptive Change—sprang from a simple question: How do we access our passion when, essentially, the shit has been kicked out of us? I wanted people to know that even when they were scared because the world around them had changed, they could find a way to make empowering choices. I used the Transitions work but added my own spin, hoping to show people how passion could be used to bring us into alignment with our best selves.

The final months of 2001 seemed like the perfect time to have these discussions. The sense of safety and security was irrevocably shattered for many of us. Terrorism had breached our shores, and the changes to come wouldn't be merely temporary inconveniences but the beginning of a new chapter in American history. As we saw with air travel, our freedoms were becoming more and more limited. The specter of war hung over us and then became reality. I wanted to support people in managing their fears so their lives were free to become an expression of passion rather than frustration or worry.

When I finally held the workshop, I looked out at about ten people gathered together, their faces lined with the stress of the past weeks but also lit up with small rays of hope. These were people looking for answers, and while I didn't think of myself as offering answers or directives (and that's still not my role), I knew I could share tools to help the healing process begin. I became a catalyst for positive change in these people's lives.

David was in the metaphorical wings as I presented, only a phone call away. I called him before I launched into the program, and he helped me clear my conversations and energy so I could be fully present for my audience.

We started by taking stock of what had happened and putting words to the emotions we were all feeling.

"What has changed in your daily lives?" I asked my audience. "Look to your feelings and everyday routines for answers. What is different for you now, if anything? For me, I've noticed that even in the last month, people are operating differently than they did during the month before September 11. Besides priorities shifting, something has settled in at an even deeper level. I've noticed there's an edge to my experience of daily life, like everything could change at a moment's notice and that it would be good for me to be ready for it. What is true for you?"

We went through a collective sharing of ideas. We looked at what was important for each of us, what our lifestyles were, and how our priorities had shifted. Several people in the audience said they had gained a deeper appreciation for each and every moment.

"Many of us were dealing with rapid change before the September 11 events," I reminded the group. "We're still attempting to maneuver through our days using the same methods and tools we have always used to cope and deal with that stress. I believe it will take something more extraordinary, an authentic shift from within, to exorcise those familiar strategies that have delivered the same results all our lives."

After we had talked about how things had changed, I shifted to talking about Capacity. I wanted to challenge the group to think about ways their future could look if they built alliances and expanded their worldview to include others.

"What would living a passionate life look like for you?" I asked.

First, I had everyone define passion and then write their answers on the board. Then, we looked at what it would take for each person to live in alignment with that possibility. Some people had trouble coming up with things they were passionate about. They could name things they liked, but drawing out the things that really stoked a fire in the belly took some more digging: "What are you passionate about? When do you feel energized? When do you feel like you're 'in the flow,' naturally motivated? How do you know you are experiencing your passion?"

To find out where passion lay, we talked about how to recognize it when it happens. We talked about the most passionate people we knew and experiences we had in which we flirted with passion. There's the loss of time, the moments of synchronicity that seem to affirm this is what you're supposed to be doing. We talked about how passion shows up in the body—the heat traveling through the veins, all nerves on alert, a glow pulsing out from deep within.

"Passion is the essence of commitment," I explained as I shared my own definition of the word. "It's that which deeply stirs us. It's the fire from within that motivates us. When passion is missing, our actions lack meaning, and we don't get the results we want. Without passion, our actions are obligatory and lack velocity. Commitment emanates from passion—passion is the seed from which commitment blossoms."

I decided to share the definition of passion I had found when I was working on creating the workshop: "The English word 'passion' comes from the Greek word for suffering. In Christianity, the Passion refers to the final few days of Christ's life, marked by violence and ending with his crucifixion. Passion doesn't just refer to something positive and wonderful; sometimes, it involves a lot of pain, too. It's okay if the things that bring you passion have an element of pain or spring from trauma."

In the end, everyone was able to come up with at least one thing they felt true passion about. And then we had to move beyond passion. Passion alone does not always bring the positive choices and change we want. "So, what else do you need?" I challenged them. "What gets in the way of you expressing your passion?"

Almost everyone agreed that they needed others to make it happen. Few people thought it was likely they'd get to passion by sitting around all by themselves. And sitting around thinking was also a problem, we decided; most people in the room could relate to getting stuck in the contemplation stage of a potential new venture. And everyone was also in agreement about what stops us when it comes to expressing passion.

"Fear!" one woman in the back exclaimed, with absolutely no hesitation. That got a lot of nods and murmurs of agreement.

That was the crux of the problem, wasn't it? Plenty of us had been fearful of following our passions before tragedy struck our nation, and now we had one more fear to add to the barricade of dread that kept us from pursuing our most meaningful lives.

At first, silence followed the recognition of fear as the largest barrier. Then a tall woman in the front talked about her sister, who had been diagnosed with cancer but had chosen to take part in a marathon anyway. We talked about how much commitment goes into a decision like that, how passion can outweigh fear.

Other people volunteered their own stories of success—friends who had overcome infertility or had opened businesses. We talked about Gandhi, Lincoln, Bill Gates, and others who had made choices and became successes despite personal and systemic obstacles. Even though all of the people we mentioned had different success stories—and definitions of success—it was clear that they had something in common, some clue we could comb over as we worked to puzzle out the idea of choice and passion.

"What qualities do successful people have in common?"

I listed the four that I knew of on the whiteboard at the front of the room:

- Focused
- Future oriented
- Results oriented
- Possessing a strong sense of responsibility (Successful people know they are 100 percent responsible for their own actions and conversations and can see that when everyone embraces responsibility, there is integrity.)

The first two were pretty broadly agreed on, but a well-dressed woman with bright red hair challenged me on the third and fourth. "It's nice to be focused on results," she said. "But we don't always get the results we want. And even if we're responsible for our outcomes, sometimes fraud or violence or something outside of our control impacts our results. And I'm confused—if we need others to succeed, how can we take full responsibility?"

That led me to ask yet another question: "How do we achieve results?"

"Action," the red-haired woman said.

"And what is the source of action?" I asked her.

There was a long silence.

"I'll tell you what I've found after exploring this idea for many years," I told the group. "Most people take action because of the conversation happening in their own heads about what is going on. Not only are your actions directly correlated to the conversations that you're in, but so are your mood and your attitude. There are lots of conversations going on, some of them disagreeing with each other, and they affect what you do and how you feel—the results you see."

Some people were nodding along at this point, but some people were less sure.

"Think about it this way," I told them. "You signed up for this workshop. And that action probably was caused by a conversation you had in your head."

I held up two hands and used them as puppets to illustrate the internal conversations we all have:

"We should do something about our lives, we should go."

"No way, we've tried changing and nothing has helped."

"There's hope for us yet. We should go."

"Who is this Lori person? Maybe she can help."

I put my hands down. "Most of us aren't even aware of these conversations; they happen so quickly and automatically. But they affect what we do. Say that you tell yourself you're tired, depressed, or anxious. No doubt your reality reflects that, and we gather evidence to prove those conversations 'true.' Maybe it's a gray and rainy Wednesday afternoon, and as you look out the window of your office, you tell yourself that you're sooo tired. Your body, ever obedient, supplies giant yawns and drooping eyelids to support that story. Pretty soon, your body is acting as though it's about to drop, and you tell yourself, 'See? I really am tired.' Whatever you're telling yourself right now, it shows!

"Here's the problem," I told the group. "Those conversations we have with ourselves do a lot more than just tell us to come to Lori's wonderful workshop." Everyone laughed. "Those conversations also tell us how we're going to handle obstacles and other people—not to mention personal responsibility. One person says, 'Because I don't have a degree, I can't be a successful businessperson,' where another person says, 'Because I don't have a degree, I can really get in touch with the average customer and become a *great* businessperson.' I don't want to make anyone wrong, but what if we consider the ways our internal dialogue makes us react to obstacles and other people? What happens when we take responsibility for those internal talks? I would suggest it changes the way we react to others, to obstacles, to everything around us."

Once the talk died down, I continued. "If I were to break down the internal dialogues that people have into two major categories, I would say you can differentiate between conversations that are 'conditioned' and conversations that are 'creative.' Conditioned conversations leave you with what you already have, the status quo, limited possibilities. Creative conversations, on the other hand, offer new possibilities, open you up to the opportunities all around you."

I asked for examples of conditioned conversations, and the answers came almost faster than I could write them down.

"I'd like to, but I don't think I can."

"I don't have enough time."

"I'm too old.

"I'm not enough."

"I don't have the education."

"I'm just not that smart—or smart in that way."

Once the stream of answers had slowed to a trickle, I turned back to the room. "Great job. Now, what are some examples of creative conversations you have with yourself?"

There was a long silence. People avoided eye contact with me and stared instead around the room, hoping their fellow participants had answers. I gave the question plenty of space, and after nearly a minute, someone in the back spoke up.

"I feel strong today?" one woman eventually volunteered. "I think that way when I get to the gym."

"I feel good," someone else volunteered.

The energy in the room had shifted. Many people who had called out their negative self-talk had trouble coming up with creative conversations. They seemed almost shy about offering any words.

After dinner that night, I kept thinking about how difficult it is for some of us to be compassionate toward ourselves. Why is it so easy to criticize and so hard to be kind? And if we have such a hard time coming up with nonconditioned responses to ourselves, what hope do we have of being giving and creative with others? How can we enter a Clearing of Capacity when we're so stingy with ourselves?

That evening, I sat down to journal about it. As I wrote, I realized that I wasn't always as generous with myself as I could be. Even though I taught this stuff, I had to remind myself to enter creative conversations. When I started to think about the conversations I had had with the participants, I immediately began with conditioned conversations: Had I not explained the ideas well enough? Was *I* not enough?

I had to redirect my language toward a more creative conversation: When we met again, how could I better support this audience? As soon as I wrote those words down in my journal, I realized the workshop was me stepping into a Clearing for Capacity. I had taken a moment of immense collective pain and had reached out to others, scaling my gifts. What had started as a workshop became an event I had created for my community.

I realized it wasn't just that audience—and it wasn't just me—who could stand to be more creative and generous, first with ourselves and then with the world around us. When I was in college, I often discussed Ram Dass with my classmates. There's a wonderful quote from him that has always stayed with me: "We're all just walking each other home." It's such a simple but beautiful image of generosity, helping, and community. No matter who we are and where we are in life, we're headed home—and it's our job to offer an elbow or a hand to those around us, to make sure they make it home safely, too. In my life, I want to be able to say, "Yes, I helped walk my fellow humans home, and I supported them when their journey got hard or long."

That's not to say it's always an easy stroll. Few people acknowledge how uncomfortable it can be and how much of a challenge it sometimes is. If we're all walking each other home, as Ram Dass says, there are certainly people who are pleasant to walk alongside and some who are less so. If it were easy to love everyone, we wouldn't have locks on our doors. Sometimes people challenge us. They are different or make choices that we don't agree with. Some people don't have honorable motives and seem to enjoy harming others. Even if we can nonjudgmentally acknowledge that they've made different choices than we have, it can still be a challenge to interact with them the same way we connect with the selfless and the hardworking and the kind. The idea of loving everyone is truly one of the most demanding ideas out there, despite its simple language. Most of us have conversations inside our heads about why we can't connect with this or that person, why that work would simply be too difficult. Sometimes, caring is the biggest challenge we have.

We can meet that challenge to interact in many ways. The process can be self-directed: we can be more generous and kind in our conversations with ourselves. It can be directed toward individuals in our immediate circles: we might offer support to a lifelong friend or a colleague to whom we've never spoken before. And connection can also work on a larger scale, directed toward communities that can range in size from a one-block neighborhood to the global village.

It was this third tier of generosity that I stepped into when I first started learning about ethical business and socially conscious leadership. I wanted to create a Clearing for Capacity that went beyond finding mentors or even supporting others; I wanted making a difference to be part of how I lived my life. Adjusting to these new ways of thinking wasn't a simple stroll for me, especially at first. I met people who were so passionate about what they did, and while I admired them a great deal and was intrigued by their work, I was also, to be honest, really intimidated. The people I met who were making big contributions were talking about things I'd never heard about. I felt like an imposter, posing as someone who actually gave a shit about the environment, social capital, diversity, and inclusion. I didn't *not* believe in those things, of course, but I rarely had passionate discussions about them. I didn't even recycle back then. At the time, I was focused on transitioning from my dancing and DURC. Where did inclusion, social justice, and social capital fit into that? What did dancers have to do with the environment, anyway?

I felt like I had been plopped down into a world where people talked about the earth as if it were their lover. Everything inanimate came alive, had a soul. The tiniest steps had a big impact, and we were all in this together—or so I was told. At the start, I hung around the edges, learning more about people in my community and in the world who were dedicated to growth, not just for themselves but for global consciousness. Heady stuff, and powerful.

I listened to hair-raising stories of racism and economic inequality. I spoke with people who were on the front lines of fighting injustice. These people were exploring ideas that were naturally attractive to me, but they were *huge* ideas. How could I make a significant impact on racism when I was just one person? It was even more intimidating when I was talking to or reading about someone who had done something truly meaningful in the fight against racism, had been thrown into jail or beaten for standing up for others.

One of the biggest lessons I learned by talking to people passionate about change and justice, though, is that you don't have to be on the front lines. You can make small contributions wherever you are, and those do make a difference. Cutting down on the amount of paper waste in your business or being conscious about how you relate to your family are significant changes toward larger goals, even if the actions feel incremental. Eventually I found and fell in love with the philosophy "The way you do anything is the way you do everything." I would live my life by those words, but it was a long journey.

There have been many opportunities to walk people home, and not just in my professional life. I've also volunteered my time and my skills. In 2006, for example, I worked with a group of young people who wanted to come together to make political change. They had a burning desire to make the world a better place, and their board president invited me into their meetings to help, because they were struggling. There were lots of ideas flowing around at every meeting, he told me, but they needed to get clear about their values and create a structure for their meetings so that things got done.

In the autumn of 2010, I helped launch a local Net Impact chapter and became the right-hand woman of the president. Our mission was simple: to become a regional hub for supporting professionals interested in using ethical business to create a more sustainable and socially just world. We helped corporations explore social enterprise, corporate social responsibility, and sustainability. We worked to amass resources, advertise volunteer opportunities, and set up events in our area. We held meetings and reached out to local businesses that might be interested.

In early 2014, I met with a woman who had just come out of retirement. She had a vision I was very excited about: to create a women's network for mentoring. We organized three networking events and established a network of mentors. I mentored a few of the women, including one who was an aspiring coach. The work was deeply intuitive and important for me. It allowed me to create a new set of allies with women interested in some of the same issues I was interested in. It let me feel I was making a difference in other people's lives.

• • •

Creating a Clearing for Capacity isn't always about changing the world. Sometimes, it's more like quiet ripples on the water rather than a splash. Today was an ordinary day. I woke late, had coffee with Larry, went to work. And yet, today I told Larry he was handsome and that I loved him. I met with a client and helped him realize his passion for violin—a passion he's been denying himself for twelve years because it doesn't grow his business or contribute to the bottom line. As I get ready to go to sleep, the smile on that man's face when he realized he was choosing to bring music back to his life stays with me still.

I slip under the covers of my bed and listen to Larry's deep breathing, reflecting on the day. I think of the organic food I bought and the dinner I prepared with Larry. Did my simple day make a big difference? Perhaps. It was a well-lived day that made me glad to be alive. As my eyes grow sleepy and I drift off, I send out a wish that anything I have done out of kindness today will find ground, like a seed carried aloft, and grow roots.

Chapter 15

putting it all together

I met Madison because she needed someone to help her get to the C-suite. Or at least, that's what she thought at first. Over the three months we worked together, Madison found that her journey was about a lot more than her ambition.

Madison worked for a national chain of catering companies. She was part of the team involved in refocusing the company to specialize in exclusive and celebrity events. She wanted to be the company called for actresses' weddings and big events across the country.

"I need more influence," Madison told me over lunch at Marea in Manhattan. The restaurant overlooked Central Park South, and we ate our meal amid the buzz of well-heeled movers and shakers. But Madison was frowning.

"It's just so slow moving. It's been six months since the refocus! We should have more events booked by now. People should be contacting us, wanting to book our services in Los Angeles. The Emmys are coming up, and we haven't booked a single after-party."

A waiter discreetly dropped off drinks, and I nodded my thanks before turning to Madison. "You think you need to book more events to make the C-suite."

Madison nodded, her eyes downcast, fixed on her glass of sparkling water. "I have meetings all the time, and I give it one hundred percent. I feel crushed and exhausted after, like I'm wrung dry, but I'm still slogging along instead of getting to where I want to be."

My mind played over that last little bit of conversation. "You're wrung dry?" I echoed. I often used this kind of reflective listening during a first meeting, mirroring clients' words so they would be faced with their own assumptions and conclusions and challenged to respond.

"Well, of course. Each of those meetings could make or break my career. A major after-party or a really big event that will end up in *People* with our name on it—losing or gaining that sort of cachet is what it's all about."

"But you have a team that helps you? And they feel the same way—that every meeting and conversation could make or break you?"

I was impressed by all that Madison had achieved, but I could see the stress lines on her face. She was putting the pressure of succeeding entirely on herself instead of seeing it as a team effort.

"Of course. All of them help. And I do my best to support them, make sure they know they won't lose their jobs if the latest account doesn't come through."

Madison's dissatisfaction was obvious, not just from what she said, but from the tone in which she said it—sharp consonants and pinched vowels, as if she were venting her feelings on the words she chose. Madison felt that she was giving her career her all—and in many ways she was—but wasn't getting what she wanted. She couldn't figure out why the steps weren't leading to the career of her dreams.

"Can't you give me a set of practices to do?" she asked me at the end of our meeting, looking exasperated. "There must be a set of steps I can follow."

"I can come up with some steps, if you like," I assured her. I knew the default for most people was to think of transformation as a series of "steps," as though it were a linear process, but I knew that wasn't necessarily how it happened. My job was to help a person access the undercurrents of their being, to raise awareness of a deeper wisdom that already existed within them. Once a person realized that wisdom was ripe for awakening, they could experience a powerful paradigm shift, which would unfold new possibilities before them. It almost never happened in some sort of logical, ordered way. Nonetheless, I knew how to speak the language people needed to hear until they were ready for the transformations within them to bubble to the surface. "But if you feel comfortable with it, I'd like you to come up with some of your own steps. Imagine how things would work if the future worked out as you hope. What steps would you need to take to awaken that potential and possibility? Write down your idea of steps, and I'll write down mine, and we'll compare."

"Okay . . ." Madison seemed a little hesitant, clearly surprised she hadn't simply been given a sheet of marching orders. But we shook hands, and I was hopeful she would take her assignment seriously.

Over the next few days, I worked on crafting what I wanted to tell Madison about the steps she could take. As a dancer, I knew all about steps, and the way the steps often end up being more than the whole. They add up to a dance, a cohesive performance that communicates unified ideas and emotions. As a three-year-old, I had learned the first position in ballet, followed by the second, third, fourth, and fifth. Then, I learned some more steps. All the time, I yearned to be able to do the elegant dance steps the older girls did—the girls who danced *en pointe*, like real ballerinas.

Pointe shoes, with hard glue in the toe, let ballet dancers stand on the very tips of their toes—a fragile and graceful-looking pose that actually takes an enormous amount of strength. Pointe shoes were the hallmark of a real ballerina, but first I had to learn the ballet positions and get strong enough.

When the long-awaited day finally came, I was twelve. My mother drove me to the big dance store to get toe shoes fitted. In my room, I took the shoes out of the box. They were a pink silk, the toe hard and curved into a distinctive snub-nosed shape. That first day, I spent over an hour with needle and thread, sewing on the elastic and ribbons, getting the shoes ready for class. I packed Band-Aids into my dance bag, as well as lamb's wool to pad the area around my toes. I cut the bottom seams on one pair of tights so that I could easily reach my toes after dancing.

The pointe shoes may have looked beautiful, but they were torturous. I stuffed as much lamb's wool into my toe shoes as I could, but my feet were in agony at every attempt. In the studio, we'd grip the barre with white knuckles and stand precariously on our toes, wobbling unsteadily. We were ballerinas all right. Those first few months, the pointe shoes felt like cinder blocks. My legs shook with the strain of trying to stand that way, my entire body one long, taut line of pain as I worked to hide my grimaces. I had to learn how to dance all the steps again.

After standing *en pointe*, I would take the toe shoes off shakily and try to fix my feet up. I put Band-Aids on my bleeding toes and their blisters. At night, I soaked my poor aching feet in Epsom salt, trying to soothe them into healing faster.

After I met with Madison, I reflected on those early days of dance class. Each time I incorporated new skills, I had to relearn skills I thought I had mastered. Learning to dance *en pointe* was like learning to dance in my leather ballet slippers; old steps had become new again. And each time I took part in a new production, I had to learn familiar dance steps in a new context—as part of a dance.

Many of us today are used to short lists of tips and instructions—eight ways to lose weight, nine ways to save money. We expect to be able to tick off the boxes in simple A-to-B-to-C order, without doubling back or repeating a step. We like to believe that once we've done something, it's done for good: I went to a leadership workshop, so now I'll always be a perfect boss; I worked on my relationship with my husband, so now we won't have conflicts again. But real life (and real business life) is circular. We get clear about one issue, get completion, make new choices, and build capacity, but then there are new possibilities on the horizon, some with their own baggage or their own need for clarity. We start again, at a different level. It's like scaling a mountain where the path goes around and around—you pass the same side of the mountain again and again, but each time you're a little higher.

A week later, I met Madison at her office. She might not have had the C-suite yet, but her private space was spacious and elegant. A large mahogany desk took up much of one wall, with plush garnet-colored chairs for visitors. Bold abstract paintings made a statement on another wall. Even Madison's desktop showed her drive and ambitions—the desk's ornate inlay clearly visible because her desk was perfectly organized and free of even a scrap of paper.

I looked at the heavy silver frame behind her desk. In it was a picture of her whole team in front of the offices, smiling.

"I was thinking, Madison, about what you said last week," I began. "And I want to reframe what we said about steps. I know you want specific steps to get to your goals, but what if we changed what the steps mean? What if you approached every conversation and meeting not as a 'make me or break me' kind of moment but rather as a potential stepping stone to getting to your goals—a stepping stone that includes a strategy so that you succeed. So instead of making the steps a checklist, we make it about a series of commitments or choices you make in every moment, conversation, and meeting."

Madison shrugged as she recrossed her legs. "That makes sense, but I already look out for every opportunity. When I take on a new project or meet with a new contact, I'm always trying to figure out if it's going to boost me up a level."

"This is different," I explained. "It's actually not about figuring out how other people can serve you. An interaction is a stepping stone not because of what someone else does but because of what *you* do. In this way of thinking about your work, you start to show up differently with people—in service to them, curious about them. And it doesn't apply just to clients. This goes for employees, business partners, everyone. If you connect with people as authentically as you can, they'll see it. They'll feel you caring. They'll see who you are and what you are committed to, and then—" I smiled. "Well, something magical happens. When you show up inspired, others will too. It may sound theoretical, but it's not. Showing up that way makes real, tangible changes in the way people respond to you. I've seen it."

Madison tilted her head to the side, considering my suggestion. "I like the idea," she agreed after a moment. "But I'm not sure what that looks like."

"Well, to show up differently on the outside, in how we connect to others, we usually have to start by looking at how we're showing up on the inside, for ourselves. We need to examine the stories we're telling about who we are, where we are, and where we're going. So let's start by looking at how you got here." I gestured to the ornate office. "What's your narrative?"

"I started as an assistant at this company and worked my way up. We originally had three offices, but the owners had built a national chain. This is their legacy. Now I want to take the next step."

I looked over at the pictures on her bookshelf. "That's great. But that narrative's partly about the owners. What about your story?"

Madison frowned. "I'm not sure."

"It might take some time to get clear about it. So how about you really think about it and write it down, maybe in the third person. Start your story with 'she,' like you're describing a character. When we next meet, you can tell me your narrative."

It proved not to be so simple. Madison had a busy schedule, and though we met four times over the next four weeks, she told me she hadn't had a chance to do her homework.

The real issue was resistance. Meeting in the lobby of the Marriot in Dallas weeks later while Madison was in town for a conference, she shook her head when I once again mentioned the narrative. "I just don't see what my story has to do with anything. I want to go forward, not back."

"And we're getting you moving forward, but it's hard to know which way to go if we don't really understand where we've been." Seeing her doubtful expression, I went on. "Imagine if I called you and told you I'd gotten lost on the way to this meeting. What would you need to know to help me get where I wanted to go?"

"I'd probably ask you where you were, maybe what was the last intersection you'd crossed or whether you'd passed any landmarks or anything . . ." Madison trailed off and smiled at me. "Okay," she conceded. "I see your point."

Madison looked thoughtful, and I took advantage of her new receptivity. "Go ahead, just start. Tell me the narrative. Your story, no one else's. Right now. Start with 'she . . .' Where does that story take you?"

I sat back in my chair and waited. Madison fiddled with the straw in her drink and cast a surreptitious look around, almost as if checking to see whether anyone was listening. The tables closest to ours were all taken up by holiday shoppers and businesspeople engrossed in their own meetings.

I thought Madison was going to back out again, but she impressed me.

"She . . . she . . . she was a girl when she decided she wanted to make a difference. She wanted to work at something that mattered. She didn't want just another job; she wanted to be powerful and strong. But she was always told that women and girls didn't get to be as strong as men in business suits. So she worked harder and harder, determined to make it. But those stories about girls and women were like little drops of poison. Late at night, when she didn't close the deal, she wondered whether those voices were right. She got rid of that thought fast, but it would always come sliding back. She wants to succeed to show others and herself that she can do it, but she needs to get rid of the poison."

I was genuinely surprised. "That's beautiful. So this girl or woman felt her influence slipping when others told her that it was businessmen who run the world?"

Madison laughed. "Well, I know that I'm as good a businessperson as my dad or any of the company owners, and I know times have changed, but there's always that holdover—the client who treats me differently because I'm a woman, or someone who assumes that my assistant is my boss. It's frustrating."

"I definitely understand that—those experiences frustrate me, too," I told her. "But now that story is outside of you. You've taken it outside of yourself and used your imagination to make it something less personal. How does your narrative feel now?"

Madison smiled. "Pretty good, actually. I feel clearer about why I don't feel in control. But . . . I'm still not sure how to fix that."

"We're working on it," I promised her.

In our next meeting, I asked Madison to work on what loss of control felt like to her. We stood the way she stood when she felt a conversation was crumbling or when she didn't get an important account. We looked at her internal conversations.

Then we moved as she would move in the C-suite: how she would answer the phone, sit in her chair, walk to the door. I wanted Madison to look beyond the stories she was telling herself, which basically equated a certain office with success and certain outcomes with failure. I wanted her to feel in her body—without those old stories in play—what the different possibilities felt like.

Madison in conversation was in a defensive pose, standing up tall but wound so tight that I could practically hear her joints popping. She walked tall, but it seemed like bravado. In the C-suite, however, she pictured herself as more relaxed, her walk smoother. I asked her how Madison in between today and the C-suite looked. Madison walked around the office and she seemed unsure how to make the pose. Finally, she pictured it as a flurry of chaotic movement.

"How did that feel? What narrative or feeling showed up for you when you made the movement between you today and you in the C-suite?"

"The unknown. Chaos. A nebula or black hole in the night sky."

I had a hunch about one of Madison's blocks. Would you really move through an obstacle to your dream future if, at some level, you pictured it as a black hole that would gobble you up?

A week later, we met at her office again. Madison had just finished a last-minute call and looked drained, offering me an apologetic smile and almost slumping over in her chair. I suggested a walk around the local park.

Madison seemed surprised but agreed, and the two of us walked along the groomed paths between clusters of tulips and moms with strollers.

"So we have your narrative, and we know some of what might be holding you back. And we've talked about your goals: to have more influence and to get into that C-suite. Now I have a question."

I looked over at her to make sure I had her full attention. "What if you were already a woman of influence?"

Madison slowed and sat down on one of the benches, stretching her legs like a cat. "Well, I already have success. I do have some influence. But I want more influence."

She looked at me hesitantly, as though I were about to berate her for greedily grabbing for the brass ring.

"Of course," I acknowledged. "But what if all the influence you want— all of it—you already had? What would you do? How would you act? What would that look like? Take me through your day. You're in the C-suite, and you own the company. You come into work. It's morning. Now what?"

Madison crinkled her brow, thinking. "Well, I'd want to greet everyone and get them into the lounge for an impromptu meeting, first thing. I'd want to hear their ideas for how to attract celebrity clients. And then we'd get down to brass tacks—sending flowers and cards to agents and celebrities with our logo on them, creating presentations for trade shows, meeting wedding planners catering to celebrity clients, and making friends with writers who could put us in newspapers and magazines. Each of us would tackle the projects that held the most passion for us, as a team."

"That's interesting," I told her. "I don't hear anything about you hanging out in your office, sipping Dom Pérignon. I'm hearing that being an influencer means harnessing the power of your team and making everyone a resource. Does that feel right?"

Madison nodded slowly, as if warming up to the idea, and I continued.

"Well, what if you acted like that now? What if you made everyone on your current team a resource, focused on helping to build the company?"

I could see the proverbial lightbulb moment, the moment when a shift in thinking changed everything for Madison. She stood up tall, her five-foot-nine frame towering over me. "I have to get back to the office!" she blurted, a huge smile on her face.

Over the next few sessions, Madison was engrossed in our work in a whole new way. She imagined herself in the C-suite and got focused on making everyone a resource. It meant looking at everyone on her team differently, with more careful attention.

"I found out today someone I've been working with for months speaks four languages. I had no idea! It's like I'm discovering superpowers in my team!"

I laughed. We talked about the new choices Madison was making, including her choice to put four people on a project alone and bow out so she could focus elsewhere. Where before she would have insisted on taking the lead, she was now excited about letting someone else handle the reins.

I couldn't help teasing her a bit. "What list of steps would you come up with to help you succeed?"

Madison shuddered. "Steps are for wimps. I'm dancing the dance, not taking it one step at a time." I worked with Madison as she transitioned into a new way of doing business. Yes, Madison eventually reached the C-suite. But she is still working on her path, as all of us are, choosing in each moment what to focus on and how to keep moving forward, past our stories and toward community.

Chapter 16

stepping into the clearing— with hesitation

If I could, I would make sure everyone stepping into the Clearing did so with joy and certainty. I wish people could dance into the Clearing. Sometimes, though, it's more of a hobble. So many of us live our lives with doubt, uncertainties. We second-guess and subject ourselves to cross-examinations even the most ardent district attorney would hesitate to voice in a courtroom. Even I sometimes get a painful heaviness in my stomach when I worry about meeting with a client. I especially remember that tension when I first met Daniel.

In a way, it would've been odd if I *hadn't* felt tension around working with Daniel, as he entered every meeting wound tight enough for both of us. I first started coaching him when he was still in school, training to be a veterinarian.

I met Daniel because of the Peace Circles that Larry and I held in our living room. I got the inspiration from spiritual writer Marianne Williamson. Her best seller was *A Return to Love*, but I had the privilege of hearing her speak at the Naropa Institute in Colorado right after 9/11, and the initiatives she spoke of there pushed me to act. She had come up with the idea of Peace Circles as a way of embracing a different vision of the world. I loved the idea. These were gatherings where a group of friends met for meditative practice, and then each of us would speak about how we created peace in our hearts. It was a way to reconnect, to be part of something greater.

Larry and I had met Fiona through one of Larry's business friends and colleagues. She came to one of our first Peace Circles and brought Daniel with her. They made a striking couple. Daniel is tall, and Fiona is petite, with flowing brown hair and a bright smile. Daniel asked a lot of questions during the circles and shared himself easily.

On the surface, Daniel seemed to have it all. He did exceptionally well in school, was very much in love with Fiona, was close to his family. Under the surface, however, he was far from proud. Though his face was open and kind, his anxiety and lack of confidence quickly became evident.

"I'm worried about the future," he told me at one of our earlier meetings. "Veterinary school is competitive, and I'm not sure if I'm making the right choice here. My family comes from a long line of doctors. Caring for animals feels like my destined path, but what if medicine is my destined path? I'd still be helping people. And that's really important to me, no matter what I do. I want to make a contribution—maybe even beyond healing disease."

It was clear that Daniel felt a lot of pressure to make something of his life and to make a meaningful impact. That phrase came up a lot—"destined path." Once, when we were meeting in my home office, he slumped in the chair and shamefacedly showed me an exam he hadn't scored well on. Even though he consistently had a near-perfect GPA and worked hard, that one test had him stressed out. "I want to make something of my life. I should be doing better than this!"

In fact, Daniel's anxiety was so acute that it was affecting his health. Crushed under a heavy workload and hours of studying, he had developed digestive issues. He went to one specialist after another, but they were never able to find anything.

"I just went to the doctor last week," he told me at one of our meetings. "All my tests came back negative. I'm still feeling all this pain, but the doctors couldn't find anything wrong. I think it might just be stress. Maybe it's an ulcer. The problem is if I'm distressed now, how will I be when final exams start next month? I'm worried that eventually my stomach's going to get worse. What if I go to the doctor one day and get really bad news?"

One of the first things I did with Daniel was to take a look at how he moved. He was a little over six feet tall, and he moved slowly and methodically, his shoulders slightly hunched over and rounded. Daniel's slow movements and cautious, constrained steps perfectly represented his worried state.

Like many people, Daniel had habitual ways of thinking and behaving that didn't serve him and negatively impacted every area of his life. Like many of us, he wasn't as sure of himself as he wanted to be, and that uncertainty made him hesitant in not just his professional life, but his personal life as well. He loved Fiona but wasn't sure whether marriage was right for him. He was fascinated with his veterinary studies but wasn't quite sure it was what he should be doing. Constantly worrying and stressing and second-guessing himself, he was running around in circles.

So how did Daniel learn to move past this anxiety? He stopped reacting. Many of us consider thoughts to be things that simply show up, that exist utterly outside our realm of control; but in reality we get to choose. We get to generate thoughts that move us closer to where we want to be and how we want to be. Daniel, like so many of us, was a victim of his own thinking because he believed thoughts were simply things that *were*. Instead of trying to change his thoughts, he was trying to get control of the things around him (like his relationship or his grades). Once he became aware that his thoughts were something he could control and realized that he didn't always need to react to whatever his mind came up with, things started to change for him.

It's an old idea. People have been trying to separate themselves from their thoughts and gain control of the mind for centuries. Zen meditation, among other practices, tries to clear away our thoughts so that we have the space to create our own realities. As we've seen, in The Clearing I teach people to become conscious of their thoughts and to help them see they are not their emotions.

Worry and anxiety are killers; you don't have to be an avid reader of medical journals to know that. However, breaking the worry habit is difficult for most people. In order to help Daniel, I told him about the ninety-second rule.

"When we experience a strong emotion, such as anger, the brain sends out chemicals that cause physiological reactions," I explained to him during one of our meetings. "After about ninety seconds, though, the chemicals are completely gone from the bloodstream. The automatic physiological experience is over. If you continue to be angry or upset after those initial ninety seconds, it's because you're allowing the circuit to continue. What that essentially means is that after those ninety seconds, we get to choose whether we make a different response."

I then taught Daniel how to gain back control over the emotions that seem to come out of nowhere.

I started by telling him a story: "You know, Larry and I are both independent consultants. We spend a lot of time networking or going to client dinners. I love my husband, but sometimes being married to Larry is like being married to a race-car driver. We're always going one hundred and eighty miles per hour. One day recently I found myself just feeling fed up with it all. So when he came home, I turned to him and said, 'Honey, don't you know we're going around in circles?' I finally told him I just wanted to slow down."

Daniel looked interested but puzzled as I went on, as though he couldn't imagine what my domestic disputes had to do with him.

"We both got more and more upset, and we broke one cardinal rule of our marriage, which is to never go to bed angry. I woke up the next day at four-thirty because I had a meeting in Fort Worth at seven a.m. I hit the snooze button a few times, and by the time I finally crawled out of bed, I felt frantic. I jumped into the car and realized that I didn't have any gas. I had just enough to get to the gas station, so I zoomed over to fill up, and all the while, I could feel my heart racing and my muscles tightening. Finally,

I got on the freeway. Energy pulsing, the veins in my neck throbbing, I was white-knuckling the wheel. My heart rate was up. It would have been really good for me to check in, recognize that I was triggered, and ask myself what I was triggered by."

I looked at Daniel expectantly, and he answered hesitantly: "Your fight with Larry?"

I nodded, smiling to encourage him. "Yes! I was angry at Larry because I was telling myself he cares more about work than about our intimacy. I was also triggered because I was going to be late, and I had professionals waiting. My professional reputation was on the line."

"Well, that's reasonable," Daniel said. "Larry could have apologized."

"Yeah, but who pushed the snooze button? Who didn't put gas in her car? I can just own it."

"So what did you do?" Daniel asked.

"I recognized the physiological response, but I also asked myself, okay, what else might be true? When I ask that, I can talk myself down off a ledge. I can tell myself something different from what I'm telling myself. The truth is, I got to my meeting by 6:15. And after the meeting, I chose to call Larry and try to listen. I realize I'm always continuously monitoring my own internal conversation. So I need to ask if I'm really listening or whether I'm just perpetuating a cycle that should have lasted only ninety seconds.

"Look at it this way," I told Daniel. "My day seemed completely out of control. But I had to realize I was having a physical reaction, and I had to take a deep breath to calm down. Then I had to figure out what I was feeling, and *then* I could choose to think in a different way."

Daniel nodded, and I continued. "Let's look at your conversations with your family, for example. When you talk to them, do you have a physiological response when they disagree with your choices?"

"I feel stomach pains and sometimes get headaches. And my jaw aches sometimes. I'm all tense."

"Right," I said. "The next time you experience that, maybe you can try to focus on what you feel in your body and then take a few deep breaths. Think of it like a forensic science, if it helps. We're looking for clues about what's hijacking your mind and your life."

"And then I try to define my emotions?"

"Yes, just let yourself feel the emotion and try to track it down. Is it resentment? Anger?"

Daniel thought for a moment. "I think sometimes . . . it's sadness—sadness that my family won't accept what and who I am."

"And how could you reframe that?"

He seemed stumped, but once we worked on it for a few minutes, the answers started showing up: "They want me to have a legacy like the doctors of our family. They care about me and want me to be happy. They want to help, but they don't know how."

"And when you think about your family from this standpoint, what do you think and feel? Do you feel that same sadness?"

He thought about it. "I think I feel compassion. Sympathy."

"Why sympathy?"

Daniel considered. "I think that fear is a terrible thing, and they live with it all the time—lots of anxiety and worry about me, their finances, everything. That deserves sympathy, in my book."

We were starting to make headway. But there was an even bigger task ahead: stop the worrywart behaviors from showing up in the first place. Daniel got a homework assignment: come up with a list of five triggers that put him in a state of anxiety.

"Triggers are the circumstances, words, or actions that make us more likely to get into difficult emotional states like anxiety, fear, and anger." I also asked him to write out what anxiety most often looked like for him, because when we know that, we can recognize when we are being triggered.

Daniel found two triggers by the time we next met—it was clear that his parents' disapproval was a big one, as was the feeling that he was falling behind his classmates. More importantly, he determined that at the core of the triggers was the belief that he was not good enough. That belief is at the core of most people's triggers. And that belief manufactures behaviors designed to keep that belief at bay. We find ways to be successful to prove to the world we are worthy. We avoid telling the total truth to ourselves and others because we're afraid the truth will make us look bad. We find ways to be the smartest person in the room when what people really want is just to know who we are. These are all signs of cultural conditioning, and our triggers keep them in place.

Daniel also realized that when he felt triggered, certain behaviors manifested—namely, eating a lot of sugar and caffeine, isolating, insomnia, a comparison racket with other students, and withdrawal from the activities he loved. Once he had a new, conscious awareness about what his triggers were, he could be on the lookout for them. When they did show up, he had done the investigative work to know what emotion was at its core—whether it was fear, sadness, anger—and he acknowledged that emotion without judging it.

There was also a plan to ward off the anxiety-producing behaviors before they took hold and to guide his body into more healthy habits—like eating healthier foods instead of drinking down coffee like the typical vet student. When he knew a trigger was leading him down an unhealthy path and his impulse was to go home and isolate, he found he could choose to call a friend. We all have to be especially on guard for triggers when we are fatigued and overworked, and there are steps we can take to avoid getting to that vulnerable point. But it all starts with knowing what triggered us—with acknowledging the triggers, pausing, and working to reframe the situation in a different light, with different labels that have less power.

Within a few months, Daniel's stomach and digestive issues lessened and then went away. He had never been able to find any medical reason for his pain, but now he not only had a clean bill of health, but *felt* like he had a clean bill of health.

That feeling of health seemed to be a direct result of the work we did around Daniel's anxiety regarding school and his family's judgment of his professional choices. But veterinary school wasn't the only worry he had. As soon as we started talking about his possible future with Fiona, we came face to face with the past.

"I love Fiona," he explained to me. "But I'm still in school, and marriage is such a huge commitment. And who knows where we will both be in a few years? I've had relationships that I thought were going to last forever, and then they just ended. I don't want that to happen here, and it would be even more devastating if we got married and divorced."

Daniel was so scared of losing Fiona that he was worried about divorce before he had even decided to propose. Whenever he talked about losing Fiona, his posture changed, and he became more curled into himself, his fear showing in lines on his face. He was clearly drawn to the possibility of creating a lifelong partnership with Fiona, but a few past relationships were keeping him from moving forward. Ironically, trying to avoid the hurt that he had experienced with past relationships ensured that the past would repeat itself. By not committing to Fiona, he was all but ensuring that it wouldn't work out.

I tried to break it to him gently: "So you think you want this relationship to work out, but you're worried because it might not. If your reticence to commit is more about protecting yourself from getting hurt, though, is the relationship more or less likely to succeed?"

He eventually understood that by trying to avoid the pain of the past, he was setting himself up for more of the exact same. The day he realized that, he made a date with Fiona before he even left my office and ordered a bouquet of flowers as he headed out the door. He was ready to commit.

The work on Daniel's relationships started the process of Clarity and Clearing for Capacity. We got the chance to continue this work around Capacity years later when Daniel had become a veterinarian. At the time, he was running a clinic with a partner, but the partnership was not the greatest match. Daniel wanted to make a real difference and contribute to the community, but his partner did not always share that vision.

It was time to get clearer about what Daniel wanted.

After I listened to Daniel listing the pros and cons of running his own practice, I asked, "Do you remember when you accessed the part of yourself that enabled you to move forward and make the right choice?"

Daniel closed his eyes and breathed in deeply, as we had practiced all those years ago while he was still a student. "Yeah. I was meditating at the Shambhala center."

I remembered him telling me about the course he had taken at a meditation center in Dallas. "Remind me—what became available to you then?"

"I got clear about who I was and what I was meant to do and be." Daniel's breathing had changed, evened out.

"So, with that insight, what has been cleared for you?"

"I think I'm stepping into a place where I am enough. At the Shambhala center, I could see that I didn't have to do what my parents wanted of me. It was my life and I could make my own mark on it. I stepped into my own life. And that means . . ."

"Yes?" I asked the question quietly.

"I can step into that same space again. I can move away from the business arrangement I have now and run my clinic according to my vision. I can embrace that same space."

It would take months, but the bulk of the work started with that one moment. No more wavering back and forth and worrying. Daniel had stepped into a new space of opportunity for himself, and in doing so, some of the old baggage worrying him fell away. We still had to work on separating the business and consciously selecting a new model and path for the clinic, but it all began with that one step.

But in the end, he got his fairy-tale ending. He bought out his partner, becoming sole owner of the practice, and he moved to Austin, where he now lives with Fiona and their two sons. As part of his commitment to getting involved in the community, Daniel and Fiona created an art gallery in his office, and the profits they make go to local causes.

"I love the way that I'm able to impact my community," he told me one day over coffee. "It makes work not feel like work at all. This is miles away from the stress I used to feel in school."

The unique thing about Daniel, in my experience, is that he is a client I worked with for years. I watched him transition from a student to a successful vet to a husband and father. Along the way, we became friends. I danced at his wedding, and we stay in touch. Along the way, he's taught me a great deal, too. I noticed that even once someone steps into the Clearing, returning to that space is important. As a student, Daniel sought completion around his love of veterinary medicine and his family's expectations. As a successful practitioner, there were new things to get clear about: his vision for his practice and his desire to buy his partner out. Stepping into the Clearing is a lifelong dance, not just a once-in-a-lifetime excursion.

heartbreak and obstacles

There are moments in life when any clearing seems impossible. When clarity becomes obscured by grief and pain. When the stories we hoped to complete seem as though they will always hang unfinished. When it appears destruction has outstripped creation. When we forget our capacity for connection and feel utterly alone.

But I have found that struggle and sadness offer me opportunities for growth as great as my suffering. By living intentionally, I can learn, grow, and work toward wholeness even during difficult times. With my choices, I can make a stand; I can light my small, true flame against the dark.

Sometimes, of course, trying to create light in the dark can feel like an insurmountable task. Sixteen years after my mother's death, my father passed away. On the day of the funeral, we slowly drove up through thousands of white gravestones marking the sloping green hills of Arlington National Cemetery. We didn't speak—just walked in silence from the car to the hushed, solemn waiting room. On wall-mounted screens, a quiet presentation about the history of Arlington Cemetery played.

We walked to the ceremony together—Larry and me, my brother and sister, my nieces and nephews, and other members of my family. My shoes sank into the soft ground, and I took one step after another, even though my heart was heavy; I didn't want to miss this final chance to say goodbye.

It was early on Easter Monday. Several services were scheduled back to back, and we were one of the first funerals of the day. It all felt a little like providence; there had only been one funeral slot available that weekend, which was at the height of the cherry blossom season, one of the busiest times in Washington. Somehow, we had called just in time and gotten the first morning service. Clearly, that one slot was meant for Dad.

I fell into place in the gathering. The funeral director stood solemnly, one hand over his heart, and I copied the gesture. Nearby were my sister and brother and their families, with the same somber faces. Even though we had known for years that Dad was ill and would eventually be gone, no child is ready for that final wrench and break, the ache of loss. Larry was beside me, video camera in hand, and I was thankful he was capturing these moments.

There is always ritual in passing, and as I stood there in one of the most revered spots in the country, I couldn't help but remember my mother's passing so long ago, her comments about "a beautiful death." Arlington Cemetery certainly knew how to create a beautiful ritual, one that honored the dead completely. Every part of the process—from meeting with the funeral director to receiving a permanent parking pass—moved with a smooth, dignified pace.

The ease was a relief. The whole funeral process stood in sharp contrast to the months of paperwork and applications with the Veteran's Administration we'd waded through when we'd needed aid for my father's long-term care. Amy had joked about it when we met with the funeral director for the first time: "Probably the fastest response ever from our federal government."

Standing in the cemetery, I looked left, up the hill, where more than twenty-five soldiers stood at attention, in full military dress uniform, each one impeccably groomed. To the right, a lone soldier stood erect at the top of his salute.

More commands were given, and the band played "Amazing Grace." What is it about that song? In Arlington, the song's significance to our family deepened, and after the first few chords, I let my tears fall.

Dad had made no funeral requests, had expressed no desire to be buried beside his parents outside Chicago, or anywhere, for that matter. "When you're dead, you're dead," he had said. "It makes no difference to me. I'll leave that up to you."

Maybe his view came from his religious doubts, which he'd summed up for me pretty succinctly years before his death: "If God is everything I don't understand, then everything I don't understand is everywhere!" He was pretty sure that religion as he understood it was not the truth, and he preferred to live with doubt rather than accept beliefs that could never be proven. Considering he lived the last thirty years of his life in the ultraconservative Dallas suburb of Garland, I thought my father's fairly public stance was courageous.

It seemed fitting that his children chose Arlington as his final resting place, among the honored fallen and beside a band of brothers he spoke of more in his later years. This was the highest and best tribute we could offer to his memory.

My father, John Wilmerton Darley, had been a first lieutenant in the Army Air Force during World War II. He had joined at just seventeen, eager to fight against the Nazis. When I was about nine, I remember putting on one of his uniform shirts. It was made of wool in a deep forest green. Looking at myself in my parents' bedroom mirror, I imagined what he might have looked like in that shirt. I tried to picture what he had done wearing that shirt and what it felt like for him to wear it. Truth was, it wasn't much bigger than my slim child's body at the time. He must have been one very slight, vulnerable seventeen-year-old boy.

His father before him had served as a Marine and fought in the trenches during the Great War. Neither my father nor his father shared much about those times with us when we were kids, but when my father decided to write his book, *The Darley Clan*, at seventy-three, his service stories emerged as he committed them to his genealogical memoir.

The war in Afghanistan loomed near the day we buried my father, and we watched other families arrive at Arlington to bury their loved ones. One young widow walked slowly through the grass, her face cast down to the folded American flag in her hands. A small child walked beside her, barely reaching her waist and toddling along as fast as his small legs could carry him.

What I remember most about that day was its tempo. Though I had hurried to make it there at the start, once I arrived, I loved the way the ceremony allowed us to slow down and be still: the silent spaces between each sentence, the moments designed for reflection and meditation, the emptiness. I loved the slow side-step of the soldier charged with the flag-adorned casket and his deliberate nod to signal the "all clear," before the horses pulled the caisson forward in time to the drum; the slow unfolding, then the ceremonial refolding of the flag; the soldier's hands, crisply gloved fingers curled neatly into their palms, all to the same degree, all to the same angle, on down the line.

It wasn't all solemnity and sacred ritual. There was at least one moment that was both out of place and funny in a way Dad would have adored. In his final years, Dad had suffered from incontinence. During his funeral, in the middle of our walk behind the caisson to the staging area, we got a small surprise that made me smile through my tears. Horses have their needs, too, and just because they're trained to trot with the utmost dignity, it doesn't mean that's all they do. All the planning in the world couldn't have predicted this necessary interruption of our most sacred ritual, but our best laid plans came to a quiet, uncomfortable halt when the horses simultaneously took the biggest leak you can possibly imagine. This was not the delicate trickle, gently cascading down to meet the pavement, but a no-holds-barred, gigantic gush of hot horse piss that splashed and steamed its way to the ground. Thankfully, the funerary team knew how to simply wait until they were done before recommencing the slow advance. *Okay, Dad, really?*

I thought. *Is this your idea of a last laugh?* The beauty and irony of our world never ceases to amaze.

. . .

Not long after that Easter Monday ceremony, I found myself standing in front of a group of strangers at the Social Venture Network annual member conference, spontaneously telling the story of my dad's funeral. Though I hadn't planned to share this experience, in retrospect I believe my impulse was driven by a desire to practice speaking from my heart. As I choked and sputtered my way through the short story, I realized how much I was still grieving. When the session ended, a number of people came up to me to express their condolences and thank me for sharing. I was about to leave when a man with short gray hair and glasses approached me. He smiled, introduced me to his wife, and said he wanted to know more about my father.

I smiled back. "What would you like to know?"

"I'd like to know more about his military history. I thought you had to have a special medal to be buried at Arlington."

"He was a first lieutenant," I responded. "He enlisted and flew missions over Brazil and crash-landed."

My memory seemed to fail me in that moment. Thinking that the man might want to know more than my father's military history, I continued, explaining that following his military discharge, he went to Cornell for a degree in electrical engineering and Harvard for his MBA. As I rambled on, I began to hear the defensiveness and insecurity in my words. I had assumed that the man's inquiry veiled judgment and suspicion, but an assumption was all it was. The judgment, I realized, was coming from me. I'd shared my experience of my father's death to practice vulnerability and openness, but just minutes later, my ego was rearing its ugly head to earn acceptance and belonging.

I made myself stop explaining and took a centering breath. "But in answer to your question," I said, "no, my father didn't have a special medal. He got into Arlington because of his rank and rank alone."

From my perspective, that wasn't good enough, assuming as I did in that moment that his rank was purely a function of privilege, not performance. But how did I know that? I didn't.

The man thanked me, and as I watched him leave the room, I let out a sigh. After all the training I'd been through, all the coaching I'd received and all the insights into life's purpose I'd gained, I'd still felt as though I were being accused of making up stories, of using my father's story for my own selfish ends. My inner dialogue suggested that some shadowy accusation had been made about the truth of my family story, but that polite man hadn't said anything to that effect. I could have stewed about it for hours or days, but instead I found Gail Larsen of Transformational Speaking somewhere in the room. She was the one leading the breakout session, and she'd be able to help me toward Completion.

"Did you want to reconnect with that couple?" she asked me after listening to my worries.

"Yes," I told her. "There are a few more questions I need to ask."

Later that same day, I found the couple and asked the man why he was interested in my father's military history.

His answer was so simple: "I wanted to know because I served four years in Vietnam, and I wanted to know how and where he served."

He also wanted to tell me that he was a speaker, too, and one of his significant realizations was that one never knows who is in the audience. This gentleman wanted me to share more details of my father's life in the Army because he wanted to connect even more deeply to the story I was telling. That was it. No judgment. No story about how my father didn't deserve to be buried there. He just wanted to more fully appreciate the personal story I'd just shared.

Once again, I realized that the fear I'd felt in that moment—and indeed all the suffering in my life—was generated by me. And once again, I was reminded that I get to choose whether to suffer or not.

And so I chose. I faced my own vulnerability. I told the truth about my fears. I talked to Larry about the experience at the conference, and I journaled about it. The biggest step I took, however, had been in the moment—facing the man and finding out his intentions rather than letting my mind assign him nefarious motives for no good reason. I took the steps necessary to clean up the misinterpretation that, had I hung out in my dramatic monologue, might have robbed me of the most precious memories I will ever have of my father.

I tell these stories because all of us struggle with loss at some point. No matter what kind of loss we experience, in the moment many of us feel paralyzed or think we need to express our sorrow in a specific way. Many of us even have hidden stories about loss—if we loved someone we lost, we tell ourselves what an appropriate time for mourning looks like and what it *should* look like. In these cases, too, The Clearing and choice can be a powerful tool in helping us move past that initial anguish and into new possibilities.

Chapter 18

dancing naked, right where you are

One night, I dreamt of my mother in the house in Schenectady. In the dream, she is wearing a long green dress, her beautiful hair curled up in a French twist for a party. She is at the sink in the kitchen, her hands deep in soapy water. Dream-me wanders into the room, looking around the once-familiar cupboards and table, and my mother turns to me and smiles, that beautiful smile I have missed all these years. From the sink, she lifts something and hands it to me. At first I think it's going to be a white plate, but when I look down I see it is a book, its pages bright white. Then my mother winks and disappears.

I wake in the early Dallas dawn and look over at Larry, who is still asleep, his breathing even and quiet. The room is already warm, even though the sun is not up. I pull on my bathrobe and curl my toes into the thick rug on my side of the bed before making my way to the bathroom. The face that looks back at me in the mirror is sleepy but smiling. As I brush my teeth, I wonder whether my mother would recognize my face today; she's been gone so long. I think of the book in the dream, miraculously saved from water damage.

Curling up on the chaise longue in a patch of sunlight, I pick up a note-book and pen to write my morning pages. Larry is up now, and I can hear the periodic tap of the razor against the sink as he shaves. On the page, I reflect on my dream and on the book I'm writing. My writing meanders across the page, traveling through memories of Mother and her books—her journals, her love of reading and writing. As the pen leaves its inky tracks, I am full of gratitude for the moment, for the sounds of Larry in the next room. My love for my husband makes itself known in the words I write.

Finally, once my three pages are done, I put down my pen and stretch. I have been doing morning pages for years.

After I put my notebook away, Larry comes into the room and swoops down to kiss me. We smile at each other, and his eyes crinkle in happiness. I'm aware that I'm more in love with him, with life, with everyone in my life, than I ever have been.

In some ways, meeting Larry was a fairy tale—a chance encounter in a restaurant becoming a lifelong love affair. But this isn't high fantasy; this marriage is about dancing with what is right in front of us. This marriage is about intentional cocreation. We are both aware and conscious enough to know that we have to pay attention or our most important relationship will suffer. Having someone who is willing to dance and create with me is amazing.

It could all go another way. Each day, Larry could snipe at me for leaving my clothes on the floor, or I could roll my eyes in derision when he sends a plate back at a restaurant. There are days when my responses to his questions might seem clipped to someone on the outside looking in. It's a real marriage, with real problems and its own set of demons, but every day we wake and face them together. Every day we choose to be kind and loving. He picks up something I drop on the floor, and I ask how I can support him when he gets annoyed with someone. And it's not just about tolerance. Larry and I decided early on that we would always share our vulnerabilities; no hiding the snippy little thoughts that can fester in the dark. It's all out in the open, where whatever issues we have can heal.

I pull my mind back to the present, and as I get ready to head out the door, I feel a tension in the pit of my stomach. Long ago, I learned that when there's tension somewhere in my body, I'm feeling something that I haven't worked through consciously. I take a deep breath, stretch my body up and out, and remind myself that the feeling is just my brain doing its thing, just the amygdala trying in its ancient way to protect me. I refocus on the love and warmth I felt this morning, and my body relaxes.

In the car, headed to meet a client, I think of that tension in my stomach. I realize that it's nervousness. There was a time when I felt nervous before meeting every new client. Today, that tension might also be because I'm getting ready to present a new talk in the next month, and I'm nervous about what to say. I'm supposed to be talking about leadership, and I know I want to start with an anecdote about my dancing days. As I drive along, I think about how often dancing comes up when I coach. It's because the skills I learned by paying attention to dance steps and my body are things that leaders in boardrooms and business suits desperately need to understand.

Many people see leadership—at least in most traditional businesses—as something that happens from the head up. Think about it: When's the last time you saw a picture of an executive's feet? We post headshots on board of directors' web pages, and we show businesspeople hard at work at their desks, only their torso and heads visible in photos. We think of corporate work as something that involves words and numbers, something that happens between the ears.

But the body is a huge resource of information—and paying attention to the body has a much bigger impact on what goes on in the boardroom than most people realize. Being a conscious leader means being conscious of everything. And for me, that starts with being conscious about what's happening in the body.

When tiny ballerinas are just wobbling around in their first pair of ballet slippers, one of the first things they're taught is to stand up straight and to pull in the stomach. Yes, it creates a more beautiful line to the body, but it also strengthens the abdominal walls to allow dancers to eventually create the most amazing movements. Many of the moves and postures dancers execute with seemingly little effort are unnatural and require almost super-human strength right at the core.

Japanese aikido masters call the center of the body *hara*, and they teach that when the body is triggered, it's important to connect to the hara. Fo-cusing on the hara lets us connect with what's important to us and gives us a way to concentrate our energy instead of freaking out about the missing report, the traffic pileup, or whatever the trigger may be. In my Somatic Leadership training, which is based on a number of aikido practices, I learned to get in touch with my body—and how to help others do the same—to connect with a source of energy and power not tapped through any other way. Aikido helps us access something that wasn't possible before, allowing us to move through and past triggers and obstacles.

When you're triggered, it can feel as though your core is literally off balance, and there's a physical reaction: the pounding heart, the feeling of dread in your stomach, the tightening of muscles in your arms or chest. When this happens, slowing down your breath and connecting to your cen-ter and core values helps restore balance. Whether you're looking out at an audience from the stage or over at your team from across the negotiating table, you need that balance to perform.

Back when I was in Miss Danzig's studio, the constant refrain was "Backs straight!" and "Pull up! Drop your weight!" Leaders might benefit from hav-ing someone standing behind them shouting much the same thing.

In dance, we're always fighting against gravity, and when we pull up—when I literally visualize the top of my head gliding along the ceiling and then drop my weight, when I imagine the soles of my feet growing roots to the center of the earth—we create the balance needed for the complex steps of a dance.

Executives and leaders often ignore their own bodies at work because they're focused on strategy, meetings, and full schedules. But focusing on the lower half of the body and maybe doing a few squats sends blood flowing and boosts energy. At the same time, pulling up or sitting up as straight as possible creates a feeling of powerful energy. Sometimes, I tell my clients to imagine themselves in the body of a giant, reaching up toward the sky. They invariably feel empowered, which often changes the tenor of the decisions they make.

Another thing I often tell clients has to do with making small changes. Often, the leaders I meet with love the idea of big actions and grand, sweeping changes. But dancers know the power of tiny shifts. For instance, when I work out in my living room, I sometimes use a few five-pound weights. I perch on one leg, tipped forward like a teapot but with both arms, hands holding the weights at my sides and parallel to the floor, and my other leg extended out behind me so I make the shape of a capital letter *T*. My objective is to just stand there and keep balance. If I pay attention, I notice the many small, incremental shifts needed to maintain that balance. I extend the energy through the heel of my elevated leg. I pinch my buttocks together and bring my navel closer to my spine. I relax my shoulders to the extent the weights allow.

When I'm coaching clients, sometimes they want the big answers—the one magical solution that will let them tackle their to-dos, double their business, or land that client. But life doesn't come with Miracle-Gro. In most cases, it's the tiny moves that change our path. Years of quiet moments with a loved one build a strong marriage. Years of steady work build a career. And at any point in time, my clients can make tiny shifts to reset or change their course. When I feel overwhelmed, I'll sometimes make a loud, diaphragm-supported tone alone in the car. Just the small focus on breath is sometimes enough to turn around a bad day and let me move more confidently in the direction I feel I want to be going.

Dance isn't about just breathing and bodywork, of course. There's also the moment of hushed anticipation before the curtain rises and you are immersed in the magic of a performance. When all the work and all your creativity are being used, you tend to achieve a sense of flow. When you are in the flow state, you are present. Time seems irrelevant, and you are so engaged in what you're doing that nothing else seems to matter. When I danced at my highest level of performance, I couldn't have been more present to the music, the dancers around me, the lights, the sweat, and the breath. It wasn't an experience of me dancing—it was the experience of the dance dancing me. The dance and I were one.

In my coaching business, I also had to find that flow in order to help leaders. I once worked with a client who wanted to create a community to help victims of human trafficking. The work he did was an inspiration, but it also showed some of the darker sides of humanity, and it was hard for my client to stay positive. Simply exposing the horrors of human trafficking, we decided, wouldn't work. We needed to inspire and uplift, because people needed to feel that there was hope and that they could help create change. But how to create any sort of inspirational or hopeful message around a topic so grim? My client needed to look beyond the obvious painful elements to find a new whole.

Supporting him through that process meant I had to bring a new level of A-game to our interactions. One day, after we had talked through every aspect of the issue in detail and were still working on Clarity, I decided we had to move through it. I asked my client to walk around the room and picture how he felt when he saw the worst of the human condition that he encountered through his work. Then, I had him walk while he thought of the most inspirational stories from his work.

I let him walk around farther before I spoke up. "Now I want you to focus out beyond yourself and the work you do. Imagine your donors and the audience you want to reach. Move and walk the way you want them to feel. How inspired? How hopeful?"

At first, his steps were measured and careful, but within a few minutes it was like watching a volcano explode. His arms lifted up as though of their own accord, and he started moving faster and more gracefully, swirling around. His movements got more powerful and faster still until he was dancing across the floor. We had gone from painful movements full of misery to the power of the human spirit embodied in dance—and all because we looked past the sum of our ideas and plugged into our bodies while switching our focus to the audience.

Through rhythm, it all poured out of him—the pain that led him to the cause, the frustration that came with people not caring enough, and his passion that something had to change. Once he worked through the pain in dance, he turned to writing. He started freewriting around topics like hope and inspiration, sometimes just describing what he wanted members of his community to feel and the experiences that kept him going. It took months of work, but he started to build the community he wanted and even gained some inspiration for other areas of his life.

Being in that sense of flow is important for leaders of every kind. The executive in charge of a company may find that flow state when negotiating contracts or wrangling spreadsheets. For a mother heading a family, flow may mean art projects at the kitchen table or creating a nurturing home. The point is that everyone deserves that heady feeling dancers get on stage, and virtually any person can seek it out. For business leaders, it may mean focusing on the parts of business that are truly in alignment with their passions. Some executives feel that they need to "do the work" even when it's work they hate. But when we focus on jobs we love or parts of our work that bring us joy, we do a better job and really connect with people. We make a difference and experience an entirely different way of living.

As I drive to meet my new client, all these thoughts tumble through my head. When I pull into the parking lot, I pop out my journal to make a few notes. I feel better about the talk I have to give. I know this stuff, in my heart, in my gut, in my bones. I will start where I have always started: with the body. So far, it has not steered me wrong.

• • •

As a coach, I'm always evolving, learning new ideas and entering new paradigms. At fifty-eight, I'm still changing and growing. Development isn't a one-shot deal, and it reminds me of something Larry and I say to each other whenever we're faced with something that pushes us to change our views or assumptions. One of us always turns to the other and says with a wink and a laugh, "Well, it's just another FGO."

It's our shorthand for "fucking growth opportunity." My journey, Larry's journey, your own journey as you hold this book in your hands—they all come down to a chain of FGOs. What it comes down to is choosing how we tackle them—whether with laughter or anxiety or compassion. And that's the thing: we get to choose.

And we get to choose right now, because we're all starting where we are. No matter where on the journey you are, you only have this one moment and this one huge "X marks the spot" location in time. Maybe you dream of starting your own business or dancing on a stage. Maybe you already run a company. Whether you are reading this in a library, on a bus, or in a corner office, know that where you are right now is a perfect, complete moment and place. It's a time to look around you, rub your eyes, and make a choice to walk onto your stage. The performance is up to you. How do you want your symphony to sound? How do you want your dance to be danced?

When I consider my own dance, I picture myself on a boat on a rich blue lake. As the water shimmers around me, I hear the heartbeat of drums from the shore. I can see everyone who has taught me and supported me on my journey. I see my friends. I see the dancers who have held me aloft high above their heads. I see Amy, my family, the Orlandos. Miss Danzig is there and even the Germans I talked to in that hostel a lifetime ago. And they are all moving, their bodies joyful with rhythm, their smiling faces turned toward me as they wave. I am fully supported by the water under the boat, and my soul group is all around me, encircling me. They are part of the hero's journey, and while they are unique to my path, we all have our own journeys and our own soul groups. When I picture my life's adventure in this way, I don't know where the boat will take me next, but I am surrounded by love and by dance and by that steady, pulsing drumbeat. In my mind, I think maybe I am dancing naked on that boat and everyone else is, too, the pretense of our masks stripped away and our true selves beautiful and bright in the reflection of sun on the water.

This is the image I carry with me. But it doesn't have to be yours.

Wherever you are and whatever choices you make, may you pitch camp and sit with the sunlight streaming on your face. I envision you reaching your own Clearing, many times and in many ways, with your own troupe of loved ones, then continuing on, dancing along paths lined with beauty and riches. I hope we meet on that path, and if we do, I offer this invitation:

Won't you take my hand and wait for the music to start?

CPSIA information can be obtained
at www.ICGtesting.com
Printed in the USA
FSOW03n0855041016
25579FS